PIMLICO

520

CULLODEN

John Prebble was born in Middlesex in 1915 but spent his boyhood in Saskatchewan, Canada. He began his writing career as a journalist in 1934 and then became a novelist, historian, film-writer, and author of many highly-praised plays and dramatised documentaries for television and radio. During the war he served for six years in the ranks with the Royal Artillery, from which experience he wrote his successful war novel, *The Edge of Darkness*. His other books include *Age Without Pity*, *The Mather Story*, *The High Girders*, an account of the Tay Bridge Disaster, *The Buffalo Soldiers*, which won an award in the United States for the best historical novel of the American West, *The Darien Disaster*, *Mutiny* and *John Prebble's Scotland* (both available in Pimlico). John Prebble became interested in Culloden when he was a boy in a predominantly Scottish township in Canada. *Culloden* has been made into a successful television film. He died in January 2001.

CULLODEN

JOHN PREBBLE

PIMLICO

Published by Pimlico 2002

2 4 6 8 10 9 7 5 3 1

First published in Great Britain by Secker & Warburg 1961
Pimlico edition 2002

Pimlico
Random House, 20 Vauxhall Bridge Road,
London SW1V 2SA

Random House Australia (Pty) Limited
20 Alfred Street, Milsons Point, Sydney,
New South Wales 2061, Australia

Random House New Zealand Limited
18 Poland Road, Glenfield,
Auckland 10, New Zealand

Random House (Pty) Limited
Endulini, 5A Jubilee Road, Parktown 2193, South Africa

The Random House Group Limited Reg. No. 954009
www.randomhouse.co.uk

A CIP catalogue record for this book
is available from the British Library

ISBN 0-7126-6820-9

Papers used by Random House are natural,
recyclable products made from wood grown in sustainable forests;
the manufacturing processes conform to the environmental
regulations of the country of origin

Printed and bound in Great Britain by
Bookmarque Ltd, Croydon, Surrey

FOR MY MOTHER

Contents

List of Plates

Maps

This is not another history of the Forty-Five, and it is not another story of Prince Charlie's wanderings after Culloden. It is an attempt to tell the story of the many ordinary men and women who were involved in the last Jacobite Rising, often against their will. For too long, I believe, the truth of this unhappy affair has been obscured by the over-romanticised figure of the Prince. He appears in this book where he is relevant to its theme, and I make no apology for ignoring him at other times. The book begins with Culloden because then began a sickness from which Scotland, and the Highlands in particular, never recovered. It is a sickness of the emotions, and its symptoms can be seen on the labels of whisky bottles. Long ago this sickness, and its economic consequences, emptied the Highlands of people. And this book, I hope, is about people.

—JOHN PREBBLE, *May, 1961*

1

THE MARCH FROM NAIRN

"With a good will to be att them"

THE DRUMS DID not beat Reveille. The Army was to march at five o'clock that morning, and so it was awoken in its tents by the long roll of the General Call to Arms. Before sunrise, but when the light was already grey, twelve drummers of the Main Guard assembled in scarlet line before their major, their mitre caps bobbing as cold fingers fumbled with the sticks or tightened skins. A north-east wind pulled at the flame of the guard-tent lanthorn, and teased the water of the Moray Firth where Rear-Admiral Byng's warships and transports rode at anchor. To the south, across the River Nairn, mist or rain was smoking on the braes of Urchany. It was a morning that soldiers know, and Major Forrester's advanced picquets of the Royal Scots, damp and cold from a night's watch along the high ground at Kildrummie, can have felt no love for it.

The men and boys of the Main Guard drums came to the ready: left heel in the hollow of the right foot, and left knee bent so that the drum was well balanced, elbows up and buttons of the sticks level with the white Horse of Hanover on each cap. At four o'clock, from Nairn a mile away, there came the signal rattle of a single drum, and immediately the sticks of the Main Guard came down on the skins in the drag and paradiddle of the General, the left hand striking a regular, remorseless beat. The drummers moved off from the Main Guard tent, each man marching, beating, toward his own battalion streets. In Nairn the orderly drummer of the Duke's Guard, who had given the signal, strutted from the bridge to the Horologe Stone, and the noise of his sticks sounded again on the narrow windows of the town. The anger of all the drums rolled westward on the wind down the valley of the Nairn, and was heard there by the vedettes of Kingston's

13

Horse. At the alarm-pieces, set forward of the artillery park, a
duty gunner in a plain blue coat lowered his linstock to the
touch-holes. The discharge of the two guns was muffled by the
rain-soaked air: but this, too, the thankful outposts heard, and
they turned their horses toward camp, riding through the water
at Kildrummie.

The people of Nairn stirred to the impatient reveille. Inside the
Provost's house, staff-officers and generals of division yawned and
reached for their wigs, having slept in all else, including their
boots. His Royal Highness, the young Duke, was already awake,
looking from his window to where his soldiers were encamped.
Except for Howard's Old Buffs who were tented on the east bank
of the river, and for two other battalions lodged in the Tolbooth
or houses nearby, the King's Army in Scotland★ lay in ridge-pole
tents across the Inverness Road. Each battalion was a sail-cloth
town: five tents of the Quarter-Guard separated by a wide
parade from an altar of Colours, Drums, and Bells of Arms.
Behind these were six double streets of company tents for
sergeants, corporals, private men, subalterns and captains. To the
rear, and alone, were the tents of the Major and Lieutenant-
Colonel. If the Colonel of the regiment was with the battalion
this day his tent, and those of his staff, stood further back still,
upwind of the horse-lines and the sutler's wagons. Thus geometri-
cally grouped about the gaunt grey house of Balblair, where it
stood on a rise of ground, were twelve battalions of Foot, three
regiments of Horse, and a train of Artillery. There were also eight
companies of kilted militia from the glens of Argyll, Campbells
mostly, their pipes now sounding a gathering above the beating
of the drums. Of these unmilitary and unpredictable levies the
Duke had yet to say something pleasant enough for their colonel,
John Campbell younger of Mamore, to translate into the Irish
tongue of his men.

Before the drummers had finished their call the men of the
battalions were up, painting the white field of canvas with black
beaver hats and scarlet coats, facings of blue and yellow, of buff,
primrose and green. Grey smoke rolled where the butchers were
burning their garbage. The unhoused colours of each regiment,

★ See Appendix.

suddenly broken by their ensigns, spilled out in falls of silk and gold. Sky and mountains were blue-black across the Firth and down the Great Glen, and but for the white pencil of the snow-line it would have been hard to tell where one began and the other ended.

"It was a very cold, rainy morning," recalled Alexander Taylor, private soldier of the Royal Scots, "and nothing to buy to comfort us. But we had the ammunition loaf, thank God, but not a dram of brandy or spirits had you given a crown for a gill; nor nothing but the loaf and water."

The battalions must have thought sourly of the day before. Then it had been the young Duke's birthday, his twenty-fifth, and it had been his pleasure to order half an anker of brandy for each battalion so that his Army might celebrate with him. There had been some cheese, too, and meat for those regiments that had not yet slaughtered the bullocks driven up from the Spey, and for those men who had twopence to buy a pound of it. Cooking-fires had sparked the night after Tattoo, and in their glow the Duke of Cumberland had ridden by, a plump boy who would soon be obscenely fat, lifting his laced hat above his wig and pausing now and then to remind his soldiers that their life was not all brandy and cheese. "My brave boys," he said, "we have but one march more and all our labour is at an end. Sit down at your tent doors and be alert to take your arms."

They had cheered him, tossed their hats upon their bayonets, and called him their "Billy". When he rode back to Nairn for supper and a game of cards they yelled after him again. They shouted "Flanders! Flanders!" to remind him and to reassure him. The half an anker of brandy, paid for by the Duke's own guineas, had much to do with their enthusiasm, but Flanders was truly something to remember in this country where, so far, the King's soldiers had run from the King's enemies. And perhaps the talk across the copper kettles that night was of the dead ground at Fontenoy, twelve months before, over which the Duke had advanced with his infantry. He was the King's son and a German, he had forbidden gambling, flogged men for selling their stockings and threatened to hang them if they sold their issue of bread. He had banned women from the company tents and ordered sentries to stand rather than sit at their posts, but he was a brave young man with an occasional and genuine sympathy for the private soldier. He could not possibly be worse than any other general hitherto commanding in Scotland. He had a personal interest in victory, since it was his father's crown the Rebels wished to take, so his soldiers' cheers and their pleasure at his birthday, their boasting call of "Flanders!" had been sincere enough while the brandy lasted and the fires burned.

But on a cold morning, with only dry bread and water to fill a grumbling belly, past glories have no present satisfaction for a foot-soldier. There were twelve wet miles to be marched and a battle to be fought. Sluggish blood needed the pulse of the drums, and at half-past four they began to roll again in the drag, stroke, drag, stroke of the Assembly, with its warning to pack and parade. The battalions gathered by companies. The halberds of the directing sergeants straightened the ragged lines, hoarse voices calling *"Dress . . . ! By your right man, close step!"* The pipes of the Campbells still sounded, mingling with the squeal of wheels in the artillery park. In Nairn, the Duke and his staff came down the outside stairs of the Provost's house, and passed by a slab in the stone wall on which a Latin inscription offered thought for pretending princes and ambitious generals: *All earthly things by turns become another's property. Mine now must be another's soon. . . .*

When Cumberland reached the field about Balblair his soldiers were listening to the Word of God, conveyed to them by the brigade chaplains, and heard with indifference or reverence according to the state of each man's soul or stomach. Prayers precede a battle when all material needs have received attention. In every soldier's pouch there was enough powder, ball and paper for twenty-four rounds. Half an hour before sunset, the day before, company officers had made sure that all cartridges drawn from the Train were opened, examined, and made up again. Each man had produced, on demand, his turnkey and picker. Subalterns had inspected the muzzles, locks, pans and ramrods of all muskets. The watches, rings, money and other valuables of each private soldier had been handed to his officer for safety. Four days' rations of cheese and biscuits were already loaded on the bread-wagons, and now the men stood on parade, by companies and in battalion line, while the north-east wind blew away the chaplains' words. And when the prayers were done there was more to be heard.

They listened to the General Orders of the Day. Each captain held the Order Book, its marbled covers pressed back against the wind, and he shouted the orders so that no man might reasonably claim that he had never heard them. So every man, his mind on the battle to come, on the hard bread still dry in his mouth, on the night's damp ache in his bones, or perhaps in wonder at the dawn-blue hills of the Black Isle, so every man heard what must be and what was to be: "The battalion horses and the women are to march in the rear of each column, and it is His Royal Highness' order that the Commanding Officers do not allow any old soldier to go with the battalion horses, but awkward men or recruits, nor are they to suffer any women to march with their corps. If any bat-man loses his horse or baggage, or runs away with them, he will be hanged."

There had been a hanging the day before, and the Duke of Cumberland, who was to hang many of his father's subjects in order that those unhanged might learn loyalty and obedience, had authorised this execution too. A boy of seventeen was accused of spying for the Rebels, and was tried for it, standing before a court-martial on the heather. Drummers of the Inlying Picquet beat him bravely to the gallows, and he hung there for ten minutes before Macinucater Rose of Nairn won him a reprieve from the Duke. This was His Royal Highness's clemency, it being his birthday. Watching the execution was Michael Hughes, onetime student of Christ's Hospital and now a volunteer for the duration of the Rebellion. He saw the boy cut down, and saw the surgeon letting blood. "He came to life," said Hughes, "though much disordered when the Army went away."

Because he was a volunteer, moved by conviction to take an active part in this dynastic quarrel, Hughes listened to the General Orders with more attention than did the regular soldiers standing beside him in Bligh's Foot. He remembered enough of the words to put them down on paper months later. He remembered being told "that if any officer or soldier did not behave according to his duty, in his rank or station during the time of the engagement, he should be liable to the same punishment at the discretion of a general court-martial according to the nature of their default and misbehaviour".

Cold words on a cold morning. Drums to quicken a man's blood, and threats to stiffen his courage, but Hughes thought them pretty and proper. "It was quite necessary and prudent to have a regular and strict order preserved, that a finishing period might be put to the scandalous progress of these rebellious vermin." More exactly, it was essential that upon this, their third engagement with the Rebels, the King's soldiers should stand, fight and win.

The voices of the company officers were silent. It was past five o'clock in the morning of Wednesday, April 16, 1746.* And once more the drums began, the tap, demand and urgent command of the grenadier drums at the head of each line, and by battalions the Army formed into three columns of Foot. A pause, with the wind blowing still and the dawn dusk lifting, and at the head of the column on the right waited the grenadier drummers of the Royal Scots, with sticks poised high as their caps.

When the sticks came down to the first beat of the March, the drums of each battalion of each column took up the call, and the Army stepped off. Three columns, each of five battalions, faces turned westward toward Inverness, the Great Glen and the massed mountains of the central Highlands. Three columns: to the right the Royals, Cholmondeley's, Howard's, Fleming's and Pulteney's; to the centre Price's, the Royal Scots Fusiliers, Bligh's, Sempill's and Battereau's; to the left Munro's, Barrell's, Conway's, Wolfe's and Blakeney's. Among them were battalions from the French wars, still wearing the grey service gaiters in which they had marched across Flanders. These were men who had stood their ground against cannon-fire at Fontenoy, calling out to each other that the approaching balls were like the black puddings sold in London taverns. And they were also the men who had run like sheep before the Rebels at Falkirk three months before, there being no continuity of courage for a soldier.

On the left of the Foot a fourth column: three regiments of Horse, Cobham's Dragoons and Lord Mark Kerr's Dragoons, and also the volunteer regiment of Horse which the Duke of Kingston had raised from the butchers, bakers, chandlers and

* All dates are old style.

bored apprentices of Nottinghamshire. On black and bay horses they moved by squadrons, with guidons of crimson silk, silver, gold and green. Their short carbines were slung by the ring, tricorne beavers pulled down over their brows, and yard-long sabres slapped on their great boots. Not a rider was over five feet eight inches, not a horse over fifteen hands.

On the right of the Foot a fifth column: Colonel William Belford's Train of Artillery, battalion-guns and shire-horses, gunners, matrosses, bombardiers, sergeants, fireworkers and lieutenants. The teamsters yelled and the wheels squealed, and the birds rose up from the heather on the moor above Balblair.

The Army moved as the drums beat, seventy-five paces to the minute. The battalions marched by companies in column, and by tradition the honour of being the leading company went to the grenadiers, the tallest and most efficient men of the regiment. They held its flanks in battle, and they wore mitre caps instead of the black tricornes of other companies. They broke ground now in the fields beyond Nairn and they had not marched a mile before their gaiters were wet to the knee. There was no music. No fifes, no horns, no trumpets braying, just the beating of the drums. Before each battalion the standards flowered, bent forward by the wind. One ensign carried the King's Colour, the Union flag, throughout. A second carried the Regimental Colour, which was blue, or yellow, or green or buff, like the facings on the scarlet coats behind. Threaded on the standards in silk, or drawn in paint, were the devices of each battalion: a dragon for Howard's, a lion for Barrell's, a white horse for Wolfe's, and a castle for Blakeney's, a thistle or saltire for the Scots regiments, and the King's cipher for those that were Royal.

Behind the columns came the bat-wagons, bread-wagons, sutler's wagons and the carriages of the lieutenant-colonels. The women, wives and doxies, rode on the bat-wagons or marched beside them with their skirts kilted to the knees. They made no attempt to leave the rear, to move forward as they might have wished, and carry their man's musket when he tired. The Duke of Cumberland's army marched as an army, and any woman found forward of the wagons would have been whipped by the drummers at sunset.

So the King's Army in Scotland marched, a scarlet and white animal crawling over the dead brown heather at two and a half miles an hour. And blind at its centre, where each red cell that was a man saw only the greased hair and leather stock of the man in front of him. At its head, too, it was little better than blind. There, mounted men in gold lace and powdered wigs knew nothing but what they might be told by the forty troopers of Kingston's Horse and the Campbell scouts in skirmish line advanced. The grey sky seemed to press down as the daylight grew, and the raw wind was thickening with rain.

The British infantryman who marched thus from Nairn that Wednesday morning was nobody's friend. Since 1740, as a result of some fanciful political dialogue in the pages of *The Craftsman*, he had been known as "Thomas Lobster", more frequently shortened to "Lobster". In return for a solemn oath that he was a Protestant, that he had no rupture, was not troubled by fits, and was in no way disabled by a lameness not immediately apparent, he acquired the privilege of translating diplomacy into death. For this he received sixpence a day and the contempt of most of his officers. Riding among the staff of Major-General Henry Hawley this day was Brevet-Major James Wolfe, a sickly young man with a weak jaw, pointed nose, and a nervous habit of pulling at his buttons and cuffs. In view of the fame which British soldiers were to bring him on the last day of his life, his opinion of them was scarcely charitable. "I know their discipline to be bad and their valour precarious. They are easily put into disorder and hard to recover out of it. They frequently kill their officers through fear, and murder one another in confusion."

The Age of Reason may have wished its armies would behave like Hectors, and every man may indeed, as Johnson claimed, have thought meanly of himself for not having been a soldier, but the reality of the life was not that imagined by the Patriot Muses of *The Gentleman's Magazine*. It was dirty, depraved and despised. All men preyed on the soldier, and in his turn he robbed and bullied them. To his colonel he was frequently a toy, to be dressed in bizarre and fanciful uniforms that must have given battle an added horror. He stood on a no-man's-land outside the law, its victim and its guardian. When called to support it during civil riots he risked death by shooting if he refused, and trial for murder by the civil power if he obeyed. The whip, the nine-tailed cat with knots of precise size, kept him in order, and his wife or his woman could be disciplined by the whirligig. In this chair she was strapped and spun through the air until she suffered the vomiting sensations of sea-sickness. A soldier, who asked permission to marry the doxy who had loyally followed him through a campaign, risked a hundred lashes for impertinence. Flogging was monotonously common-place. Almost every day's entry in the Order Books contains the names of one, two or three men sentenced to the lash, receiving anything from the minimum of twenty-five strokes to the maximum of three thousand. Men boasted their endurance of the cat. A drummer bragged that he had received twenty-six thousand lashes in fourteen years, and his officers agreed, with admiration, that four thousand of them had been given between the February of one year and the February of the next. Life for the foot-soldier was punctuated by the lash and the pox. Battle came almost as a relief. It was often his only discharge in a war.

For his sixpence a day he was expected to march from a town where innkeepers had either refused to serve him, or had robbed him when drunk, to eat a breakfast of dry bread and water, to watch his officers indulge in chivalrous courtesies with enemy officers while the lines closed, and then to endure a murderous exchange of musketry or grape at one hundred paces. "We ought to returne thanks to God," wrote a sergeant of Foot from Flanders, "for preserving us in ye many dangers we haue from time to time been exposed unto. . . ." But thanking God was not always easy when His mercy was hard to find.

Ignored at home, the soldier was usually forgotten when sent to campaign abroad, unless his efforts produced a victory that read gloriously in the sheets. His life on the transports was "hell between decks, the pox above board and the devil at the helm". He was a pawn in the speculative game of profit-and-loss played by his colonel and the victuallers. In 1741 a fleet of transports set out from Spithead for the West Indies but got no further than Cork. The water taken aboard in England had proved to be undrinkable, the provisions uneatable. A battalion that reached St. Kitt's was discovered, some time later, to have only forty per cent of its strength fit for action, its uniforms in rags, most of the men without hats or shoes, and not one with a serviceable cartridge-box.

Twopence a day was stopped from a soldier's pay as a contribution toward his uniform, and was deducted until his officers considered the debt paid. Another sixpence a week might be stopped to supply him with shoes, linen, gaiters, medicines and other needs. Beyond his basic rations of cheese and ammunition loaf, there was beef, mutton, butter and ale which he might buy with the few pence he had left. Two years of his pay would not buy a hat, wig and stockings for a junior officer of his regiment.

From such a life he frequently deserted, and was hanged for it. Civilians were more his enemy than the soldiers he faced in battle. He aped his officers by fighting duels, and may have wondered why this method of settling disputes brought them honour and him the cat. His service ended, he became a beggar more often than not. If war had not crippled him, he simulated mutilation to make begging that much easier. He was fortunate if a certificate from the Surgeon-General entitled him to a weekly pension of fivepence for the loss of an eye or a limb in battle.

He was rarely an enthusiastic soldier. His officers could never be sure whether he would run at the first onslaught or stand and fight. Not that he could always rely on them. Marching from Nairn this morning, at the head of the division on the left, was Munro's Foot. It had been broken by the Rebel charge at Falkirk three months earlier, and its ensign, still carrying the colours, had been the first man of the battalion to reach Edinburgh. He was subsequently cleared by a court-martial, but thirty dragoons and thirty foot-soldiers were hanged for running from the same battle. Since a soldier of those wars gained little by victory or defeat, beyond immediate death or plunder, why he sometimes readily gave his life in an unimportant encounter is a problem of psychology. He seems to have rationalised the complicated politics of his time into a simple contest designed to prove whether he or a mounseer were the better man. "Our nation may boast," wrote a journalist in *The Idler*, "beyond any other people in the world, of a kind of epidemick bravery. . . . We

can show a peasantry of heroes, and fill our armies with clowns whose courage may vie with that of their general." It was a half-truth, like most observations by civilians about soldiers, but bravery can be epidemic. A soldier is as courageous as the men on his right and left flank, and danger is diluted when shared among a battalion of six hundred men.

The soldier of George II came to the colours as a result of several pressures. The most common was economic, the simple desire for food and clothing. At its worst, a soldier's life could still be better than the under-seam of London. When economic pressure, or the skills of their recruiters were not enough to fill their battalions, colonels followed their naval colleagues and used the press. London newspapers in 1744 reported that two hundred men of Southwark had been impressed into the Army. The whip and the halter, a desperate loyalty in common discomfort and distress, an odd pride that will come to a man when he is an outcast, all these combined to make the British soldier into an efficient, dogged fighter when he was well led. When he had the ability he wrote of the battles to which he was committed with a peculiarly vivid understatement: "They stood us a Tug. Notwithstanding, we beat them off to a distance; we advanced, they took the hint and run away."

If it is possible to see him as one man, he was of the standard height of five feet five inches laid down in the regulations. He enlisted for a term of three years and a bounty of four pounds, most of which was drunk for him by the recruiting sergeant on the day of his enlistment. He was frequently literate, or at least able to write his own name. The pay-rolls of Colonel Belford's artillery company at Nairn show that all but three of its 150 men were capable of signing their names. Admittedly these were artillerymen, and Captain Thomas Binning, in his gentle *Light to the Art of Gunnery*, had urged that a gunner "be educated and expert in his Profession, for Experience confirmeth, some say teacheth, Art". But there were literate men in the ranks of the Foot, too, and the bold, clear handwriting of men like Corporal William Edwards and Sergeant Joseph Napper of Cholmondeley's, is still there on the Order Books of their regiment.

The infantryman looks more comfortable in the set-pieces that were painted of his battles than he could have felt during them. He wore a wide-skirted coat of heavy scarlet, well-buttoned and piped, and cuffed and faced with the regimental colour. It rarely fitted him. Colonels of regiments were supposed to have the material pre-shrunk, but most of them were too mean or too indifferent, or claimed that it spoiled the hang of the cloth and the appearance of their men. Thus the first shower of rain to which a battalion was subjected shrank the skirts, shortened the sleeves and added one more discomfort to soldiering. Beneath this coat was worn a long, flapped waistcoat. Breeches were scarlet, too, and covered to the mid-thigh with spatterdash gaiters of white or grey. The head, beneath its black tricorne, was held upright by a tight leather stock. There was only one way a soldier was expected to look, and that was to his front, and the stock made sure that he did.

Over his left shoulder he wore a wide belt, stiffened with pipe-clay which he made from a mixture of one pound of yellow ochre to four pounds of whiting. From this belt hung his cartridge pouch. On his left side, and hanging from his waist-belt, was a double-frog for a curved hanger and his bayonet, sixteen inches of fluted steel. A grey, canvas haversack, when he carried it and was not lucky enough to have it loaded on the bat-wagons, contained two shirts, two leather neck-stocks, two pairs of stockings, a pair of breeches, a pair of buckled shoes, brushes, blacking and pipe-clay. And also enough ammunition loaf for six days.

His weapon had changed little since Marlborough's wars forty years before. The musket Brown Bess, made at the Minories in London or bought from abroad, weighed eleven pounds two ounces, and its barrel was three and a half feet long. It had a ·753 inch bore, and fired a ball that weighed one ounce and a third. Cartridges supplied by the artillery train consisted of this ball wrapped in paper with four and a half drams of black powder. The musket was an ineffectual weapon at more than three hundred paces, and only of value within that if the aim were good. Its importance lay in the controlled fire-power of a hundred or more in one discharge, in the rolling volleys of rank by rank, platoon by platoon, company by company. A regiment that stood its ground under assault, biting the cartridge, priming the pan, ramming home the ball, firing at the beat of drum and loading again, a regiment thus engaged could not, in theory, be over-run. The theory argued, of course, that no enemy would continue to advance over its own dead when they lay four deep on the ground before a British battalion in line. It also argued the ability of the battalion itself to keep its head. Like most arguments in theory it was frequently confounded in practice. British infantrymen had lost their heads before this, and to-day, on one part of the field ahead, the enemy was to climb, fight and crawl over its dead to reach the red coats and the red bayonets.

To survive such a battle a soldier required more than arguable theory. Good commanders were, as always, of considerable help, but in this campaign so far the soldier of the line had not been favoured with them. Thus Edward Linn, private soldier of the Royal Scots Fusiliers and marching with the centre of the Army, had God in his mind as he moved westward at seventy-five paces to the minute. When it was all over he would write to his "beloved spouse", asking her to "give praise to Almighty God" for the fact that he had no wounds, and he would ask her to urge the Minister to remember Edward Linn in his prayers the next Sunday.

The British Army, marching toward its third and final battle with the Rebel forces of Prince Charles Edward Stuart, consisted of 6,400 Foot and 2,400 Horse. It moved to the south-west, flanked by the Moray Firth and the valley of the Nairn. For the first two or three miles it passed across fields, and its artillery rolled along the Inverness Road. The noise of its drums and the protest of its wheels could be heard for ten miles. Sailors in the rigging of Admiral Byng's ships watched its slow movement and shouted word of its progress to the decks below. Rain was not yet falling, but it was coming, and the wind was cold enough to turn it to sleet. When it came it would fall on the backs of the marching men and upon the faces of the enemy if they chose to fight. It was for mercies such as this, perhaps, that the chaplains of brigade had prayed. The ground rose and took the Army upwards toward the sloping plateau of the moor, and now the earth was broken and ribbed, soft with bogs, with here and there a tiny lochan as dull as pewter this morning. The marching men were wet and muddied to the thigh, and the guns sank and tilted as they left the road for the heather. To the left of the Army, across the Nairn's green valley, were the high hills of Cawdor, bare, treeless and matted with dead heather. To the right was the Firth, and across it the blue peninsula of the Black Isle. Ahead, seen only by the grenadier companies in the van of each division, or by the advanced vedettes of Kingston's, was the Great Glen, its mountain walls still capped with snow. So on the marching went, and upwards, with birds starting from the heather at the sound of the drums, the creak of wheels and the ring of bridle-chains.

At nine o'clock the Army passed Kilravock House, and the Duke halted there with his staff to watch it pass. There were no cries of "Billy!" or "Flanders!", but the soldiers turned their heads to see him. He sat on his horse very well indeed, and looked less fat than he did on foot. His tricorne was pulled well down on his brow and at a rakish slant. His scarlet frock-coat had lapels of blue edged with gold, and his saddle-housing was scarlet, blue and gold, too, heavy with golden tassels. His face, above the white foam of lace at his throat and within the white curls of his wig, was fat and red, his eyes black and protruding. He seemed well-satisfied with himself, the day, and his Army. The Laird of Kilravock, coming from the door, approached the Duke with suitable deference and some alarm. Not many hours before there had been another king's son at Kilravock, and the Laird wondered if the Duke knew this.

He did. "We marched about four miles," remembered Michael Hughes, "and there met five deserters who, being examined by the Duke, gave account that the rebels were waiting for us two leagues off, and that their intention was to surprise us at night in our camp." But the night attack had lost itself beyond Kilravock before it could be launched, and now the Duke could afford to be jovial about it.

"So," he said, looking down from his saddle at the Laird, "I understand you had my cousin Charles here yesterday?"

"Yes, please Your Royal Highness," said Kilravock, as uncertain as any man with life and property standing between two armies. "Having no armed forces I could not prevent him."

"You did perfectly right," said Cumberland, and rode on.

The Royal Army changed direction to the south, seeking the top of the moor. Eight miles out of Nairn, and at eleven o'clock, when the division on the right discovered that it had marched into a bog, the Rebels were sighted. Not by the main body, but by the cavalry and Campbell scouts ahead. The Quartermaster commanding them sent word that the enemy was forming in line across the spine of Drummossie Moor, climbing up from the policies and parks surrounding Culloden House. Word of this passed down the columns from battalion to battalion. It brought no joy to Belford's artillerymen whose cannon were hub-deep in the soft earth and tumbrils almost immobilised. There was a rumour that a threadbare Highlander, brooding by the roadside, had offered his help to Belford as a guide, led the guns into a bog, and then disappeared. Cumberland ordered up bat-horses from the rear, and he told the right-flank men of the Royals and Cholmondeley's to sling their muskets and put their shoulders to the guns. And the whips cracked and voices swore, and the cannon were heaved out of the marsh that was known as the White Bog.

All over the moor where the Army marched the earth sank and gurgled beneath the buckled shoes. "We waded to the knees in mud and dirt," Edward Linn told his wife, "through the moor several times that day with a good will to be att them, and no wonder considering the fatigues we have undergone this winter by hunger and cold and marching day and night after them."

So Private Linn bent his body to the climb, with Alexander Taylor of the Royals, Sergeant Joe Napper of Cholmondeley's and Volunteer Hughes of Bligh's, with all the marching Foot. Trooper Enoch Bradshaw, of Cobham's, was wishing he had a flitch of bacon from his brother's farm in Gloucestershire. The back of Private McColmon, lately a sergeant of Battereau's, was still raw and corrugated from the eight-hundred lashes he had received for looting, and he felt friendship for no man, least of all his confederates John Denison and Andrew Mallaby. The Duke had pardoned them, saying they had been influenced by their sergeant. The rain fell on them all, and hail drummed on the crowns of their hats. They pulled up the skirts of their coats and covered their muskets, and one of them would write home after-wards "It rained very sore as I ever seed, both hail and rain and strong wind. Strong on our backs and the enemies face."

And soon the enemy was close enough to be seen by Michael Hughes. "We marched on a mile or two before we could discern the terrible boasting Highlanders, and upon first sight of them we formed into line of action, which was done with great beauty of discipline and order."

If this were indeed done with beauty and order, on rough heather and a rising ground, in a storm of sleet and rain, it was to the credit of the directing sergeants, harshly shouting on the company flanks. The move from column into line was the only major manoeuvre of an infantry regiment, bringing it from its order of march into its order of battle. The Army was proud of it, and on cool summer evenings in St. James's Park the Household Brigade would perform it for the entertainment of strolling Londoners, firing volleys by platoons when it was done. Yet here was no stone-dust parade at the Horse Guards, but a sloping moorside thick with dead heather and pocked with bog-holes.

When the order to form came, the three divisions closed up and halted, drummers falling to the rear and flank of each battalion. A cautionary cry of "*Take care!*", a drum-tap and the order "*Wheel into line!*". The companies moved half-right through a quarter of a circle, still facing their front, and thus the line was made, with the sergeants shouting "*Dress! Close steps!*". And when the line was formed the columns of battalions moved forward, breaking, separating to form three lines of battle. The second battalion of each of the three columns moved up to the left of the first battalion and thus formed a line of six. Similarly the fourth battalion of each of the three columns moved up to the left of the third battalion to form another line of six, leaving the fifth battalions of each column to form a rear line of three. The King's Army in Scotland completed this manoeuvre in ten minutes, and halted, waiting for attack.

In the front line, under the command of the Earl of Albemarle, who was beginning to think himself too old for this sort of thing, the six regiments from the right: Royal Scots, Cholmondeley's, Price's, the Royal Scots Fusiliers, Munro's and Barrell's. In the second line, commanded by Major-General John Huske: Howard's, Fleming's, Conway's, Bligh's, Sempill's and Wolfe's. In the rear, under Brigadier-General John Mordaunt: Pulteney's, Battereau's and Blakeney's.

And into each of the five spaces between the battalions of the first line the gunners and matrosses of Colonel Belford's company pulled and manhandled two three-pounder guns, helped by the flank men of the battalions. While the infantry waited, the gunners piled fascines of heather and saplings before their guns, broke open their shot and brought up their powder. They blew on their slow-matches and stared through the sleet at their target and saw little of it but a distant line, more than a mile away, a turbulent flurry of plaid and steel, the black clumps of standing men.

The infantry stared, too, as it waited in line, three ranks to a battalion, with bayonets fixed. Platoon flanking platoon, company by company, with the grenadiers on right and left, and the colours in the centre. Each man and each officer had his place. The lieutenant-colonel to the rear and behind the colours, with his orderly drummer beside him, a boy blowing on his fingers to give them courage and skill. Major and adjutant on the flanks of the battalion, captains to the flanks of their companies, subalterns and sergeants with the platoons. And drummers in the rear with their sticks ready. Colour flowed and eddied along the lines, scarlet and pipe-clay, green, buff and blue, the black roof of hats and the dull grey light on steel.

To the left of the Army, Major-General Hawley's regiments of Horse awaited orders, which would come when Cumberland understood what the enemy might be about to do. But that distant cloud, from which came wild cries and the skirling of pipes, made no movement forward. It seemed, as best a man could tell in the distorting rain, to be moving to its right to outflank the Royal Army. So Cumberland ordered his men back into column and into the advance again. They went forward up the moor, with bayonets fixed and advanced, and they marched nearly a mile in this manner and in great discomfort. "We marched up to our knees in water," said Michael Hughes, "over a bog that brought us to the perfect sight of them. We kept advancing with drums beating and colours flying, with fixed bayonets till we came within gunshot. We then halted a little for the boggy ground hindered the bringing up of our cannon."

There was no silence. The company drums beat incessantly, bouncing on the thighs of the boys and the men, and the voices of the sergeants cried *"Dress . . . ! Close step, by your right man, dress!"* Across the valley of the Nairn a black-brown coat of heather lay on the shoulders of Ben Bhuiddhe. To the right the Moray Firth was barely visible. And the fall of the sleet was hard on the necks of the men.

Within half a mile of the Rebels, and still seeing no movement forward from them, Cumberland once more ordered his regiments into line. "We spent about half an hour after that," an officer wrote to the *London Magazine*, "trying which should regain the flank of the other. . . ." The two armies were like wrestlers shuffling for a hold, one to its right, the other to its left, and finding no opening. Now only five hundred yards separated them at their closest point on the Royal Army's left, and, from the right, word came to Cumberland that the bog which had protected that flank was now passed. Firm ground stretched away from the Royal Scots, down the moor to the north. The artillerymen, blue coats muddied to the shoulders, were once more pulling their battalion-guns into the line, and throwing up fascines again, when Cumberland ordered two hundred of Kingston's Horse and sixty of Cobham's Dragoons to cover the right flank of the Royals. He also told the Campbell militia to stay back with the baggage, thereby making plain his opinion of their effectiveness, but four companies ignored the order, or claimed that they had not understood it. They had been scouting ahead on the left all the way from Nairn, and now they heard the pipes sounding the gathering of ancient enemies, the ranting reminders of old injuries. Red-shanked and with broadswords drawn, they moved forward in a feeling advance on the enemy's left.

Still nothing was certain, except that the Rebels had agreed to give battle. There was time for a last appeal to a man's pride, a Crispin-day's speech of warm words to take the chill out of the sleet. This was an army that had run before when faced by the pipes and a swinging rush of steel. Cumberland rode slowly along the lines.

"My brave boys," he said, or is reported to have said, "your toil will soon be at an end. Stand your ground against the broadsword and target. Parry the enemy in the manner you have been directed. . . ."

This, perhaps, was something they understood, despite its blunt indication that volley-firing alone might not be enough to-day. In every battle against the clans that the British had experienced, men had been cut down by the broadsword while their bayonets were caught, held and brushed aside by the ox-hide shields of their opponents. In the weeks since Falkirk, however, the infantryman had been trained to thrust his bayonet at the exposed under-arm of the clansman attacking his comrade on the right, and to trust, presumably, that his comrade on the left would do the same service for him. Officers had been told to smother and deride any old soldier's story of the fury of the Highland onslaught "which there is nothing so easy to resist, if officers and men are not prepossessed by the lies and accounts which are told of them".

A soldier's emptiest moment is that before a battle begins, and his courage may grow from anything that helps him to feel that he is not alone. Generals know this, instinctively or by experience. So the boy Duke rode before his Army, his head bare in salute. "Be assured of immediate assistance," he said, and perhaps that is all he did say, there being time for little else, but when his words reached the pages of the London magazines two weeks later there were many more of them. "I promise you that I shall not fail to make a report of your behaviour to the King, and in the meantime if any are unwilling to engage, pray let them speak freely, and with pleasure they shall have their discharge, for I would rather be at the head of one thousand brave and resolute men than ten thousand amongst whom there are some who, by cowardice or misbehaviour, may dispirit or disorder the troops."

If he said that, not one man of the fifteen battalions stepped forward to take advantage of his handsome offer. If he said that, probably none of them believed him, having memories of comrades flogged or hanged for desertion. More likely the speech, passing through the improving hands of a correspondent, was coloured by a reading of *Henry V* before it reached its readers.

No man can maintain rhetoric in a high wind and a fall of sleet, but what the Duke did say was enough to bring a cheer from his men. They raised their hats on their bayonets and they yelled, "Flanders! Flanders! We'll follow you!"

Cumberland passed by the last of the battalions, his hat still in his hand, in the stiff-armed gesture that military painters found so dramatic. He rode to the right, standing his horse to the rear of the Royal Scots, between the first and second lines. His staff waited about him, squinting through the rain over the black hats of the Royals. They made a brave show of scarlet and blue, gold lace and white shirt-cuffs. Most of them were as young as their commander-in-chief, and some his particular favourites, like Charles Cathcart, ninth baron of the name. He was twenty-five, too, an officer of the Foot Guards who had been severely wounded in the face at Fontenoy. A pistol-ball had struck him in the eye, and now he wore a piratical black patch over the scar. There was Colonel the Honourable Joseph Yorke, who was only twenty-two and the son of the Earl of Hardwicke to whom he wrote as frequently and as fully as possible, so that the great lawyer might be better informed about the Rebellion than most of the King's Ministers. Captain the Honourable Henry Seymour Conway had received his first commission of Foot when he was a boy, ten years or so before, and scarcely into his teens. He had been a member of the Irish Parliament and of several pocket boroughs in England. He had fought at Dettingen and Fontenoy, and he, too, was of the same age as his commander.

And there was George Keppel, Lord Bury, aged twenty-one and son and heir to the old Dutch Earl of Albemarle who commanded Cumberland's first line to-day. Bury had become an ensign in the Coldstream Guards at the age of fourteen. He was a dandy, a rake and a gambler, a professional soldier for what purchase and privilege might bring. According to his friend Horace Walpole, who admired him, he was always "young and in high spirits". His regimentals were as splendid as those of his commander, his saddle-housings as rich as a general's, a resemblance that nearly took his life before this battle had begun.

One of these young men, remarking on the delay and the absence of forward movement from the enemy, said that since it was now past noon would His Royal Highness permit the men to dine before battle?

"No," said the Duke. "No, they'll fight all the better on empty bellies. Remember what a dessert they got to their dinner at Falkirk."

The young men laughed at this, for the defeat at Falkirk had been the error of Henry Hawley, the foul-mouthed brutal old man who had fought under Marlborough but who, in the opinion of all, had less ability in his whole body than the young Duke had in one finger-nail. Yet the lack of action from across the field was puzzling. Nobody could see the enemy very clearly. They were clumps of men, half a mile from the Royals on the right, and not the serried ranks of white and blue to which the Flanders veterans were accustomed. They were wild figures, their outlines broken by the whip and whirl of plaid and kilt. Above the noise of their own drums, which never ceased beating, the British soldiers could hear the pipes. Cumberland asked young Bury to ride out a way between the two lines and to discover what the Rebels had in mind, if anything.

When the battalions had been forming line for the second time a Highlander had come over the heather to them, throwing down his broadsword and his pistols, his musket and his target, and declaring himself the Duke's prisoner. He was passed through to the rear, and there he wandered from battalion to battalion, clutching at sleeves and asking where he might find the Duke and surrender. Lord Bury rode by him, and the Highlander stared with bright interest at this man in rich and expensive regimentals. He wrenched a musket from the nearest soldier and presented it at the young man's back, believing that he could now kill the Duke and do his Prince a service. He pulled the trigger and the shot missed, the sound of it lost in the beating of the drums. But a soldier called Newman turned in the ranks of Sempill's, and he shot the clansman dead.

The first man had died in the battle of Culloden. With the arrogant and confident indifference of his rank and class, Lord Bury rode across the moor until he was midway between the two armies. There he halted his horse and calmly stared at the Rebels.

"Their idle and antient way of life"

WHAT LORD BURY saw, across the heather and through the sleet, was the last feudal army to assemble in Britain. He can have felt no more kinship with it than an officer of Victoria's army would later feel when surveying a Zulu impi or a tribe of Pathans. To an Englishman of the eighteenth century, and to most Lowland Scots, the Highlands of Scotland were a remote and unpleasant region peopled by barbarians who spoke an obscure tongue, who dressed in skins or bolts of parti-coloured cloth, and who equated honour with cattle-stealing and murder. The savagery with which the Lowland Scots and the English were to suppress the Rebellion is partly explained by this belief, it being a common assumption among civilised men that brutality is pardonable when exercised upon those they consider to be uncivilised.

The Highlanders were a constant threat to the people of the Lowlands, or were believed to be. In England very little was known of them. Their mountains were a week or two weeks from London by fast horse. The Government was as prejudiced and as ill-informed as the people, although in a man like Duncan Forbes, Lord President of the Court of Session, it had a sober and sensible adviser on Highland affairs, did it choose to use him. From the windows of his noble house at Culloden, below Drummossie Moor, he watched the mountain people with a critical eye, and only occasionally looking down his long nose. He was sincerely concerned with the need to bring to them the soft and civilising influence of the south, and when he was severe in his judgments it was with parental disapproval. One day in the summer of 1746, when the Rebellion was over and the Government was taking steps to see that there should not be another, Duncan Forbes sat down and penned a thoughtful essay on what was and what might be now that the blood had been let. It contained a sharp picture of his wild neighbours.

"What is properly called the Highlands of Scotland is that large tract of mountainous Ground to the Northwest of the Forth and the Tay, where the natives speak the Irish language. The inhabitants stick close to their antient and idle way of life; retain their barbarous customs and maxims; depend generally on their Chiefs as their Sovereign Lords and masters; and being accustomed to the use of Arms, and inured to hard living, are dangerous to the public peace; and must continue to be so until, being deprived of Arms for some years, they forget the use of them."

The feudal framework which the power of the chiefs gave to the Highland way of life enclosed a tribal system much older in time. The ties of blood and name were strong among the people, and pride of race meant as much to a humbly in his sod and roundstone house as it did to a chieftain in his island keep. All claimed lines of gentility, and the meanest of them believed himself the superior of any soft-breeked creature living south of his hills. By 1746, however, the clan society was dying, and, for once, history was to show an appreciation of dramatic effect by ending it abruptly and brutally. For more than a hundred years the politics and the economy of the south had been entering the glens. Military roads, driven through the Highlands from garrison to garrison, and sea to sea, broke cracks across the hard geography of the land, but still the past lingered behind its defence-work of the Irish tongue, the memories kept alive by pipes and the songs. The clan remained a man's only identity, and the broadsword his only understandable law outside it.

"A Highland Clan," wrote old Duncan Forbes, "is a set of men all bearing the same sirname, and believing themselves to be related the one to the other, and to be descended from the same common stock. In each clan there are several subaltern tribes, who own their dependence on their own immediate chiefs but all agree in owing allegiance to the Supreme Chief of the Clan or Kindred and look upon it to be their duty to support him at all adventures."

No law of the country, none put down on sheepskin anyway,

determined the right of a chief to his title, nor need he have title to an acre of ground. "Some Chiefs there are that have neither property nor jurisdiction, and the cutting off of the present Chief does no more than make way for another." For a Highland chief's right to the name sprang from a dawn of society before the writing of laws. So the difficulty of imposing the Law on a race of tribesmen, who had not the understanding or will to accept it, was a matter of extreme concern to men like Duncan Forbes. For him the Rebellion, and the constant feuding forays in the hills, were sad obstacles to the progress of civilisation. But to soldiers like Cumberland, and his rough general of division Henry Hawley, there was common sense in the argument that if men are all the better for a little blooding so must nations be also. If the Law and loyalty could not be brought into the hills by persuasion and argument it must be brought by the musket, the bayonet and the gibbet.

Still Forbes persevered. "It has been for a great many years impracticable (and hardly thought safe to try it) to give the Law its course among the mountains. It required no small degree of Courage, and a greater degree of power than men are generally possessed of, to arrest an offender or debtor in the midst of his Clan. And for this reason it was that the Crown in former times was obliged to put Sheriffships and other Jurisdictions in the hands of powerful families in the Highlands, who by their respective Clans and following could give execution to the Laws within their several territories, and frequently did so at the expense of considerable bloodshed."

Great chieftains, men ennobled by the Crown like the Campbells of Argyll and Breadalbane, were thus responsible for the Law in the hills, and by the execution of it would have been less than men if they had not thereby increased their own power and property. They could put the greatest number of broadswords in the greatest number of hands, and dress the settlement of ancient feuds in the livery of the King. The Government had not solved the problem by acknowledging and confirming the Hereditary Jurisdictions of the chiefs, it had merely given quasi-legal authority to the primitive savagery of Highland life. Although, in 1746, Europe and America were within half a century of revolution and the Rights of Man, North Britain still slumbered in tribal twilight four hundred miles from London.

The social system of a Highland clan was fixed, and the barriers were crossed emotionally only. A chief's son, wet-nursed by the wife of a humbly, would never call his foster-brother his equal, but the milk shared by them imposed a life-long obligation that could and often did compel the one to give his life for the other. And if the compulsion were not strong enough, if the clansman were reluctant to come out with sword and target when needed, the chief would feel himself justified in burning the roof of his milk-brother's hut.

The geography of their land determined the economy of the clans. It was, and is, a hard land. Before Man, the moving floors of ice cut the glens, and so flayed the earth of skin that at its best the rock is covered by shallow soil. In such harsh and unrewarding surroundings men could be herdsmen only, raising black and shaggy cattle, hardy sheep and goats. And being tribal herdsmen they became warriors to protect their flocks, until in the end history stood on its head and they were men of war rather than minders of cattle. Forays against the herds of their neighbours became affairs of honour, and only the people south of the mountains saw it as robbery. A quarrel between men of different tribes might be settled by a dirk-thrust at night, by single combat, or by whole clans pulled out on to the heather by the fiery cross. One cattle-raid would be answered by another, year after year, and the bards of the clans composed heroic poems about each bloody incident, the pipes played rants in honour of men dead for centuries.

The land, once held by the tribe in common, had by the eighteenth century become the chief's, his title to it sometimes no more tangible than the approval of his tribe, a situation that proved most awkward for some of them when the great chiefs of Argyll, or Seaforth, or Lovat, discovered that a sheet of sheep-skin could be a more effective weapon than a broadsword or a Lochaber axe. Yet, though the land was the chief's, the clan's interest in the soil was deep and strong. Part of it was "mensal land", used by and for the chief himself. Parts, too, might be given in perpetuity to families of officials of the clan, men like the Bard, the Harper and the Piper. The rest was held by tenants under "tacks" or leases granted by the chief. Thus the tacksman, though not of the chief's family, was a man of importance in the tribal society, and his rank entitled him to be a junior officer or senior non-commissioned officer when the clan formed itself into a regiment for war. In their turn the tacksmen sub-leased part of their land, and so each social stratum was formed, each man owing economic allegiance to those above him, and all bound in fealty to the chieftain whose direct and known progenitor had been the strong-loined hero who had started the whole tribe.

The chief was a man of contradictions, a civilised savage whose interests and experience were often far wider than most Englishmen's. He could speak Gaelic and English, and very often French, Greek and Latin as well. He sent his sons to be educated at universities in Glasgow and Edinburgh, in Paris or Rome. He drank French claret and wore lace at his throat. He danced lightly, his own Highland reels and southern measures. He swore oaths in which God and Celtic mythology were mixed. He would boast, as did the MacGregors, that Royal was his race, or that he bore a King's name if he were an Appin Stewart, but his allegiance to Kings was quixotic. In his glens he was king, and there was no appeal higher than to him among his clan. A woman was once brought before Macdonald of Clanranald and accused of stealing money from him. He ordered her to be tied by the hair to sea-weed on the rocks, and there she stayed until the Atlantic tide rolled in and drowned her. Although Clanranald's people may have trembled at the violent justice of their chief, none could have questioned the punishment, for who stole from the chief stole from the clan.

The chief protected the clan and the chief punished the clan. At the best, offenders were driven from the glens, at the worst they might be sold to the merchant captains who called at Inverness, looking for servants for the Americas. Seven years before Culloden Sir Alexander Macdonald of Sleat and his brother-in-law Macleod of Dunvegan, chiefs of the Isles, drove one hundred of their people aboard ships for deportation to Pennsylvania, and swaggered their way out of the uproar this caused in the Lowlands when the ship was discovered and the deportees released at an

Irish port. No protest was heard or recorded from a Macdonald or a Macleod clansman.

Although now and then a chief might whet his talents on the politics or society of the Lowlands or England, most of them, once their youth was past, stayed in their hills, where they were not known by their surnames but by their land, by the glen or loch, the strath or clachan that was their home. And the wife of a chief, whether or not her husband would have been plain Mister in Glasgow or London, was always Lady. A chief's amusement came from the land and the culture of his people, from bardic poems and wild pipe music. More actively, when he was not away on a cattle-raid, he hunted. The high mountains, at one time, were running with the stag, the wolf and the cat, and the hunting of them was a fine and barbaric spectacle even after the fire-arm came to the Highlands. Sir Ewen Cameron of Lochiel, chief of a clan that was "all gentlemen" by its own estimate, once organised a splendid deer-hunt for the pleasure of his guests. He called out hundreds of his men and stretched them over the hills at the head of Loch Arkaig. They moved forward, shouting and crying, sounding the pipes and beating sword on shield, so that the deer bounded from cover and ran toward the mouth of a narrow glen. There stood Lochiel and his guests with broad-swords in their hands. By the swinging and the cutting of the long blades they slew many animals, and the Cameron Bard and the Cameron Harper made an epic of it. Tacksmen and humblies, because they were blood of blood with Lochiel, felt that some of his valour and some of his pride was theirs, too. So where he went they would go, and if he passed by their door they would have a plaid for his head and brawn for his dogs.

Duncan Forbes, in his painstaking efforts to enlighten a usually obtuse Government in London, once numbered the fighting-men of the Highlands, naming them clan by clan, from Macdonald of Glencoe's 130 broadswords to the 4,000 well-armed kerns whom Campbell of Argyll and Campbell of Breadalbane could put into battle if they wished. Altogether, Forbes estimated that the warrior strength of the mountains was 31,930, and he regarded this as a conservative figure. Had all these found common cause they could have tumbled the House of Hanover from the throne merely by assembling and marching down to the Lowlands. Less than 6,000, advancing south to Derby under Prince Charles four months before Culloden, had forced George II to think seriously of immediate retirement to Hanover. But, in fact, there had never been unity in the Highlands, nor could ever be. Religion, feuds, the political ambitions of chiefs, the natural jealousies of men who live remote and primitive lives, made common cause impossible. Each clan was enough to itself, and the world ended beyond the glen, or with the sea that locked in the islands.

The patriarchal system of clanship, the fact that there was never at one time more than half the people of the Highlands profitably employed, the ancient stories of valour and combat, all fostered the warlike spirit of the clans. Thus a chief was judged by his attitude toward military matters, by his courage, and by his sensitivity in affairs of honour. As soon as a chief's son came to manhood he was watched carefully by his father's people. If he were quick to revenge an insult by tugging out his dirk, if he were always ready to lead high-spirited young men on a cattle foray, then he was greatly esteemed and accepted as worthy to succeed his father. If, however, his brief encounter with softer living in the Lowlands, or on the Continent, had turned his mind to more sedentary interests, he would be despised, and the allegiance of the clan might turn to a younger brother. The milksop might remain the chief in name, none could take that from him, but hard sinews and a fine cunning in war were expected of the man who led the clan in battle.

Every man and boy old enough or fit enough to carry arms was automatically a soldier in the regiment of the clan, his rank fixed by his social position. The chief, or that man of the chief's family named by him, was the colonel. The chief's brothers or sons commanded the flanks and the rear. The head of each family was an officer or a sergeant, bringing in his brothers, sons and tenants to form companies or platoons. Each family, too, stood in line of battle according to its importance in the clan, so that the common humbly, the raw-thighed, half-naked sub-tenant of a sub-tenant would find himself in the rear rank of all, and think it no more than his right. Brother fought beside brother, father by

son, so that each might witness the other's courage and valour
and find example in them.

The clan gathered when the fiery cross was sent across its
country, two burnt or burning sticks to which was tied a strip of
linen stained with blood. The cross was passed from hand to hand,
by runners in relay. One of the last occasions on which it was
sent was when a Campbell, the Earl of Breadalbane, rallied his
people against the Jacobite clans in 1745. It travelled thirty-two
miles about Loch Tay in three hours. A clan that had been
gathered by the cross was moved by deep and distant super-
stitions. An armed man it met with by the way was a portent of
good fortune and victory. A stag, fox, hare or any beast of game
that was seen and not killed promised evil. If a bare-footed woman
crossed the road before the marching men she was seized, and
blood was drawn from her forehead by the point of a knife. All
this and more. Every tribe had its slogan, a wild and savage
exhortation to slaughter or a reminder of the heroic past. It was
cried for the onslaught, in the confusion of a night alarm, and it was
as much a part of the clan's identity as the badge of heather, gale,
ling, oak or myrtle that a man wore in his bonnet. The slogan
was yelled, the rant played and the badge worn, be it for a battle
such as that now facing the Jacobite clans, or for a dark-of-night
creach when young men fell upon a neighbour's cattle and sheep.

Because there were no laws to protect a clan against a chief's
rights, the past had established a compensating balance. If he had
the right of life and death over his people, he was equally responsible for their welfare, and most chiefs honoured this obligation.
As landlord, father-figure, judge and general-at-arms his power
was great, but it was not always absolute, and on occasions he
would debate major issues with the leading members of his family
and clan—the settlement of serious disputes between one man and
another, the support of children orphaned, the declaration of war
and the acceptance of terms for peace. This was something from
the tribe's past, when men held things in common, and there were
chiefs who felt themselves strong enough in their feudal power
to disregard it. They would not ask their council's advice, or
would ignore it if they did, and, if they felt their following
among the clan to be weak, they would burn a few cottages to

encourage the laggards. From boyhood, from the moment his foster-mother weaned him, a Highland chief began to understand, or at least to enjoy, his peculiar position in life. He was of the same blood and name and descent as his people, but he stood halfway between them and God.

His prosperity or poverty depended upon the industry of his clan, and it would have been unnatural if all chiefs recognised this in terms of their responsibility toward their people. A chief's tenants, tacksmen and humblies, followed his standard, avenged his wrongs, supplied his table with the produce of their crofts, reaped his corn, cut his fuel. They paid their rents to him loyally, even when he was an outlaw or in exile. For nine years after Culloden, Macpherson of Cluny lived in a cave on his mountains, nourished by his clan and protected from the soldiers. A chief was not distinguished by the degree of his fortune or by the splendour of his dress, though some walked like peacocks in tartan and silver. His power and importance rested in the cattle on his braes, and in the number of pretty fellows he could have in his tail when he went abroad. Thus did a Macdonald of Keppoch boast that his rent-roll was five hundred fighting-men. In such a climate of pride and sensitive honour the hospitality of the Highlands was more often manifest vanity. When this same Keppoch was told by a guest of the great candelabra to be seen in the houses of England he ringed his table with tall clansmen, each holding aloft a flaming pine-knot. Keppoch grinned at his guest and asked where, in England, France or Italy, was there a house with such candlesticks.

Edward Burt was a heavy-footed Englishman with no sense of humour but a rewarding taste for sociology. He went to the Highlands early in the eighteenth century to help Marshal Wade build his civilising roads, and he found the pride of the Highland chiefs quaintly archaic and faintly alarming. "I happened to be at the house of a certain chief, when the chieftain of another tribe came to make a visit. I told him I thought some of his people had not behaved toward me with that civility I expected of the clan. He started, clapped his hand to his broadsword and said, if I required it, he would send me two or three of their heads. I laughed, thinking it a joke, but the chief insisted he was a man of his word." Honour was honour, it clothed a man better than a fine jacket before the eyes of his neighbours, and the heads of three of his tribe were well-expended if they kept a chief decent. Burt must have talked the Highlander out of the bloody offer, for he does not say that he received the heads, and he was too meticulous a chronicler to have ignored the fact. He had a bumbling respect for this primitive code of honour, and for the simple and barbaric way in which the Highlanders gave their word on any sacred matter. "This oath they take upon a drawn dirk, which they kiss in a solemn manner, consenting if ever they prove perjured to be stabbed with the same weapon." And while, like a good, civilised Englishman, he deplored the mountain habit of cattle-lifting, "I cannot approve of the Lowland saying 'Show me a Highlander and I will show you a thief'. I do not remember that ever I lost anything among them but a pair of doe-skin gloves."

Another Englishman who was inclined to accept the Highlanders' claims to gentility was Daniel Defoe. "We see every day the gentlemen born here: such as the Mackenzies, McLeans, Dundonalds, Gordons, Mackays, and others who are named among the clans as if they were *Barbarians*, appear at Court and in our Camps and Armies, as polite and as finished gentlemen as any from other countries, or even among our own, and if I should say, outdoing our own in many things, especially in arms and gallantry as well as abroad as at home."

Any Mackenzie or Mackay would have agreed that Defoe was giving them no more than their due.

Edward Burt studied the clans more closely than Defoe, and saw more of the common people among them, and in all that he wrote of them there is curiosity and distaste, a wonder that such a society should exist on one island with men as civilised and as humane as Edward Burt. He never fully understood the peculiar relationship that existed between chief and tribesman. "The ordinary Highlanders esteem it the most sublime degree of virtue to love their chief and pay him a blind obedience although it be in opposition to the government, the laws of the kingdom, or even the law of God. He is their idol; and as they profess to know no king but him (I was going further) so will they say they ought to do whatever he commands."

On the other hand, the love and veneration of his clan was sometimes a trial to the chief, since he was expected to behave at all times with superior courage and superlative hardihood. Burt tells a story of a chief who was once taking his men over the hills in a winter foray against another clan. The raiders sheltered for the night in a high corrie, and when the chief rolled snow into a ball, placing it beneath his head for a pillow, his followers looked sourly at him and murmured among themselves, "Now we despair of victory, since our leader has become so effeminate he cannot sleep without a pillow."

Burt also left on record the picture of a Highland chief making a peaceful journey abroad from his glens, a proud strutting fellow with his wealth and honour in his tail. The tail was a raggle-taggle of clansmen, each as prickly proud as the man at their head. First the chief's henchman, his immediate bodyguard and his foster-brother, joined to him by the mystic union of one woman's breast-milk. Next came the Bard, a man with his own peculiar pride and honour, since on his skill and invention rested the chief's only hope for immortality. Bardship was hereditary, and carried with it a grant of land. The Highlands had no written history, and a man's reputation and memory might mount or fall on the tongue of the Bard. The songster of the clan was rarely a warrior, the fellow could not have time for the broadsword and the epic poem at one moment. He sat on a hillock when the clan went into its charge, noting individual valour, and keeping a particular and critical eye on the chief and his family. He was also the clan's principal genealogist, and if set to it could outmatch the Book of Genesis. All clansmen had this taste for naming the begotten of those who were begat. "They have a pride in their family," said Burt with wonder, "almost everyone is a genealogist."

Behind the Bard came the Piper, ready to fill his bag and finger his chanter at a nod from the chief. He too was a gentleman among gentlemen, who held his post from his father and who came from a long line of pipers. His name could sometimes live longer than the chief he served. The greatest of all pipers in all the Highlands were the MacCrimmons, who could make men weep or fight like the gods just by an inflated bag and a flute of bone.

The piper sat on no hill when the clan was for the onslaught, but marched behind the chief with the drones spread, and his wild music calling up the rant and the red reminders of past valour.

Fourth in the tail was the Bladier, the chief's spokesman, a silver-voiced man of debate and argument, who knew each precedent in every quarrel, and every promise in each dispute, and who took from the chief's shoulders the arduous responsibility of compliment and enquiry before the claret was poured and the board cleared. And behind these four was a gillie to carry the chief's broadsword and buckler, another to carry him over fords if his brogues were new and his hose of silk, a third to take his bridle on rough hill-paths, and yet another to carry his baggage. To some chiefs even this wild tail would not be enough to impress his neighbours with his importance. Behind might come a dozen swordsmen, axemen, bowmen or musketmen, in kilt, plaid and naked thighs. And whomsoever the chief visited would house, bed and feed this wild and touchy tail without protest, knowing that next time it would be his turn.

To Englishmen unfortunate enough to find themselves abroad in the Highlands, or to Lowlanders confronted on the Glasgow cobbles by a Highlandman, the most savage and outlandish thing about the hillmen was their dress. Burt attempted a description of it, stepping none too certainly across the stones of objective reporting and disgust.

"The common habit of the Highlander is far from being acceptable to the eye. With them a small part of the plaid, which is not so large as the former, is set in folds and girt round the waist to make of it a short petticoat that reaches halfway down the thigh, the rest is brought over the shoulders and fastened before, below the neck often with a fork, and sometimes with a bodkin or sharpened piece of stick, so that they make pretty nearly the appearance of the poor women in London when they bring their gowns over their heads to shelter themselves from the rain. This dress is called the quelt, and for the most part they wear the petticoat so very short that in a windy day, going up a hill, or stooping, the indecency of it is plainly discovered."

He illustrated what he meant with a story of a Lowland lady

of his acquaintance who had followed a Highland gillie up a hill in a strong wind.

The long plaid, which could be belted into a kilt and draped over the shoulders in a shawl, was the poor Highlandman's only dress. Elaborations were for his betters, and when gentlemen of high degree dressed themselves in splendour it was with a savage and vivid magnificence. A chief, since he preferred to ride a shelty rather than walk, wore trews of skin-tight tartan and not the kilt. His hair was tied back with a ribbon, and powdered if he had acquired the fashion abroad. His bonnet was trimmed with the eagle-feather that marked his rank, and he wore a tartan jacket and a tartan waistcoat, a tartan plaid that fell from the silver and cairngorm brooch on his left shoulder. If he chose to wear the kilt and not trews, a silver and leather sporran hung from his waist, and his calves were covered to the knee with hose of tartan fret. Tartan from shoulder to brogues, plaid, kilt and stockings often of a different sett, so that his clothes burned and glowed with green and yellow, blue and scarlet.

He armed himself with claw-handled steel pistols, known as Highland dags, two of them dangling from his belt. His round, bull-hide target was studded with silver bosses, and was frequently mounted with a steel spike twelve inches long. On one hip he carried a basket-hilted broadsword, double-edged, a yard long, and two inches wide. On the other he wore his dirk, its haft richly-wrought with silver, its scabbard pouched for knife and fork. Thrust into the top of his hose on one calf was a tiny black knife. And thus he stood in magnificence, a savage man who might speak French and Latin, who could distinguish between a good claret and a bad, who believed in the blood feud and the Holy Trinity, who would bargain like an Edinburgh chandler to secure a profitable marriage for his daughter, who could sell his tenants to the plantations but who would touch his sword at the slightest reflection on his honour. A man of wild and ridiculous poetry, harsh and remorseless principle, and a man who was, by 1746, an uncomfortable anachronism.

"They walk nimbly," said Burt, "with a kind of stateliness in the midst of their poverty." And it was the wretched and squalid poverty of the Highlands that most impressed visitors from the south. Where villages existed they were nothing like the aged stone and orderly thatch of England. They were, to Burt, like so many heaps of mud when seen from a distance down the glen, mean cottages of sod and heather and stone, each consisting of one room only, divided by a wicker curtain. In the middle of this room a peat-fire smoked beneath an iron cooking-pot. About the fire and the pot the inhabitants crouched listlessly during the winter nights.

"They have no diversions to amuse them, but sit brooding in the smoke of their fire till their legs and thighs are scorched to an extraordinary degree. To supply want of candles they provide themselves with a quantity of sticks of fir, the most resinous being lightened and laid on stones."

As in any tribal society, the women did most of the work. The men were indolent, according to Burt, and sat by their fires, talking of past forays, creating from the smoke the godlike images of their inspiring ancestors. The author of *An Enquiry into the Causes that facilitate the Use and Progress of Rebellions in Scotland* thought that he had found one cause in the fact that half the Highlandmen were without work of any kind, that is, what an Englishman would regard as work. "Many," he said, "are supported by the bounty of their acquaintances or friends and relations, others get their living by levying blackmail and the rest by stealing." The blackmail was the old Scots tradition of demanding "mail", or tribute, at the point of a sword. Lowland farmers living on the edge of the Highlands paid it hopefully, if not graciously, in return for the safety of their cattle.

A community that scraped the barest living from the hard hills lived a pendulum existence between semi-starvation and gluttonous feasts. On the braes about and above a Highland village grazed great herds of black cattle, tiny, shaggy ponies belonging to the tacksmen. Wooden ploughs broke bitter furrows across the stony earth, in which the people grew their corn. When times were bad, when food was scarce, they bled their cattle at the throat, and mixed the blood with oatmeal into little cakes that could be fried. For all but the sons of chiefs and prosperous tacksmen there was no schooling, nor did the people need any. In their pipes, their songs and bardic legends, they had a hard and relevant culture that matched and explained their life to them. Their Irish tongue sang sweetly on their lips, and spoke their emotions through its lilting cadences. God had found a way into the mountains long before Christianity came to the south, and had declared an amicable armistice with the Celtic mythology of giants, witches, precognition and stones that spoke with the voices of men.

As with all barbaric peoples, there was something in their savagery that stirred the imagination of more civilised man, and would leave him restless until he could take it and turn it into sentimental romance. This is what he did with the parti-coloured cloth which the Highlanders wore and which they called the *breacan*. Before the nineteenth century it is doubtful whether any one particular sett, one pattern, had a more than casual connection with one clan or family. This was the romantic nonsense to be invented later. A Highlander's name, his clan, his tribal allegiance were declared by the slogan he shouted in battle, by the sprig of plant he wore in his bonnet or tied to the staff of his standard. Each plant had its mystic meaning, was a charm against witch-craft and disaster, or had its origin in the sober utilities of life like the badge of the MacNeils. This was the sea-weed, and it was with sea-weed that the MacNeils manured the barren fields of their western islands.

Such a society, feudal and tribal, accepting the dynastic rule of absolute chieftainship, believing in the redressal of family wrongs, but, above all, such a military society was inevitably the one to which the exiled House of Stuart would appeal for support. The Stuarts had been Scottish kings before the Union of the King-doms, and although to most clansmen kings meant less than their chiefs, a Scottish king made more sense than a German. The Stuart concept of the rights and privileges of kingship differed in degree only from the Highland principle of clan leadership. So a clansman could, with less difficulty than a Suffolk farmer, sym-pathise with a young man who landed on the Inverness coast, asking help for the restoration of his rights.

There were other contributory factors. There was, of course, politics, and to many chiefs the Act of Union, which had joined

England and Scotland under one Parliament, was still a betrayal, though while the Parliament of Scotland sat in session they had shown little respect for it.

And there was religion, camp-follower in most wars. The Reformation and the joyless teaching of John Knox had touched the Highlands, Kirk and the Law walking hand in hand through some of the glens, in the Campbell country of Argyll for example. But most of the clans were tolerant Protestants or defiant Catholics, and the latter were bound to have sympathy for a Catholic prince come back from exile. Non-Jurancy was strong among the Protestant clans of the west, the Camerons and the Stewarts of Appin. They were a dissident sect, and their clergy had been ordained by the bishops who had refused to take the oath of allegiance to the new kings once the Stewarts were driven into exile, arguing that an oath to one was not transferable to another.

Religion was not an issue in the Highlands until the south made it so. There were Catholic clans with Protestant chiefs, Non-Jurant meeting-houses on the lands of the jurants. The Chisholms of Strathglass, the people of the Gordon country, the Macneills of Barra, the Macdonald men of Glengarry and Glencoe were Catholics, with the significance of the mass and confession laced tightly into their own peculiar notions of man and his purpose.

In 1745 the Catholic church was very busy in the Highlands. Fourteen years before, Hugh Macdonald of Morar, step-brother to the chief, had come from Rome as Vicar-Apostolic to the Highlands, dispatched thereto by the Pope and with His Holiness's particular blessing. He came with a little band of priests, all Highlandmen born of chief or tacksman. He came to open seminaries for the training of boys to the priesthood, to say mass in the ruined churches of Badenoch once more, and all this he organised from his island headquarters in Morar, now and then travelling about his scattered parish, disguised in plaid and bonnet. Catholics and non-jurors mixed with a tolerance that might have deeply disturbed His Holiness, but which certainly made Whig clans like the Campbells twitch nervously at the scent of idolatry and treason. For the suspicion of treason they had cause. Bishop Hugh welcomed Prince Charles when he landed, and, having found that the young man was determined to stay, blessed his standard for the battles to come.

Where there were deep glens, protected by the broadsword or the earth itself, Catholicism flourished. In Lochaber it was due to Father John Macdonald, known as *Maighstir Iain Mor*, a holy man whose ancestors had been warrior chiefs of Clanranald. He had been in Lochaber for a quarter of a century before the Prince arrived. In Strathglass, the Chisholm country, Father John Farquharson dressed in kilt and plaid for the common days of the week, but on Sundays he put on sacerdotals to celebrate mass in the old meeting-house at Balanahoun. The Government knew he was there and made some attempt to root him out, dispatching soldiers one day and catching him at the altar. But his congregation took arms against them, would have killed them and buried them beneath the floor of the church, had not Father John argued against it. The soldiers did not come again until after the 'Forty-five, and until then the Father went on celebrating the Mass and baptising the new-born of the Chisholms from a natural font in the rocks.

There were other priests: James Grant in Barra, Alexander Forrester of the Scots College in Rome who came to South Uist, Aeneas MacLachlan in Knoidart, and Alexander Cameron, Catholic brother to Protestant Lochiel, who came to Lochaber. The great Catholic centre was Scalan in Glenlivet, fifteen hundred feet above sea-level. If the waters of Glenlivet were later to give Scotland a fine whisky, in the eighteenth century it was the place from which it was hoped that the true faith might once more grow and flower. There, on the Crombie Burn, was a little seminary training a dozen or two dozen Highland boys for eventual graduation to Catholic colleges abroad. Several times before the Rebellion of 1745 soldiers came to the glen and burnt the seminary and the cottages, but each time Bishop Hugh's priests put stone upon stone again and continued with their work and their prayers, living a harsh and comfortless life in their house beside the burn.

When the Catholic prince landed with his seven followers, and told those chiefs who bluntly advised him to return home that he *had* come, the Catholic priests of the Catholic glens became his most enthusiastic recruiting sergeants. Father William Duthie, a one-time Episcopalian minister, but now Superior at Scalan Seminary, sent a message of joyous exhortation to all Catholics in the Highlands, urging them to join the Prince. Other priests set an example, belting on broadsword and dirk and joining the clan regiments as chaplains with the rank of captain. In Gordon country, other priests got into the saddle with pistol and riding boots, to trot with the tenantry of the Duke's lands. In Strathavon Father Grant and Father Tyrie cast lots between them, to see which might have the honour of going to war with their communicants, and which the disappointment of staying at home. Father Tyrie won, and went off to march to Derby and to stand in line with sword and target when it all ended at Culloden.

The whole melancholy affair was a confusion of politics and religion, tribal loyalties and clan jealousies. Brother fought brother because of disagreements over the Act of Union, and co-religionists took arms in opposition because of their preference for this king or that. The English were involved as the principal military force and the Parliament of the kingdom because it represented the Law in challenge, but the Scots engaged themselves in a bitter civil war over a young man whose grandfather had been king sixty years before. Honour, even Highland honour was capable of cunning interpretation as fathers stayed at home and sent one son to fight for King George and the other for King James, thereby securing their estates whatever happened. Few were like Donald Cameron, younger of Lochiel, who committed everything he had, clan, family and property, to the cause of the red-haired young man whom he had earlier advised against coming.

When that young man landed, eight months before Culloden, the chiefs, for all their Jacobitism, non-juracy, or Catholicism, were reluctant to come out. It was nearly thirty years since the clans had last taken to the heather. Old issues had become mildewed, old passions tired, and the hope for armed support in England was something a madman would dream. The boy's army, when he finally gathered one, was never more than a few thousand of those thirty thousand clansmen of the mountains, drawn there by chiefs charmed by his nature or committed by rash promises. The other chiefs remained in their hills, fingers still smarting from the last burning they had received in the Stuart cause, or else they allowed a few of their clan to go out as a gamble, while blandly disowning the rascals to the Government.

And the clansmen: they came out when told, most of them, pulling broadswords from the sod where they had been hidden since the Disarming Acts that followed the last rebellion. They dug up Lochaber axes and steel dirks. They primed muskets and dags, and told their wives to watch the winter fields. They came out through no particular attachment to the Stuart cause, and their approval of the Prince, when he put himself ahead of them in trews and plaid, was personal rather than political. They came out because their chiefs called them. And this not always willingly. Romance, lusting after fact, conceived a picture of the Highlandmen springing to arms like a stag from the heather as soon as they heard that the bonnie laddie had come to their hills. Lowland ladies, writing sad songs thirty years later when the bonnie laddie was a middle-aged man in drink, were responsible. The number of clansmen who came out reluctantly and under duress was probably a minority, but it was sizeable enough to show both the character of Highland society and the sad waste of it. When the Government had thousands of Jacobite prisoners in gaols from Perth to Carlisle, from York to London, many of them advanced, as a plea for mercy, proof that they had been forced into service by their chiefs. The plea was largely rejected, the Courts arguing that, so far as they could see, there had been nothing to stop a man running away when once forced out. This argument, reasonable enough to an Englishman, was ridiculous within the context of Highland society, for where could a clansman run once he had disobeyed his chief?

The common persuasion used to bring a man out with the clan regiment was the threat to burn his roof over his head, a threat that was put into effect where necessary. This made, for many of them, the Rebellion a choice between two evils. Along Speyside able-bodied men were told that their cottages would be burned if they did not answer young Lord Lewis Gordon's demand for recruits. If they did answer, then their houses were most certainly burned when the Duke of Cumberland's soldiers passed that way.

After the Rebellion was over, the Reverend James Robertson wrote a humble petition, asking mercy for fifteen men of his parish at Lochbroom then lying in prison at Tilbury on the Thames. He said that, in March, Macdonald of Keppoch had come by, snatching men from their beds and dragging them from their ploughs. "One I did myself see overtaken, and when he declared he would rather die than be carried to rebellion, was knocked to the ground by the butt of a musket and carried away all blood."

Another minister, Mr. Gordon of Alvie, declared in petition that of forty-three of his parishioners who went away to join the Prince three only could be said to have volunteered for the adventure. The rest had been forced by the burning of their houses, by the slaughtering of their cattle, and by the breaking of their heads.

Donald Cameron, the "gentle Lochiel" of Jacobite romance, was indeed a man of honour and sensibility, but he was also a Highland chief. In August of 1745, when Lochiel had committed his clan to the Prince, several tacksmen of his estates went from house to house through Rannoch "to intimate to all the Camerons that if they did not forthwith go with them they would instantly proceed to burn all their houses and hough their cattle; whereupon they carried off all the Rannoch men, about one hundred, mostly of the name of Cameron".

Some weeks later, according to the deposition made by a clansman before the authorities in Edinburgh, Lochiel's brother, Dr. Archibald Cameron, passed through Cameron country "declaring to all men of the chief's name that if they did not come off directly he would burn their houses and cut them in pieces". Before the same authorities and on the same day another Cameron clansman declared that he had been forced out in this way, and that when he and some of his comrades had tried to escape service with the Prince "Lochiel beat them severely with his whip". Yet a third Cameron deposed that he had consented to go out only after four of his cows had been killed by Dr. Cameron.

The chiefs and the tacksmen who beat up their following in this manner saw no wrong in it, for within the context of the clan it was the reluctant Cameron who sinned and betrayed his ancestors.

A chief's declaration of war, agreed to by his elders and his tacks-men, was binding on all the clan, and disobedience was dishonour. But the fact of such frequent enforcement marks the common suffering, and the common indifference to the political issues, between the pressed clansman and the pressed soldier of King George.

But forced or not, the clansmen who stood on Drummossie Moor that Wednesday were on the last defensive, standing in arms for a society that was now as obsolescent as the cause of the young man who had brought them there. Their furious valour, the wild charge which was their only battle tactic, had taken the Jacobite cause down into the heart of England before the impetus died, and its leaders found themselves like dream-walkers awoken on a window-sill. Through the winter the retreat had continued, back to the hills. A battle flung and won against Hawley's unsuspecting camp at Falkirk, and then the retreat northwards again, with the young Duke of Cumberland in pursuit. Northwards, and still northwards, with winter passing into spring, and then a final decision in a final battle.

'*The ground on which they stood was plain*'

FOR TWO MONTHS the Rebels had been at Inverness. They had retreated thither from Aberdeen, through a storm of snow that all but froze the enthusiasm of young John Daniel, a volunteer captain from Lancashire. Three hundred carts and tumbrils tangled the march of the clans, or were abandoned in the storm. "Here men were covered with icicles hanging at their eyebrows and beard," remembered Daniel, "and an entire coldness seized all their limbs. . . . And very easy it now was to lose our companions, the road being bad and leading over the snow." But the retreat continued, until the harsh weather halted Cumberland's pursuit. The Rebels laid siege to Fort Augustus and Fort William, and harried Government detachments in the glens, capturing thirty small posts in one day on the braes of Atholl. They chased the Earl of Loudoun's Highlanders far north across the Dornoch Firth, and they held the coast southward toward Aberdeen. All this, for a while, took away the harshness of the fact that many of the Macdonalds were deserting. They were mostly Glengarry men, sullen and dispirited still by the shooting of Angus Og, their chief's son. He had been accidentally killed after Falkirk when one of the Macdonalds of Clanranald was clearing his musket, and although the Glengarry men had demanded, and received, a life for a life according to custom, they had lost their enthusiasm for the Rebellion. Nor were Clanranald's people happy about the summary execution of one of their clan, and some of them, too, were slipping away home to Benbecula.

So, by Inverness and the mouth of the Great Glen, the Highland army waited until, on April 14, the Duke of Cumberland came to Nairn. The white sail-cloth of his tents was spread about Balblair, his transports were anchored in the firth, the vedettes of his Horse could be seen on the heather, and the sound of his drums came down on the wind.

At dawn on April 15, when the chanters sounded the gathering, the Jacobite Army awoke in its camp among the parks and policies of the Lord President's fine house at Culloden. At six o'clock the Highlanders marched up the braeside to the south, and took their position in line of battle across Drummossie Moor, their faces to the north-east and their eyes searching the troubled roll of heather for the first sight of Cumberland's infantry.

Nobody had thought fit to consult the Lieutenant-General about this choice of battlefield. Angered though he may have been by this, Lord George Murray could not complain that it was unexpected. Son to the Duke of Atholl, and aged 46, he was a good soldier and deserved his general's commission, but the Rebels were led less by good generals than by a wilful Stuart. As his adventure moved toward its sunset, this Prince fell more and more under the influence of Irish admirers like the aged tutor Thomas Sheridan, whose last experience of battle had been at the Boyne, fifty-six years before. The man who decided that a fight could be made on Drummossie Moor was another Irishman, the Quartermaster General John William O'Sullivan. When upset, he would retire to bed for frequent bleedings, and so, in Lord George's opinion, he was an idiot who fought wars in his nightcap.

"I did not like the ground," said Lord George, recalling the moor afterwards. "It was certainly not proper for High-landers. . . ." He sent officers to reconnoitre more favourable land across the water, but Mr. O'Sullivan had gone to Inverness, or to bed, and saw nothing to change his mind. The decision was made to fight on the moor that Tuesday, the Prince agreed, and Lord George may have thought the battle lost thereby. He asked only that he retain command of his Athollmen and the right of the Army. It was to be Prince Charles's battle, the first in which he had commanded during the Rebellion. He was a young man, a few months older than his cousin Cumberland at Nairn, a boy living a desperate and exciting adventure, a boy more easily swayed by Irish flattery than the hard reason of his Lieutenant-General.

There was no battle on Tuesday. Cumberland remained at Nairn, and his soldiers drank brandy and ate cheese in honour of his birthday. The Rebels waited in line until eleven o'clock, when the Prince told them that they might refresh themselves with sleep "or otherwise". If, by this, he meant food, the advice was bitter. The meal, which the clans were accepting in lieu of pay, was still at Inverness, nobody having assembled the carts to carry it six miles to Culloden. This nobody was John Hay, the Prince's secretary, a weak and silly man who answered Lord George's angry protests with hysterical cries of "Everything will be got!"

But nothing was got, and the clans went hungry while their chiefs, their generals, their Prince and his Irishmen argued what should be done next. Lord George, when asked, again declared the unsuitability of Drummossie Moor. Across the Nairn Water, he said, the ground was rugged, mossy and soft where no Horse could be used, and everyone knew how little the Highlanders liked cavalry. The moor on which the clans now stood was an ideal field for regular troops like Cumberland's, exchanging and receiving fire until the moment arrived for an orderly advance with the bayonet; but it was not a field for the clans. Their warfare was the warfare of mountain people, the wild burst from cover or night, the yelling rush down the braeside on a stumbling enemy. They had no discipline and no restraint to wait as they were waiting, on a flat plateau, with bellies empty, broadswords bending beneath the weight of tired bodies. But the Prince would not listen to counsels of retreat. The night before he had spent with his Irish and favourite officers, his eyes bright with excitement and his conversation foolishly wasted "in boasting unworthy of a Prince", according to one who heard him. He was, in those last hours he had an army, very much a Stuart.

Throughout the 15th nothing was certain, and to fret Lord George's patience still further was the knowledge that the army was wretchedly under-strength. Some of the clans were away in the hills, on raids, or on pressing personal business in their home-glens where the Campbells were loose. Keppoch's Macdonalds had not come in, nor recruits to fill the gaps in Glengarry's regiment. The MacGregors were to the north in Cromarty, and although the Macphersons and most of the Frasers were marching on Inverness it was not thought that they would arrive in time. Lord George went to the Prince, and told him and the assembled

officers, that he was now willing to lead an attack on the camp at
Nairn such as Charles had previously proposed. But he suggested
a night attack, not the onslaught at dawn the Prince desired. The
clans, he said, should march at dusk that day, pass round the
town of Nairn and fall upon the soldiers in the darkness, and
while they were drunk, as drunk they surely would be after
celebrating their commander's birthday.

The plan was accepted. Lord George would give no orders
when asked for them by O'Sullivan, saying every man of the
clans knew what to do, and perhaps privately thinking that the
less the Irish knew, the better for all.

From the beginning it went wrong. By seven o'clock in the
evening many Highlanders had drifted away from the field at
Drummossie, straggling back to Inverness, declaring that they
were starving, and declaring further to the horsemen who
galloped after them that, though they might be shot for it, they
were not returning until they got meat. A third of the Army
straggled away in this manner. The ration for the day had been a
biscuit to a man, and some had not received even this. Thus it was
nearly eight o'clock when the Army moved eastward toward Nairn,
with Lord George in the van and in a black and bitter mood that
was not lifted even when the Prince put an arm about his neck and
cried "This will crown all! You'll restore the King by it! You'll have
all the honour and glory of it! It is your work . . . !" And so on.

Lord George took off his bonnet, bowed coldly, and said
nothing. The march went on. In the van, with the Camerons,
Appin Stewarts and Athollmen, and guided by officers of Clan
Mackintosh whose country this was, the Lieutenant-General kept a
good pace. But behind him the rest of the weary Army under an
irresolute Prince dragged its feet and broke away to be lost in the
foggy darkness. Men who made the night-march remembered
it more vividly than the battle of the next day. They remembered
the trackless moor, the sudden quagmires, the earth that moved
and the horses that squealed as the earth moved. Exhausted
men flung themselves on the heather and swore that they would go
no further. "But, oh for Madness!" wrote John Daniel, remembering it too, "what can one think, or what can one say here!"

When a halt was made O'Sullivan and Lord George argued

bitterly, each making stilted references to honour and loyalty, until a chieftain spoke up out of the confusion and said what was in all the Highlanders' minds, that if they were to be killed would it not be better in daylight when a man might see how his neighbours behaved? And so the surprise march went on, with more halts and with more bitter quarrels, until finally came first light and Nairn not reached. From the distance ahead rolled the drums, the battalion drums beating the General call by the tents at Balblair. Attack was impossible.

In the dawn the Highlanders went back to Culloden House, this time taking the road that skirts Drummossie Moor to the north. Charles, thinking himself betrayed by Lord George and by Cameron of Lochiel, who had decided on retreat, rode among his men crying "March back! We shall meet them later and behave like brave fellows." But the brave fellows had been marching to and from elusive battle for nearly two days now, with nothing more than a biscuit and water to give them strength. They had an hour, two hours of sleep in the policies about Culloden House, and then once more the pipes sounded to drag them up into line of battle on Drummossie Moor. For some, a thousand or more, even the rant of their clan, squeezed from the bag, was not enough to waken them. They slept where they had fallen, in the ditches and by the walls, in the open fields, and they were to sleep through the battle that followed, and were to sleep until well past noon when Cumberland's dragoons came down upon them.

But at seven o'clock on the morning of Wednesday most of the clansmen were back on the moor in roughly the same position they had taken twenty-four hours earlier. They were bitter, confused and angry. Some broke from the ranks and went foraging, seeking meal in the poor cottages above Nairn Water, cattle that they could slaughter. Below, in Culloden House, senior officers drank the last of the sixty hogsheads of claret that had been found in the Lord President's cellars. Duncan Forbes' steward, who had prepared a roast side of lamb and two fowls, told the Prince that they would be on the table soon. "I cannot eat," he said, "while my men are starving."

He rode to the moor on a grey gelding and at the head of the Camerons. His face was pale. He had had no sleep, having spent the two hours after the return from Nairn by riding into Inverness in an effort to bring up meal for his army. There was a cockaded bonnet on his red hair, and a light broadsword at his hip, and his body was slender in tartan jacket and buff waistcoat. "Go on, my lads," he cried in his lisping Italian voice. "The day will be ours!"

The clans raised their bonnets to him, where they had the will and the energy. The Macdonalds—Glengarry's, Clan-ranald's, Glencoe's, and Keppoch's who had come in now— grumbled and muttered as they pulled their way upward toward the left of the line. The right, they believed, was theirs by tradition, and had been since Bannockburn, and they thought little of this proposal to place them elsewhere. Enough Macdonald officers thought this serious enough to report it to the Prince, and beg him to alter the line and put their clansmen where they should be. In his turn he had pleaded with them to bear with him, for he had already granted the honour to Lord George Murray's Athollmen.

So there was no good humour anywhere among the fatigued and desperate men. Among the senior officers there was a growing feeling that it was madness to stand and fight at all. Lord George was sunk in pessimistic resignation, but the Prince continued to behave prettily, riding among his men and calling upon them to be brave and strong for the King his father. Taking a sword from one of them he tested its edge, grimacing and saying merrily, "I'll answer this will cut off some heads and arms to-day!" He seemed certain of victory. He seemed to have forgotten the night before when the Marquis D'Eguilles, France's elegant ambassador to the Rebels, had gone down on his knees to implore the Prince not to risk a battle.

At eleven o'clock some men of Clan Mackintosh and of Lochiel, posted in advance of the Jacobite Army, first saw the coming of the Royal soldiers and first heard their drums. Over the curve of the moor and through the sleet marched three columns that halted suddenly, and thickened into a red wall. The scarlet and white, and the silk of the standards, glowed against the dark sky. The Mackintosh men and the Camerons waited, and when the wall came on they slipped back to the Highland line, where the clansmen had been waiting for nearly five hours. Once more the Rebel pipes sounded, and the drums beat, the officers called. Men who were asleep where they stood, or who lay asleep in the ranks, were pulled to consciousness. They lifted their heads, and the bitter rain and hard sleet struck their faces. And they saw the enemy.

"We began to huzza and bravado them in their march upon us," said John Daniel. "But notwithstanding all our repeated shouts, we could not induce them to return one: on the contrary, they continued proceeding, like a deep and sullen river."

Riding with the baggage to the rear of Cumberland's Army was James Grainger, a surgeon's mate of Pulteney's regiment and a young poet with a taste for Latin verse. He heard the shout of the clans, and marked the answering silence of the Royal Foot. He stared forward at the enemy, over the bent shoulders and bayonets of the line, and because he had been in other battles, and had developed a critical eye for such things, he was pleased by what he saw. "The ground on which they stood," he wrote to his brother William, "was plain, and the field seemed adapted in every way to decide the fate of the Rebellion."

The ground on which they stood was five hundred feet above sea-level. Between the Moray Firth and the valley of the Nairn is a fold of land that stretches some twelve miles, south-west to north-east, in a descending gradient from Loch Ness to the town of Nairn. In April 1746, it was bleak and treeless, the land falling away to the south and the north, and a man standing there could feel himself suspended, with the sea behind him and the saucer-rim of the mountains before. This was the country of Clan Chattan, the Mackintoshes principally, and the few people who had built their sod-houses and dry-stone walls on its brown pelt were tacksmen or tenants of the Laird of Mackintosh at Moy Hall. One of these was a man called Macdonald, and his wife was making bread this Wednesday morning, hearing the pipes and the drums in the weather outside. The moor supported the sheep of the three parishes during the summer, but it was good for little else, except a battle. It was always windy up there, June or December, with nothing to break the breath of the North Sea as it passed through the throat of the Great Glen. On the slope to the north was Duncan Forbes's estate, its parks and fields stretching upwards from the quartz-stones on the firth shore to the heather below the moor. In the lee of Nairnside were a number of small stone buildings, the farms at Urchil, Leanach and Culwhiniac. Culwhiniac was the largest, and stood within a stone-walled enclosure, six or eight hundred yards in width, and near to a thousand in length from the River Nairn below to the moor above. It was on a curve of ground between the north wall of this enclosure and the furthest reach of the Lord President's estate that the two armies finally met.

Both had been edging toward the northern dyke at Culwhiniac, seeking to rest a flank upon its stones, or to secure it against the other. Most of the men, standing or marching across the moor, did not know that the enclosure was there. They saw what was to their front only. But the Athollmen knew, for it was on their right, and away on the Royal Army's left the men of Barrell's also knew. The grenadier company on the left flank of the "Old Tangereers" splashed and floundered and shivered in a stream of water that welled from the ground at the north-east corner of Culwhiniac, and ran idly along the foot of the wall. Whoever took the enclosure, and manned its northern wall to enfilade and flank, would win the battle, or so hindsight seems to argue. The Rebels made no serious attempt to take it, perhaps seeing it only as a welcome protection from the cavalry all Highlandmen feared. The fault was John William O'Sullivan's. In his double role as Adjutant-General and Quarter-Master, he was responsible for the order of battle, and he should at least have had that north wall pulled down, giving the right of the Army some room to manoeuvre. But frequent bleedings the day before had not cleared his wits.

Noon brought no lift in the dark clouds, and the sleet still fell on the faces of the clans.

"O, come here on flesh to feed!"

WILLIAM ROSE, who held a farm at Meikle Leanach, stood at his door that morning, looking through the mist and listening to the noise of the Rebel Army as it gathered once more upon the field. In later years he told his children and his grandchildren that some of the Jacobites sang as they waited. They were singing the words of the Twentieth Psalm: *Jehova hear thee in the day, when trouble He doth send.* . . . In the heather, along the northern slope, lay half a dozen schoolboys, playing truant from their tutor at Petty on the firth shore. They were the sons of chiefs and tacksmen, and they had come to watch their kinsmen in battle. Among them was Archibald Fraser, who was nine and a half years of age and the youngest son of Simon, Lord Lovat, chief of the Frasers. Archibald's brother, the Master of Lovat, was somewhere on the field with the clan, or marching to it with reinforcements. There was the son of Mackintosh of Farr, and there was Arthur, son to the Laird of Inshes. All night the boys had lain in their plaids, and heard the ring of weapons, the movement of feet, the cry of the parole *"King James!"* They saw the Rebel Army march out for its night attack on the camp at Nairn, and they watched its return at dawn. Then young James Mackintosh saw his father, Angus, pass by at the head of a company in the Clan Chattan regiment. He did not call out a greeting, nor rise from the heather, for he could not. The boy was fourteen only when he saw this, and he lived to be ninety, but he never forgot the look on the face of Angus Mackintosh of Farr because it was the last he ever saw of his father.

There were many boys upon the field, some standing in the clan regiments with their brothers and fathers and men of their name. They were, said an Englishman, "perfect hurd boys, without arms, stockings or shoes, about fourteen to sixteen years of age . . . ". There was William MacLean, who was fourteen, and who was one of those who had been forced into service from the parish of Lochbroom. There was Dougal M'Lea, sixteen, who stood with the Mackintoshes. And there was Alexander Mather, aged fourteen also, a baker's son from the Earl of Airlie's lands. At least one boy had been brought there that morning by a sudden impulse for adventure. Murdoch MacLeod, aged fifteen, was a pupil at the Grammar School in Inverness, but when the word spread that there was to be a battle he ran away. He armed himself with broadsword, dirk and pistol, taking them, perhaps from the sleeping men below the moor, and he walked down the line, seeking men of his name with whom he might stand.

Many people came to watch the battle, from Inverness and the country about. There were the women of the Clan Chattan regiment, gathered in tartan groups on the brae of Creagan Glas across the Nairn. There was Elizabeth, daughter of Duncan Campbell of Clunas. The man she hoped to marry, when the King enjoyed his own again, was MacGillivray of Dunmaglass, lieutenant-colonel of Clan Chattan. To the south-east of the moor was a ragged brood of beggars, men, women and children, corbie crows who would loot the dead whoever won, and while they waited they screamed and fought among themselves. Many people had come to watch the battle, ministers and merchants of Inverness, and some of them were to wish that their curiosity had not been so compelling.

According to its Muster-master, Patullo, there were less than five thousand men of the Rebel Army on the field. All were tired, hungry and dispirited. Since the retreat from Aberdeen they had also been mutinous, angered because they were being paid in meal and not in money. For many of them their homes were a mountain's width or a day's march away and they were sick with longing to be there. They can be divided, generally, into three classes. First, and largest, were those who had come out, or been forced out, under the clan system, and who were formed into clan regiments. Second were those liable to military service under the land tenure of their lairds, and the compulsion

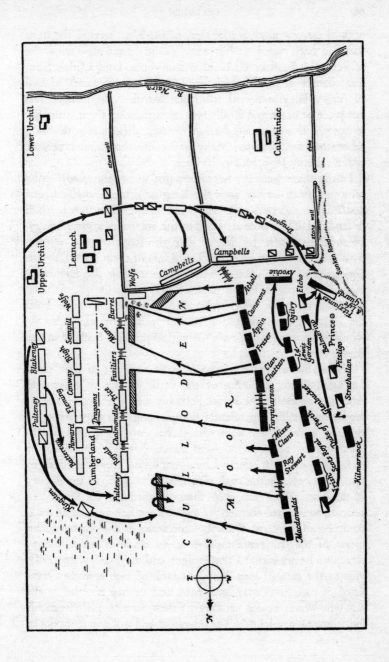

upon these was more feudal than tribal. They formed the units that had been raised on his family's land by the attainted Duke of Perth, by Lord Lewis Gordon and young Lord Ogilvy from the tenantry of their fathers, the Duke of Gordon and the Earl of Airlie. They were not tribesmen like the mountain people, but pride of name and family was strong among them, although it was not always strong enough to bring them out in rebellion when the laird ordered. Many had come there under protest, rather than see their roof-poles burn.

Finally there were the volunteers (for want of a word), exiles returning from service with the King of France, Lowland men and English deserters who owed no traditional service to chief or landlord. They were attracted to the Stuarts by sincere loyalty, by sudden impulse, by disgust with the Royal Army, or even by a drunken dream of adventure. Some of them served in clan regiments of their choice, with friends among the Highland-men. Some, the exiles, in units of their own. Others marched with the regiment which John Roy Stewart had raised from the Edinburgh wynds and Perthshire valleys by methods that would have excited the envy of any impressment officer in the Royal Navy.

"None but a mad fool would have fought that day," said old Lord Lovat, thinking of the battle before his execution. And mad or foolish the Prince probably was, as he rode his gelding along the lines, petulantly complaining that they were too slow in forming. By noon the Rebel Army stretched north-westward over the moor from the Culwhiniac enclosure, its front line—its only effective line—consisting almost entirely of clan regiments. Before each clan stood the chief, or the deputy of the chief. With him were his henchman and his Piper, and a small bodyguard formed by two of the best men from each company of the clan. With the companies in line, captained by cadets of the chieftain's family, or by chiefs of smaller septs, were two lieutenants and two ensigns, and they, too, were chief's sons or the sons of sons. The first rank of each company con-sisted of men who may have held land or had no land at all, but who were, in the geology of their society, placed among the strata of gentlemen. They were armed with long firelocks and steel dags, with broadsword, dirk and target. Behind them stood those with lesser claims to gentility, and behind again yet another rank, so that in some clans the ranks were six deep. In the rear of all stood the wild and bearded humblies, naked of thigh and chest, and scarcely armed at all. But these common men, too, disposed themselves by families, brothers and sons about the father, for it was in the tradition of their hills that the oldest and most respected should stand closest to the enemy, and that inspiration and courage should pass through father, brother, son, tenant and servant.

Orders issued by the Prince's command, two days before, demanded that "each indevidual in the Armie as well officer as souldier keeps their posts that shall be alotted to them, and if any man turn his back to run away the next behind such a man is to shoot him. No body on Pain of Death to Strip the Slain or Plunder till the Battle be over. The Highlanders all to be in kilts. . . ."

And in kilts they were, in the fret and the check, the burning scarlet or faded green; hose, plaid, kilt and jacket all a different sett. In their blue bonnets they wore the ancient badge of their clan, if there had been time to gather it from the country about. In their bonnets, too, they wore the white cockade of the Stuarts, a large knot of five bows in silk or linen, on which was printed a laurel wreath and the words *With Charles our brave and merciful P.R. we'll greatly fall or nobly save our country.* Cumberland's young aide, Joseph Yorke, picked such a cockade from the field afterwards, and sent it home as a souvenir for his father, the Lord Chancellor. If it was an example of them all, they had probably been stitched in hundreds by the sempstresses of Edinburgh, Glasgow and Manchester. The cockade and tartan sash, basket-hilted broadsword and spiked target, were the brave equipment carried by all Jacobite soldiers, Highland or not.

Lord George Murray commanded the right wing of the first line, the Athollmen, the Camerons. and the Stewarts of Appin. The men of Atholl had that place of honour which Lord George had secured for them at the expense of Macdonald enthusiasm, the extreme right of the line with their flank resting on the dry-stone wall of the Culwhiniac enclosure. They came from the glens and braes of Lord George's own country, and they must have been a sad worry to him, for they had taken more trouble to recruit and suffered more from desertion than any other unit. There were some five or six hundred of them from the small clans of Atholl, Robertsons of Struan, Menzies of Shian, Murrays, and maybe some MacGregors who were not away elsewhere with their chief Glengyle. They are a puzzle, so many melancholy and reluctant heroes who might have run understandably at the first volley firing, but who stayed and who charged with an extraordinary fury.

On their left stood the Camerons, Lochiel's men from Lochaber, perhaps seven hundred of them, although at this time and distance it is difficult to be sure, since nobody, not even Mr. Patullo, was keeping a correct tally on that hysterical morning. The Cameron gentility was at strength. Their chief, John, was not there, having surrendered the leadership of his clan to his son, Donald, the "gentle Lochiel". All Cameron gentlemen were brothers, sons or cousins, and made a military family of touchy sensibilities. Lochiel might have found his loyalties confusing this morning, had he not had a single-minded devotion to the Jacobite cause. Both his wife and mother were Campbells, and further down the line from his men stood the Mackintoshes, with whom the Camerons had been feuding and fighting for longer than either could remember. It was a matter of pride to the Camerons that their pibroch had been the first heard when the Prince set up his standard at Glenfinnan. That pibroch was sounding now in the sleet: *You sons of dogs, of dogs of the breed, O come, come here on flesh to feed!*

The Stewarts, on the Camerons' left, were Appin men from that sweet and green peninsula in Loch Linnhe to the west. Among them were some MacLarens, who were their ancient allies from Balquhidder. These Stewarts were gentle men, or were said to have been, but they had been drawn into the Rebellion as much by a bloody hatred of the Campbells as by their old attachment to the Kings of their name. Their chief was a child still, and at home in Appin, and the clan was led by his tutor, Charles Stewart of Ardshiel, a tall, pretty man with a great reputation as a swordsman. He was a great plotter, too, and had signed his name to a promise to come out long before the Prince left France. He had nearly three hundred men in his regiment at Culloden, a high proportion of them officers with claims to an acre or acres of land on the hills above Loch Linnhe and Loch Creran. And behind them stood the common men: McColls, Carmichaels, Livingstones and MacLeays. They wore a sprig of oak in their bonnets. Above them flapped and snapped their standard, the yellow saltire on a blue field, and their Piper played the pibroch that had been composed a hundred years before by the great Patrick Mor MacCrimmon.

The centre of the first Rebel line was commanded by Lord John Drummond, a "tall, jolly man of dark brown complexion, neither fat nor lean". In his command, standing to the left of the Appin men, was a battalion of Frasers, perhaps three hundred. They claimed to be Norman in origin, or at least their chief did, his name a derivation of the French for strawberry. Whatever cunning game of political dice Lord Lovat was playing, and would continue to play in an unsuccessful attempt to save his life, his Frasers were committed to the Rebellion, and he had sent his first son, the Master, to be their colonel. A high-spirited boy of nineteen, he was not on the field (or, if he arrived in time, his clan kept it a secret afterwards) and the Frasers were commanded by Charles Fraser, younger of Inverallochie. He held the rank of lieutenant-colonel as the nearest in blood to the chief, after Lovat's own family, and he was within a month of his twenty-first birthday, which he was not to reach.

By far the most restless of the front line under Lord John Drummond, and formed next to the Frasers, were the five hundred men of Clan Chattan who had not yet fought an action on the Prince's behalf. Clan Chattan, the clan of the cats, was an ancient confederation of many tribes holding land to the east of Loch Ness. On the moor to-day they were mainly Mackintoshes, MacGillivrays and MacBeans, Non-Jurant Protestants who had been raised by Lord George Murray's cousin Lady Mackintosh, the "Colonel Anne" of Moy Hall. Her husband had gone off to command a company of militia for King George, and no sooner had he gone than Colonel Anne thumbed her nose at him and raised his clan for the Prince. By persuasion or threat, a kiss or a frown, she had called up the men from the glens and given each a white cockade with her own hand. She was twenty years of age, and when she took her husband's men to the Prince she rode at their head, a man's blue bonnet on her hair, and her riding-habit of tartan. The lieutenant-colonel of Clan Chattan was Alexander MacGillivray of Dunmaglass, his home fifteen miles to the south-west of Drummossie Moor, below the sandstone knot of Garbhal Beg and Garbhal Mor. Where most Highlandmen were small, he was a giant, strong-limbed and able to swing a broadsword like a switch of oak. He was feminine in face, and one of his clansmen, remembering him long afterwards, said, "He was a clean, pretty man, he stood six feet two inches in his stocking soles, his hair was red and his skin was white." And the girl he proposed to marry was the daughter of Campbell of Clunas.

Because the moor was within a short walk of Clan Chattan's walled burial-fields, it was to be said afterwards that the Mackintoshes, MacGillivrays and MacBeans were "much obliged to the soldiers, for by their means many of them died on a spot nearer by one half to the usual place of their burying than if they had expired in the arms of their wives".

Leftward of Colonel Anne's men, and separated from them by four ineffectual and ill-manned cannon of uncertain calibre, there were mixed clan units, the exact composition of which cannot be determined now. There were some Farquharsons of Monaltrie, and some of Balmoral, although because they, too, were of the great cat confederation they may have fought with Dunmaglass' command. Their chief, Finla, was a mental defective, and at home in his house and his simple dreams, and the clan was led by Farquharson of Balmoral, his uncle, and by the yellow-haired Francis Farquharson of Monaltrie. The Farquharsons were proud, their name meant *the dear ones*, and they did not argue with the description.

There may have been some MacLeods among the mixed clans, but it is also said that those who were at Culloden, and not at home with their shuffling Laird, had been used to fill the deserted ranks of Glengarry's Regiment, among Clan Donald on the left of the line. Certainly there were Grants with Glengarry's

Regiment, from the Jacobite lands of Glenmoriston and Glen Urquhart, though their supreme chief, the Laird of Grant, was a Whig and would take a mean revenge upon them very soon. Young Grant of Glenmoriston had brought his clansmen to the Prince early in the Rebellion, and when reproached for entering the Royal presence dirty and unshaven had answered proudly, "It's not beardless boys will do Your Highness' turn!"

The MacLachlans and the MacLeans formed one regiment to-day, though they had served as two until now. Old Lachlan MacLachlan, whose son was the Prince's aide, came from a family that had held land in Argyll for over five centuries, and he could even produce a piece of mellowed parchment to prove it. He brought one hundred and eighty men of his clan into the Rebellion as soon as it began, and he had as many with him to-day on Drummossie Moor. Charles MacLean of Drimnin was the lieutenant-colonel of the united regiment, and his sons served as his captains. It was said of him, too, that "he came from Morven with nine score MacLeans to the rebellion, of whom returned but thirty-eight". Drimnin, who had served with the Royal Navy for some time, was a kind and generous man, but he had a hot temper where his honour was concerned, and it once caused him to strike the Laird of MacLeod across the face in an Edinburgh street, and once to thrash a schoolmaster for impudence (so he thought). All the MacLeans, hearing the pibroch of the Argyll and Breadalbane Campbells across the moor, had a particular and personal interest in the battle, regardless of whom it made King. While they had been away from Morven and Ardgour, and from their lonely homes on the Isle of Mull, the Campbells had come down on their glens, burning houses and stripping women of their clothing, driving away cattle or slaughtering them in the byres.

John Roy Stewart's Edinburgh Regiment stood by the MacLeans. He was a man to inspire Robert Louis Stevenson, an adventurer, braggart and plotter, good soldier and bonny fighter. His Jacobitism, which had led him in and out of treason plots, was heavily larded with the ancient hatreds of his clan. Skulking in the hills he once wrote a parody of the Twenty-third Psalm: *The Lord is my target, I will be stout with dirk and trusty blade; though Campbells come in flocks about, I will not be afraid.* He was forty-six years of age at Culloden, and in his time had been many things. He once had served King George as a lieutenant of the Scots Greys, but, when he did not get the commission he desired in the Black Watch, he transferred his military talents to King Louis and bravely fought the English at Fontenoy. The regiment he raised for the Prince came mostly from the Edinburgh slums, from romantic apprentices caught up by his drums, from men he had impressed in Perthshire, and from men who had deserted from the Royal Army. The regiment was the only non-clan formation in the first line of the Rebel Army. There had once been five hundred of them, but two hundred only were on the moor.

There were not many Chisholms at Culloden, less than a hundred probably, and, so far as one can be certain about anything in the battle that day, they took a position to the left of the Edinburgh Regiment. They were Catholics, of course, from Strathglass, and their priest was with them, in kilt and plaid at the head of a company, his hand in the basket-hilt of a broadsword. MacIan, chief of the Chisholms, was too old, or much too circumspect to be with his people. His family was divided cannily between both sides, so that whatever happened his land and title would not become forfeit. Two of his five sons, John and James, were officers under Cumberland, standing with the Royal Scots on the right of the line. The youngest son, a boy called Roderick Og, led the clan for the Prince, with six hundred yards of heather between him and his brothers. Ian Beg, Piper to the Chisholms, stood behind the young colonel, carrying the tribe's legendary Black Chanter. It was known as *The Maiden of the Sandal*, brought from Rome by a chief, and bound with hoops of silver by successive chiefs. It was supposed by all, by all Chisholms at least, to have wondrous powers. If a member of the chief's family was about to die, no man, not even a MacCrimmon could finger a note from it. It should have been silent this morning.

The left wing of the Rebel Army, all Macdonald regiments in the front line, was commanded by Lord James Drummond, styled Duke of Perth. He was a sickly man, having been crushed by a barrel when he was a child, but he was brave and resolute, and at this moment very worried about his Macdonalds. They were three regiments, Clanranald's, Keppoch's, and Glengarry's, perhaps a thousand men in all, though they might well have been less, for many had drifted away in hunger or in anger or in bitter exhaustion. Their surly complaint was the position in which they found themselves. When Angus Og, father of the Lord of the Isles, gave Robert the Bruce sanctuary, the King had promised that from thenceforward the Macdonalds would stand on the right of the line in battles fought by him or for his descendants. Admittedly the Macdonalds had yielded this honour once or twice over the years (to the MacLeans at the battle of Harlaw, for example), but it had been an act of courtesy, and when the issue had been put to them by a Highland gentleman who had the tongue for it. No gentleman, Highland or otherwise, had asked their permission to-day.

The Duke of Perth stood before them, his back to the enemy and his bonnet taken from his head. He called out to them as loudly as his weak lungs could manage. He said, "If you fight with your usual bravery you will make the left wing a right wing!" There is no indication that they accepted this double-talk, and, in any case, an honour was an honour and should not be turned upon its head to suit another man's pleasure. Nor, perhaps, were they moved by Perth's promise that if they did well to-day he would "ever afterwards assume the honourable name of Macdonald".

Clan Donald was the largest of all the Highland clans. The lands filled with people of its name and loyalty, ruled by its chiefs and sub-chiefs, stretched down the west from Lewis to the Mull of Kintyre. The Isles, and the blue water between, the sea-lochs and the wide glens that broke from them, were Macdonald. Their greatest chief had been Lord of the Isles, descended from Conn of the Hundred Battles, and in their dreams the Macdonalds saw their ancestors as wondrous figures cast in iron, bronze and gold. Their pipe-music sang of more battles, laments, salutes and gatherings than that of any other clan. There were a hundred or more septs within the tribe, and the chief of each, though he be small of land and rent-roll like MacIan

of Glencoe, was as proud as if he commanded the hundred white
sails of the Lord of the Isles. They had blood-feuds, active or
passive, with every tribe that bordered their country, and, when
these failed to be of sufficient entertainment, they brawled just
as heartily among themselves. Against the Campbells, of course,
they had a long-standing grudge, which the chiefs of Argyll
and Breadalbane had slily neutralised by marrying their daughters, sisters, nieces and kinswomen to as many Macdonalds as
possible.

The regiment of Clanranald had been the first of the clans to
come out when the Prince landed. Three companies of it had
stood on the shores of Loch Shiel when the Stuart banner first
went up in the wind. Its colonel was Ranald, the hot-headed
son of its chief, who had said that he was prepared to advance
on London even though the army consisted of himself and the
Prince only. For his major he had Alexander Macdonald of
Glenaladale, and his captains, lieutenants and ensigns were all
his kinsmen. One of them was Charles Macdonald of Drimin-
darach, chief of one hundred and fifty men, a mighty man who
had broken down the gates of Carlisle with a sledge-hammer
some months before. His reward for this had been the right to
half an hour's plunder in the town, but he was a modest man
and contented himself with two gold candlesticks only.

Keppoch's regiment was commanded by the chief, he of the
human candelabra and the rent-roll of five hundred fighting-
men. But there were only two hundred of them with him to-day.
He was an old man, as ages were marked in those days. He was
a matriculated student of the University of Glasgow, he had
fought in the Rebellion of 1715, and he had served the King of
France. His brothers, sons and bastard were with him, and
at home in Keppoch, that week, his lady had just presented
him with yet another new-born. Keppoch did not wish to
fight to-day, although his objection had nothing to do with
where he thought a Macdonald should stand in the line. He did
not like the field and had argued against it, sharing Lord George's
opinion that there was better ground for the clans across the
Nairn Water.

Glengarry's Regiment were Macdonells, but the spelling is

unimportant, they were all Clan Donald. There were five hundred of them, and might have been more but for those desertions. The chief, John Macdonell, had taken no part in the Rebellion, no active party anyway. His sons, by his first and second wives, led his men, and when Angus Og fell by a Clanranald musket after Falkirk the colonelcy of the regiment came to James, eighteen years of age and son to Glengarry by his second wife.

Chiefs of smaller septs joined one or other of these three regiments of Clan Donald. Alexander Macdonald of Glencoe took his company of proud and quarrelsome cattle-stealers into Keppoch's. Coll Macdonald of Barisdale led his father's men as a company in Glengarry's. The Macdonalds of Kinloch Moidart and Morar were with Clanranald's.

There was a Lowland gentleman standing with Clan Donald, though his proper duty would seem to have been with his company of the Duke of Perth's Regiment in the second line. He was the Chevalier de Johnstone, son of an Edinburgh merchant, and if his happy memoirs do not explain how he came to have that "de" he was as proud of his kinship with Scots nobility as any Highlander. He had been on the night-march to Nairn, and when it came back he rode on to Inverness for sleep. "But when I had already one leg in the bed and was on the point of stretching myself between the sheets, what was my surprise to hear the drum beat to arms and the trumpets of the picket of Fitz-James sounding the call to boot and saddle." He got back into the saddle, his eyes half-shut, and rode to Drummossie Moor. There he sought his friend, Donald Macdonald of Scotus, a captain of Glengarry's, and said that he would fight beside him that morning.

The first line of the Rebel Army, which was all of the army for any effectual purpose, stretched away obliquely, its right five hundred yards or less from the Royal troops, its left wing eight hundred or more. Time, perhaps, the nervous disorder of John William O'Sullivan, ignorance, or a combination of them all prevented this irregularity from being corrected, and it was to prove calamitous. The line was long, longer perhaps than Cumberland's front, though it contained less men. A regular soldier was allowed twenty inches in the ranks to load his musket and use his bayonet with comfort, but a clansman needed thirty inches or more in which to swing his broadsword. The Highland line stretched across the moor for more than a thousand yards, despite its captains' desperate cries of "*Close up!*"

Behind this front of clans, and separated from it by a hundred yards of flattened heather, was a second line of unhorsed cavalry and unhappy Lowlanders. On the right the Angus Regiment, whipped up from the tenantry of the Ogilvy lands, and led by the Earl's son, a boy of twenty with a long, straight nose, a heavy jaw and a calm eye. Five hundred men, by one account, and it seems a very generous accounting. They were paraded in two battalions, behind the Camerons and Athollmen, and on their left stood the battalions of Lord Lewis Gordon, a one-time lieutenant of the Royal Navy and the third son of the Cock of the North. He had ridden with whip and spur through the country of his father, the Duke, to get these men, raising them from shires and towns more accustomed, historically, to slamming their gates in the face of the Dukes of Gordon and their sons.

On the left of Lord Lewis was another Gordon regiment, that raised by John Gordon of Glenbucket, a craggy man of seventy or more, his body twisted by rheumatism. He was a man of little property in Strathbogie, but he liked the Highlanders and had married his many daughters among them. The men he had recruited from the Duke of Gordon's estates considered him a more terrifying press-officer than John Roy Stewart. He drove in every able-bodied man and boy he could find, and he took every horse, not excepting those belonging to the Duke. He had two hundred men with him at Culloden, and he sat in front of them on a grey Highland pony. Close by was the priest and chaplain of the regiment, Father John Tyrie, who had won the toss in Strathavon.

The Duke of Perth's Regiment, standing with Glenbucket's behind Clan Chattan, had been drummed up from the Duke's own country, men of his name, some Robertsons, even some MacGregors. There were some English deserters among them, too, still wearing their red coats. Since the whole of this regiment appears to have been a sorry force, Johnstone's preference for the fighting company of the Macdonalds may be understandable.

The Scots Royal, in red-faced uniforms of blue, were men of a regular French regiment raised for King Louis by the exiled house of Drummond, titular Dukes of Perth. Recruits for it were found among the Scots in France, or among the disaffected and adventurous in the hills at home. They were principally Jacobites, and many of them had volunteered and received furlough to fight for the Prince. Perhaps three hundred and fifty had come since the Rebellion began, but even they had been thinned by desertion, and there were not more than three hundred of them at Culloden. Their commander was Lord Lewis Drummond, son of the attainted Earl of Melfort, and a domiciled Frenchman.

Exiles, too, were the Irish Picquets who held the left of the second line, formed on the flank of the Scots Royal. Originally, when it had been proposed to send them to Scotland, they had consisted of units of fifty men drawn from each of the six great Irish regiments in the French Army—Lally's, Ruth's, Clare's, and Dillon's, Bulkeley's and Berwick's. The British Navy had prevented most of them from reaching Scotland, and the hundred and seventy-five who were at Culloden had come from Dillon's, Ruth's and Lally's only. They spoke French, they had French manners and French homes, but their names were as Irish as the peat—O'Brien, Molloy and Sullivan, Cusack, Sweeney and Sarsfield.

Lieutenant-Colonel Walter Stapleton, an officer of Berwick's Regiment, and a "Brigadier of the Armies of the Most Christian King", was the commander of the second Rebel line, and he thought bitterly of the odds. "The Scots," he said, "are always good troops until things come to a crisis." It was his opinion that the crisis had been reached.

There were cavalry with the Prince, though Cumberland's three regiments of dragoons would have guffawed at the use of the word. They made a third line of sorts, grouped about the Stuart standard. Most of them were without horses, like Kilmarnock's. Once this small regiment had been known as The Horse Grenadiers, and then The Perthshire Horse, and then again Strathallan's Horse, but titles will not make a horse-soldier when he has neither horse nor saddle. By the time Culloden was reached, Kilmarnock's had handed in its last horse and stood on foot. Its commander, William Boyd, Earl of Kilmarnock, was with it, and may or may not have known that his son was not far away with Cumberland.

Behind the Irish Picquets was another one-time troop of horse, Baggot's Hussars these, raised from farmers' sons about Edinburgh, but now, without horses, and almost without men, there was scarcely any point in it being there at all. Pitsligo's Horse, which stood with the standard, had given up its horses, too, and the few Banffshire men remaining in the regiment were on foot with their commander, Lord Pitsligo.

The regiments that had received the last horses from these sad troops were the Prince's Life Guards and Fitz-James's Horse. There was little more than half a troop of the Life Guards left, and they served as a bodyguard for the Prince. They were gentlemen of property, or the cadet sons of such gentlemen, supplying their own horses, arms and equipment. They wore uniforms of "blue turn'd with red", and when the Rebellion began they had hoped to become a Corps d'Elite. Fitz-James's Horse was at squadron strength. It was over-officered and formed by French and Franco-Scots. In France it had existed as a regular unit of the French Army, named after the Duke of Berwick, natural son of James II. Most of the regiment, sailing in French ships, had never reached Scotland, and those men who did arrive were under the command of Sir Jean McDonell and a redoubtable Irish captain called Robert O'Shea.

There were also some scattered remnants of Horse that had once been raised by the young and impetuous Lord Elcho, and by Lord Balmerino, an old, philosophic man whose life was rapidly running out. John Daniel served in Balmerino's.

Prince Charles sat on his grey horse beside his standard. "The pipes will play when the cannon begin," had said the Orders of the Day. But the pipes had been playing for some time, each piper the rant of his clan, while the wind pulled at the drones. And above the noise of the pipes there were still the anxious cries of "Close up! Close up!" The clans were ready, they had tied their kilts high between their thighs, and some had thrown off their plaids to free their sword-arms. There was no answer to their shouts from the red wall across the moor, and no answer to their pipes but the beating of the battalion drums.

The Jacobite artillery had always been an embarrassment to the Army. It was often too large, and frequently too small for the role required. There was nobody with sufficient knowledge to train it, or the discipline to maintain its fire. The Duke of Perth's Regiment usually got the thankless job of looking after it, and the Chevalier de Johnstone remembered this part of his adventures with no pleasure at all. "I was frequently obliged to pass the night in the open air, without any shelter, in the most severe weather in the midst of winter when any of the waggons happened to break down. . . ." The Royal Artillery could have told him that this was a gunner's life.

On the right, left and centre of the Rebel's first line were a number of four or six-pounders, but most of those who had called themselves the Prince's gunners had run away, and the pieces were now manned by Highlanders who knew little or nothing of the work. Somewhere among these guns was John Finlayson, a "Mathematik instrument Maker" from Edinburgh, and it would seem that he was Master of the Ordnance for the moment. Perhaps it was he, on his own impulse or upon order from another, who decided on the first shot.

Certainly Lord Bury provoked it, sitting there between the lines with casual calm. From the centre of the Rebel line, and almost opposite him, there broke a balloon of white smoke, whipped back quickly by the wind. Now had begun the cannonade, without which, the Duke of Cumberland said, a battle was a dance without music. The Rebel ball passed over Lord Bury's indifferent head, over the hats of Price's and Cholmondeley's regiments, over Fleming's and Conway's in the second line, and came down somewhere in the rear, cutting a soldier in half. The Jacobite guns were not to improve upon that.

Lord Bury turned his horse and slowly rode towards the Royal troops. The Rebels cheered him. For the first time Cumberland's battalions answered with a short and hoarse hurrah.

2

DRUMMOSSIE MOOR

"My Captain has a stream of blood!"

BREVET-COLONEL WILLIAM BELFORD waited for the order to fire his guns, standing with his staff to the left of the King's Army. He wore a blue double-breasted surtout that was cuffed and lined with red. He wore a gold-laced hat and white spatterdashes, and he carried a brass-hilted sword in his hand. He was the commander of the Train, and he had entered the Royal Regiment of Artillery upon its formation, serving with distinction at Carthagena, Dettingen and Fontenoy. He was thirty-four years of age and he was not like the officers of Foot and Horse to whom military service was often an exciting extension of their social life. He was dedicated to his profession and close-mouthed about his art, believing, like most men who are the servants of machines, that they imposed upon him certain spiritual obligations. These he had read when a cadet, as they had been set down by Captain Thomas Binning who asked of a gunner *"that he be one that feareth God more than his Enemy, that he be Constant and not given to Change, that he be faithful, True and Honest"*.

During winter, when civilised wars stood at ease for the comfort of all, Belford trained his gunners in the use of shoulder-arms and in infantry drill, believing that even though their pieces might be over-run they were still bound to fight as soldiers. This coming battle would be of particular interest to him, since it was the first time in nine months of riotous rebellion that the clans had faced cannon manned by regular and disciplined artillerymen. He was to get little credit for his company's decisive role in this affair, and he may have been much chagrined by it, for he was a sensitive fellow where the honour of his corps was concerned. At Carlisle, four months before, when the town was taken from the Rebels, Colonel Belford had shocked the Dean and Chapter with a peremptory demand that the cathedral bells be surrendered to him. This, he argued, was a gunner's traditional right, and the bells would make good cannon. The Dean appealed to Cumberland, who shrugged his shoulders. The Dean then threatened to appeal to the Lord Chief Justice, by which time Belford and his cannoneers had moved on to Scotland, leaving the bells still in their tower.

The company of Royal Artillery at Culloden was Captain Archibald Cunningham's command, though that gentleman had been dead for two months, to nobody's regret it seems. Below Belford was Lieutenant John Godwin, not long out of Woolwich, six other officers, three sergeants, three corporals, eleven bombardiers, sixty-six gunners, sixty-two mattrosses, and three drummers. It had ten three-pounder battalion guns placed in the front line by pairs, and some other three-pounders and cohorn mortars that may have been set on a slight brae to the rear and the left. It had trail-carriages, tumbrils, forge-carts and carpenter's wagons, elevating-screws, hand-spikes, ladles, sponges, wadhooks, rammers, tarpaulins and harness, shot, grape, powder, match and fascines. It had draught-horses to pull the guns, and enough blue-coated men to manhandle them once those horses were led to the rear.

The battalion guns had been ready since Lord Bury rode out on his casual reconnaissance. The wheels of each were matted with heather and mud, but the iron barrel, a yard and six inches long, was swabbed and clean. When the tompion was removed from the mouth it was fed with a pound and a half of powder on a copper ladle, carefully rammed home by a wooden plunger. Next the three-pound shot of iron, rammed home too. A dribble of powder from the touch-hole, and the gunner stood ready with his linstock in his hand. This looked like Mercury's serpent rod, a stick about which curled a cotton rope that had been soaked in saltpetre, lead acetate and lye. When lit, it would burn four inches in an hour. Lieutenants or fireworkers sighted each gun, using the quadrant, a carpenter's square, one end of which they put in the bore. But on the left the enemy was so close that sighting was scarcely necessary.

The order came to Belford, was passed to Lieutenant Godwin, and on to the fireworkers and non-commissioned officers at each battery. The cannon fired in one great roll. The bombardiers yelled as the guns jerked back, bouncing on their wheels. *Sponge!* and the lambskin mops swilled the barrels. Powder . . . *Ram!* Load and . . . *Ram!* Ready and . . . *FIRE!* The high moor shuddered, the Rebel lines were at once hidden by the smoke, and the gunners could see their black shot passing smoothly into the fog. The cannonade was terrible in effect. Each battery loaded and fired at will, so that there was no great crash but a continual noise like ten iron doors clanging, one after the other. The shot came bouncing toward the first Rebel line with deceptive slowness, or travelled in lazy trajectory over it to strike the second, tumbling men like skittles. At the Rebel guns, four on the flanks and four in the centre, the gunners and unskilled clansmen manning them fired ineffectually. They seemed to be aiming not at the front of the scarlet battalions, but over their heads, seeking to kill Cumberland. But he was never in one place for more than a minute or two. Nine minutes after John Finlayson trained and fired his first gun from the centre nothing more was heard from the Jacobite artillery.

But the Royal guns continued. Above the rolling, rumbling discharge, and the screams of those who had been hit, officers of the clans shouted desperately *"Close up! Close up! . . ."* And the clansmen closed the gaps the round-shot made, but they looked over their shoulders to the rear, or cried back at their officers, demanding the order to charge. For more than an hour they had stood with the bitter wind and sleet on their faces, and now they still stood, and were expected to stand while the Royal guns played upon them, and the smoke of Belford's powder burnt their throats. Most of those who died in the battle were killed at this time, by the round iron coming among them, their limbs parted and thrown among their comrades.

Now Belford ordered some of his gunners to raise their elevation and to drop their shot to the rear of the clans. Through his glass, as he stood on the little brae, he had seen a knot of horsemen about the Stuart standard, and believed them to be the Prince and his Life Guards. Sir Robert Strange, the young engraver who had designed plates for the Prince's currency, was among these horsemen, and he was disagreeably surprised as the Royal shot came over the clansmen's ranks, or scythed its way through them. "One Austin, a very worthy, pleasant fellow, stood on my left; he rode a fine mare which he was accustomed to call his lady. He perceived her give a sudden shriek, and, on looking around him called out, 'Alas, I have lost my lady!' One of her hind legs was shot and hanging by the skin. He that instantly dismounted and, endeavouring to push her out of the ranks, she came to the ground. He took his gun and pistols out of the holsters, stepped forward, joined the Foot but was never more heard of."

John Daniel, of Balmerino's, was also among those receiving Belford's particular attention. The colonel had been right in assuming them to be grouped about the Prince. "The whole fury of the enemy's Artillery," said Daniel, not altogether accurately, "seemed to be directed against us in the rear; as if they had noticed where the Prince was. By the first cannon shot, his servant, scarcely thirty yards behind him, was killed."

Most of the fire upon the Prince and his Horse was coming from the glens which Bedford had placed on the brae to the left, and their aim was coldly sure. The Prince decided, under appeals from his staff, to move to the right with Fitz-James' Horse. He had turned there when a ball struck the ground beside him, covering him with earth, and this was something of the battle that he seems to have remembered most vividly, and would tell of it weeks later when he was skulking in the hills. "I was riding to the right wing, my horse began to kick, at which I was much surprised, being very quiet and peaceable formerly, and looking narrowly to him to see what was the matter with him I observed blood gushing out of his side. 'Oh, oh!' says I, speaking of the horse, 'if this is the story with you, you have no less reason to be uneasy.' Whereupon I was obliged to dismount and take another."

And he rode off to the right, leaving behind the body of his groom, Thomas Ca, cut in two by one of Belford's shot. John Daniel went with the Prince, carrying a battle ensign. "Frequent turns and looks the Prince made, to see how his men behaved, but alas! our hopes were very slender. . . .We had not proceeded far when I was ordered back, lest the sight of my standard going off might induce others to follow." So he went back to where he had first stood, and he heard the clans crying for the order to charge. Some of the Highlanders, if they were not to be allowed to charge themselves, wished that the enemy would advance and end the terrible trial of the guns. Little knots of them ran out from their line, and stood before the Royal troops, clashing their broadswords on their targets and yelling taunts until shot down.

Surgeon Grainger, still to the rear of Pulteney's, watched the cannonade with admiration. "The cannon gave our men infinite spirits. The enemy renewed their charge not only from their first battery but from two others to their left. They only made our gunners fire the faster, and really complimented the enemy at least twenty for one. The wind drove the smoke in the teeth of the enemy; their batteries were silenced. . . . The thunder of our cannon was perpetual, and if they had stood much longer where they were our mattrosses would have done the business."

Cumberland, pleased by the way his guns were thinning the Highland ranks at no expense at all to his own army, would have agreed with Daniel that the Rebel hopes were slender. But he had heard enough of the Highlanders to believe that they would not stand for long, and that when they broke it would not be in retreat but forward in desperate charge. So he made fresh dispositions in his line to be ready for them. He had no intention of sending his battalions forward in advance, not while his artillery was so effective, and it is the common experience of war that an attack usually suffers more than a defence. He ordered Pulteney's men up from the rear, to stand on the right of the Royals in the first line, for there was no protecting bog there now, and the ragged regiments of Macdonalds outflanked him. He ordered Battereau's from the rear, too, to stand by Howard's on the right of the second line, thereby leaving himself with no third line at all, except Blakeney's men in scarlet and buff. He did not think a *corps de reserve* would be needed, and he was to be right. If he was not a brilliant soldier, nor even a very good one, he was a methodical and careful young man who had learnt his lessons well, and he knew that a general should take every advantage of the stupidities of his opponents. He had not overlooked the Culwhiniac enclosure, nor failed to see it as the bolt on which the battle might swing.

He sent Joseph Yorke away with orders for Major-General John Huske, commanding the second line. This leathery old man was yelling above the noise of the guns, telling his men what to do when the Highland assault came, and if it broke through the first line to them. "He gave us this charge," said Michael Hughes, "that if we had time to load so to do, and if not, to make no delay but to drive our bayonets into their bodies and make sure work." Yorke's orders were that Lieutenant-Colonel Edward Martin, of Wolfe's regiment, should march his men away from the left of Huske's line and place them *en potence* with Barrell's on the left of the first line. That is, they were to so wheel that their right flank made a right angle with Barrell's left, their backs to the stone wall and their front facing down the field. If any of Wolfe's men, with water up to their calves as they took up their new position, and with a fine view of the cannonade, wondered what His Royal Highness meant them to do there, they were very soon to discover.

And then the enclosure. . . . The Rebel generals, in the hour before the cannon had begun, had argued the best use that might be made of this. O'Sullivan had a hare-brained scheme for garrisoning the farm, though it was two or three hundred yards from the field. "The walls are between you and them . . . !" he said idiotically to Lord George, forgetting that what stones one man may have put together, many others may pull down. There was still argument and quarrel when the first fire of Belford's guns cut through the clans. Then word came from the Athollmen that they had seen dragoons in the enclosure, riding the steep slope which O'Sullivan had sworn no Horse could cross. The skirl of Campbell pipes was heard and the Argyll men were seen running before the red coats and black boots of the dragoons. Lord George Murray realised that he was to be taken on the flank as he had feared.

Since dawn some of the Campbells had been in the van and on the left of the Royal Army. As scouts, they had been out all night with the picquets of the Royal Scots and the vedettes of Kingston's Horse. When the Army marched, they were away along

Nairnside with targets slung and red legs leaping, moving nimbly as deer. "We were advanced about one-eighth of a mile before the left of the Army," one of their captains wrote to his chief, "and thus we moved from village to village along the water of Earn till we came into hollow ground where we were out of sight of both armies except six squadrons of dragoons. . . ."

Like the Rebels, the Campbells were dressed and armed with kilt, plaid, musket, broadsword and dirk, but in their dark bonnets they wore Clan Diarmid's badge of myrtle and a red or yellow saltire that declared their allegiance to King George. They had been raised, not without the usual difficulties, from the clansmen and tenantry of the nobles of Argyll, Loudoun, and Breadalbane. Their "Colonel Jack" was the young son of John Campbell of Mamore, a Major-General of such militia, a King's man and a kinsman of the Duke of Argyll. The ordinary men of the Campbell clan were not, perhaps, particularly concerned with who sat on the throne, but they were as subject to tribal compulsions and obligations as the Rebels they opposed. In this sense, Culloden was a clan battle to them, an opportunity to avenge past and present injuries. If the MacLeans were remembering the recent raiding by Campbells in Morven and Ardgour, the Argyllshire men had good cause to think of what the Camerons and Stewarts of Appin had done when they harried the Campbell glens.

Colonel Jack had not protested when His Royal Highness told him to take the Campbell militia back to the baggage, though he cannot have liked the order. During the march from Nairn his command had been equally posted on the flanks, and, when ordered, the right-flank companies went to the rear with him. Four companies on the left, however, one hundred and forty men, were away ahead of the dragoons and did not retire. They were captained by high-spirited young gentlemen of Achnaba, Achrossan, Netherlorne and Ballimore. They had heard the pipes of their enemies, and seen their tartan in the sleet of the morning. The alchemy of dark superstition had been at work in their imagination for some days and they knew that a fight was inevitable. In the company of Colin Campbell of Ballimore there was a "half-witted fellow" (or so he was taken to be by reasonable men with no belief in the old Highland talent for the second-sight). One morning recently this fellow had turned to his friends and said, "What is the reason my captain has a stream of blood running down his brow!" His vision, which was the kind of vision seen before most clan battles, was told by one man to the next and repeated through the company until it was heard by Ballimore himself. He was an intelligent young man whose imagination had been sobered by civilised contact, and he laughed and made light of the whole thing.

The four companies moved ahead of six squadrons of dragoons until, wrote Captain Duncan Campbell, "we came to a high enclosure that extended to a great way to the Right, and quite to the water of Earn to the left. From this place we sent to acquaint General Bland that the Horses could go no further. . . ." They had come to the dry-stone wall of the Culwhiniac park, a third of its way down the Nairnside slope, and there they waited until the English generals decided what should be done next. The wall was about four feet high, and the Campbells could have gone over it with ease, but it successfully blocked the cavalry, as O'Sullivan had hoped it would. The Argyll men squatted on the earth with the rain on their backs, and, high above them on the moor they saw the smoke-blue sky and the sleet pulled taut across it. They heard the sound of drums and pipes, and because there was a fight coming, and a Campbell pibroch was therefore as necessary as any Cameron rant, their own pipers tucked the bags beneath their arms, threw the drones over their shoulders and sounded the war-songs of Clan Diarmid. Some way to their rear, in the lee of high ground at Urchil, waited the squadrons of Horse, uneasy on that slope, and their boots filling with rain. They were big, heavy men, and young, with the blunt faces of English rustics. They, too, had covered their carbines with their scarlet coats, and punched down their tricornes to keep the rain from their necks. They looked more valiant than they probably felt, and certainly more than they were to behave. There were two hundred of Cobham's Dragoons and three hundred of Lord Mark Kerr's, commanded by old Humphrey Bland who had been a soldier for forty-two years, and by the young Earl of Ancrum who had received his first commission less than ten years before. The general of all cavalry was Henry Hawley, and when he was told of the wall he probably swore, since he rarely said anything without putting it in a parenthesis of oaths. But he also said "Pull it down!"

The Campbells did this with pleasure, pulling slab from slab, and making a gap wide enough for a squadron abreast. The four companies of Highlanders went through first, running obliquely up the slope to the north wall and the Rebel flank. After them came the dragoons, dock-tailed horses of black and bay slipping on the wet rise of ground. Their officers yelled that pistols were not to be drawn from the holsters until the enemy was broken and in flight, but they were scarcely heard above the metal clangour of Belford's cannon. The Argyll men moved across the enclosure until they came to another wall that also ran north to south, dividing the Culwhiniac enclosure into an east and west park. They broke a gap in this wall, too, and went running through it, with the cursing troopers behind.

"The Dragoons went out and formed at a distance, facing the rebels," reported Captain Duncan Campbell, "and we were ordered to attack them." The Campbells took their position along the north wall, flinging their muskets across it, while Hawley's Horse edged westward, seeking the Rebel flank and rear, and there they found that Lord George Murray had done the best he could to receive them. As soon as the Campbells and the troopers' black tricornes were seen in the enclosure, he ordered some of Lord Lewis Gordon's men to face to the south behind the Athollmen. This was the battalion which Harry Gordon of Avochie had raised in Strathbogie. Lord George also ordered the Life Guards and Fitz-James's Horse to wheel to their right at the rear of his wing, and so counter the threat of Hawley's dragoons. All this was done while Belford's guns still played on the Rebel lines, although the rain and the sleet were mercifully slackening.

Some reports of the battle, in Home's *History* for example, say that the Rebels had posted men in the enclosure, about a hundred or so, and that these had gone down under Campbell broadswords when the Argyll companies came up the slope. But Duncan Campbell, commanding one of these companies, said nothing of this in his report to Lord Glenorchy, the son of Campbell of Breadalbane. It is unlikely that the slaughter of a hundred Athollmen or Camerons or Stewarts, or whoever they might have been, would have been ignored by a Campbell singing the valour of Campbell men.

The advance of the militia and the Horse had outflanked the Rebels, and Hawley's men were hovering at the rear, but geography can often neutralise the best of manoeuvres when the land is unknown. Between the dragoons and the Prince's scanty riders there was now discovered a deep ravine or sunken road, with walls so steep and so slimed with heather and mud that neither side could plunge down them to attack the other. There was some pistol-popping and carbine fire across the gap and Trooper Bradshaw's horse took a ball in the left buttock. "Twas pritty near Enoch that time, but, thank God, a miss is as good as a mile, as we say in Gloustershire."

By this time the clans had broken into the charge.

"They came running, like troops of hungry wolves"

CLAN CHATTAN BROKE away first, the Mackintoshes, MacBeans and MacGillivrays running forward into the smoke and hoarsely yelling *"Loch Moy!"* and *"Dunmaglass!"* The sustained fire of Belford's ten battalion guns had lasted for nearly half an hour, and by it some of the clan regiments had lost a third of their men. Because the fool O'Sullivan had not insisted that they stand in ranks of three instead of six, or because this would have been too much of a change in ancient practice, one ball only, bursting through the body of a man in the front rank, mangled four or five others before bouncing on toward Stapleton's second line. "Most of the shots took effect," said Surgeon Grainger, with military rather than medical approval, "and laid numbers of them sprawling on the ground." This was not how Highlandmen could endure or fight a battle. Their weapon was the broadsword, and their only tactic was to bring it to work as soon as possible. Above the firing of the guns and the playing of the pipes, the beating of drums and the yells of Belford's gunners, the clansmen called upon their chiefs as children to a father, asking for the order *"Claymore!"* that would put them to the onset.

They had seen little or nothing of the Royal Army since the firing began, nothing to their front but smoke stabbed with crimson, and from which the round-shot came rolling. Because they were nearest to the enemy, three hundred paces from Sergeant Edward Bristow's guns on the flanks of Barrell's and Munro's, the Atholl Brigade and the Cameron men suffered most. Lochiel, a pistol in one hand and a sword in the other, stood angrily before his men, and heard the balls whispering past to kill them. He sent a kinsman to Lord George, saying that he would be able to hold his clan in check no longer, they were "galled by the

enemy's cannon and were turned so impatient that they were
like to break their ranks". Lord George, no less angry with his
vacillating Prince, sent an officer to Charles, urging the order to
advance.

The Prince was alone with the command he wanted, and all
responsibility his, and the responsibility for the delay and the
men killed waiting was his too. He was on a rise behind the right
wing, surrounded by a guard of Horse. When Lord George's
appeal came to him he sent his aide, young Lachlan MacLachlan,
to pass down the line with the order for a general advance on
the Royal battalions. But a round-shot killed the boy before he
reached the front, and the delay went on. Now the excitable
O'Sullivan clutched Lord George's sleeve with orders "to pray
him march directly on the enemy". And Walter Stapleton,
His Christian Majesty's Brigadier, had hurried to the Prince to
say that his line of Gordons, Ogilvies, Scots Royal and Irish,
could stand no more.

Then the Clan Chattan men were away, their kilts pulled high to
the groin, their bonnets scrugged down over the brows. A Lowlander who was in the line with them remembered how each
man's face was twisted with rage and despair. They ran forward
with their bodies bent and their feet kicking at the heather, and
they did not know that the rain and the sleet had now stopped.
Their pipes screamed the rant until the bag was handed to an
attendant boy, and the Piper pulled out his sword and ran forward
with his tribe. Belford's men, hearing the clans come, changed
from ball to grape. No powder was ladled into the barrels this
time, but a paper case rammed home and containing charge,
leaden balls, nails and old iron. The case was pricked through the
touch-hole and powder laid in the channel above, ready for the
linstock. Partridge-shot, an English officer called this grape when
writing home, thinking of a beat across the Yorkshire moors,
perhaps.

Once Colonel Anne's men were away, Atholl and the Camerons
started after them. Appin Stewarts too, with Ardshiel at their
head. He was sometimes said to have been a lethargic man, and
disinclined to effort, but at this moment he ran four or five
paces ahead of his clan. Because of the slant of the Highland line

the clans did not run directly upon the enemy, but obliquely and to the left. They came, thought Colonel Yorke, where he could see them in the smoke, in three great wedges, bearded, ragged, angry men, with their mouths open in yells that merged into one unintelligible shout. Their right arms were lifted, holding their broadswords high, and behind the front ranks there chopped and swayed the axes held by the common men. In mid-field, Appin Stewarts and Camerons collided with Clan Chattan, and for a moment the charge halted. Or perhaps it was halted by the first murderous discharge of grape, the balls and the iron whispering and whistling their killing way. Father stumbled over son, brother over brother in the sudden slaughter. Then the charge came on, but now the Appin men and Camerons swung to their right like animals shying in alarm, and they drove for the left of the Royal line, pushing the Atholl Brigade toward the dry-stone wall and toward Wolfe's men *en potence*. They threw away their muskets and pistols without firing them, and this, more than anything, shows their temper and their despair, for it was their custom in the charge to advance, to fire a volley, and then run in with the sword and the axe.

Clan Chattan continued its charge to the left, and perhaps it was the first to see the Royal Infantry. Years later John Grant, when he kept the inn at Aviemore, would tell how he advanced with a Mackintosh company, and how he saw nothing at first, nothing but the smoke of the guns until a pull of the wind lifted it. And there, ahead of him, he saw a long line of legs, white-gaitered to the thigh, with black buttons running down the calves. Such small things do men remember of battles. Clan Chattan ran toward the Royal Scots and toward Cholmondeley's regiment on the right of Cumberland's centre. In the front rank of a platoon of the Royals waited Alexander Taylor, once a good and peaceful servant to a gentleman of Ayr, and what he saw at that moment he put into a letter to his wife the next day: "They came running upon our front line like troops of hungry wolves."

Belford's guns were still firing grape, and the clans still advancing over their dead when the British infantry began their long roll of musketry. In each of the six battalions of the front line the preparatory orders had begun before Clan Chattan broke. The drums tapped, the word passed from captain to subalterns to platoon sergeants. *Make ready!* And the first of the three ranks brought its muskets to the recover, each man going down quickly on his right knee. *Present!* And the brown muskets came up to scarlet shoulders, right cheek pressed to the butt, right eye sighted from hammer to muzzle. Then as the leaping, kilted figures came screaming through the smoke, *FIRE!* Each man sprang up quickly when he had fired, a strong spring on the left leg as he had been taught. Behind the front rank the second was firing, and behind this the third was taking a pace to the right, and firing when the first rank went down on its knees once more, loaded, primed and cocked. And so it went on, company by company along the six battalions, front rank and flanking grenadiers firing first, second and third ranks following, the volleys swaying and rippling along the line. Bayonets shone in a wave as muskets were brought to the recover, ramrods rattling in the barrels. Men bit savagely at the cartridges for a dribble of powder to prime their pans, until their tongues, their lips and their cheeks were black with it.

"'Twas at the twinkling of an eye that the fire of the small arms began from right to left," wrote Andrew Henderson, Master of Arts, author, bookseller, and eyewitness by his own claim, "which for two minutes was like one continued thunder equalling the noise of the loudest clap."

Less literary was Edward Linn, writing to his beloved spouse the next day and giving the picture as he had seen it from the Royal Scots Fusiliers. "We kept a continual closs, firing upon them with our small-arms. . . . We gave them a closs with grape-shot which galled them very much."

Of twenty-one officers who ran forward with Clan Chattan only three survived the charge. They were killed, most of them, with hundreds of their clan before they got within twenty yards of the infantry. Thus Farquhar MacGillivray, who was nineteen and who died with all his father's people of Dalcrombie. And thus, too, James Dallas of Cantray, "a loyal, kind, brave young man who had raised his company at great expense". And Donald Dallas also, a lieutenant in the company of Cantray. Yet, despite the grape and the musketry, some of Clan Chattan broke through the infantry to the second line, or ran past the guns to reach it. None of these survived, for there the second line, as it had been ordered by John Huske, drove home with the bayonet. And on the bayonets of Fleming's or Howard's or Bligh's died Angus Mackintosh of Farr, a mile or less from where his son lay watching in the heather.

Gillies MacBean, major of Clan Chattan, passed through the Royals or Cholmondeley's like a reaper, and advanced on Fleming's. He was stabbed several times by the bayonet, in the body and in the arms, and his head was opened from brow to chin by the cut of a hanger. His right thigh had been broken by grape, but he ran on until he was thrust down by the bayonets of the second line. Big John MacGillivray got a pistol-shot beyond the first line, killing twelve soldiers, and he was running on Blakeney's solitary battalion in the rear when he was killed. Clan Chattan's colonel, the red-haired MacGillivray of Dunmaglass, was the first to reach the infantry and the first to pass through it, leaping over the bodies of the men he struck down. Half-blinded he ran to his right, and struggled there with Bligh's or Sempill's. When he fell he was not dead, but was able to crawl, through the stamping ammunition boots of the infantry, until he found a spring of water to the rear. And there he died with his face in the water.

"The brunt of the battle fell upon Clan Chattan," said John Hossack a few days later when writing to friends, and he should have known, for he was baillie of Inverness and once its Provost, and he had many friends and kinsmen among the clan whose deaths he mourned, though he was a loyal Whig. All of the clan's field officers, all of its captains and most of its lieutenants who closed with the Royal infantry were killed by them. Those of the clan who did not break the line stood fifteen paces from it like enraged animals, unwilling to advance into the musketry or bayonets, too proud to retreat. They were shot down where they stood, and they slashed at the empty air with their swords. "They threw stones . . ." reported Cumberland to his father's first Minister, with a soldier's amused contempt for such amateur soldiering. And so they did, having tossed away their fire-arms in the charge. They bent down, tugging stones free from the heather roots, and they threw them at the infantry until at last they fell back.

They would not leave their standard. The young Mackintosh cadet who had carried it behind Dunmaglass had been killed early in the charge. The banner was seized by a private soldier, a young man from the Flemington estate, and he held it in the air until the clan began to retreat. Then he tore it from its staff and wrapped it about his body. If he ran anywhere it was away from his home, for this was eastward behind the Royal Army. But in time he came home, and from that day he was known as *Donuil na Braiteach*, Donald of the Colours. And his sons, when they were born, were called Angus and Charles of the Colours, never by any other name.

The little regiment of MacLeans and MacLachlans went forward, too. They cried *"Another for Hector!"* and *"Death or Life!"*, if they had the breath for it, but they never reached the Royal line. They had even further to run than Clan Chattan, and they fell rapidly under the grape and the musketry, choking in the smoke and stumbling over their dead. The fire against them from the Royals and Pulteney's was so thick that some of them held their plaids before their eyes, as if they were still facing the rain and the sleet. Old Lachlan MacLachlan, whose son was already dead, died himself before he had run many yards, and most of his clan fell about him there. MacLean of Drimnin was halfway across the moor when Clan Chattan, or what was left of it, came back from the charge, their faces sullen, and they were like a wave which, receding from a beach, halts and turns the one following. Drimnin saw that his clan was no longer advancing with him. He stopped and called to them, waving his sword, and to his side came his son, Alan, bleeding from a wound. Above the noise of the relentless volleying, Drimnin asked for news of another son, Lachlan. Lachlan was dead, said Alan, whereupon Drimnin turned toward the enemy again, saying the boy would be avenged.

Alan MacLean pleaded with his father to come away, but the old man shook off his hand. *"Allein, comma leat misse, mas toil leat do bheatha thoir'n arrigh dhuit fheinl"* Alan, he said, don't think of me, take care of yourself if you value your life. He must have run across the front of the Royal line and toward its right, for out of the smoke there appeared before him two troopers of Kingston's or Cobham's. He cut one from the saddle with his sword, and he wounded the other before more rode up and killed him.

The Chisholms of Strathglass were in this confused charge, far to the left, but their colonel did not lead them. Young Roderick Og had been struck down by a round-shot before the onset, and was being carried to the rear by his henchman, Donald MacWilliam when another ball struck them both, maiming MacWilliam and killing Roderick. And perhaps Ian Beg was able to finger a pibroch from *The Maiden of the Sandal*, and perhaps he was not, but the rest of the Chisholms went forward, to founder and to break many yards from the front rank of the Royal Scots where stood Captain James Chisholm and Captain John Chisholm, sons of their chief.

The smoke lifted a little from the centre of the moor. "I never saw a field thicker of dead," said Fusilier Linn.

"Those on the right with their glittering swords"

BARRELL'S MEN WERE old soldiers and a Royal regiment. The howl of a clan, coming to the onset, was nothing strange to them and they had met it, and repulsed it, at the Battle of Falkirk, almost the only British regiment that day to keep its face to the Highlanders. They had been cool, "quite cool, as cool as ever I saw men at exercise," according to their brigadier. The valour a soldier has displayed in one battle becomes surety for his behaviour in the next, and this morning Barrell's were perhaps less unnerved by the yells and the pipes than any of the battalions along the line. It was the misfortune of the Highland Army that its greatest shock should fall upon the one regiment least likely to run from it. Down on the three hundred and fifty men of Barrell's was now charging the whole of the right wing of the clans, Atholl, Lochiel and Appin. Lord George Murray was among them, riding a restless horse that shied and bucked before the heat of the cannon. But he kept it in rein, and he yelled *"Claymore!"* as he waved his own sword.

"Those on the right," said *An Eye-Witness to the Facts*, "with their glittering swords ran swiftly on the cannon, making a dreadful huzza and crying 'Run ye dogs!' "

The Athollmen never reached the battalions. Forced to their right, and against the dry-stone wall of the Culwhiniac enclosure, they were enfiladed by the hundred and forty Campbells on the other side. They stumbled past this and across the front of Wolfe's regiment, waiting *en potence* to Barrell's. Rank by rank this battalion fired into the flank of the Athollmen. Thirty-two officers of the brigade died there, falling quickly, and the men of Atholl about them by the tens, until those who still stood halted their charge, and cut at the heather in desperate anger before falling back.

Lord George's spirited horse took him on ahead of the clans, galloping past the battalion guns to the rear of the Royal Army, and there he fought to control the animal. His wig and hat had been blown from his head, his sword was broken, his coat torn by grape and bayonet thrusts. He dismounted and fought his way back to where the Camerons and the Stewarts were now breasting Barrell's bayonets. He saw little but enough of the struggle to realise that help was needed. He ran back across the moor, yelling for the second line to come up.

Barrell's and Munro's had held their fire until the bobbing, yelling faces were within twenty yards of them, and then there was time for one volley only from each rank. Sergeant Bristow, at his guns between these battalions, fired grape from both, one discharge and then he was chopped down by a Cameron sword, as were Bombardier Paterson and Gunner Edward Hust. All three crawled beneath the wheels of their guns, with terrible wounds from which they were not to die until two months later. Fifty yards from these guns lay Lochiel, both ankles broken by grape-shot, and he leant on his hands and watched his clan. Camerons and Stewarts, though they too had been winnowed by the fire from Wolfe's, ran on to their front, yelling that they were sons of dogs come for meat. They climbed over their dead, which soon lay four deep, and they hacked at the muskets with such maniacal fury that far down the line men could hear the iron clang of sword on barrel. Many had thrown away their targets on the night march to Nairn, and now they had nothing to protect themselves from the thrust and lunge of the bayonets, the fluted steel coming not from the man to their front but from his comrade on the left. The fight was confused and bitter and the line swayed, Barrell's lion standard of blue dipping at the centre. Lord Robert Kerr, captain of grenadiers, received the first charging Cameron on the point of his spontoon, but then a second cut him through the head to the chin. Stewarts and Camerons flooded through the gap of the guns and cut at the grenadiers of Munro's as well as Barrell's. Some ran to the rear where Lieutenant-Colonel Rich of Barrell's was standing on foot. He held out his slender sword to parry the swing of a broadsword, and both hand and sword were cut from his wrist.

Munro's were fighting as doggedly as Barrell's, though they had shown no courage at all at Falkirk, and perhaps that was why. Only their left flank platoons were met by the clans. On their right the musketry and the grape stopped the Frasers short of the line. Munro's were a surly, quarrelsome regiment, with more than an English battalion's usual share of reluctant Irishmen. At least three men among them had backs still raw from the lash, and there were many more with healed scars. They suffered nineteen killed and sixty-three wounded during the few minutes that the Camerons and the Stewarts closed with them. The yellow facings of the first rank were soon as scarlet as their coats, and behind each levelled bayonet was a face black with powder. Their old Huguenot colonel, Louis Dejean, stood on foot to the rear of the colours, shouting encouragement in French and in English. "I had the honour to command the grenadier platoon," wrote a captain of Munro's to the London press. "Our lads fought more like devils than men. In short we laid (to the best of my judgment) about 1,600 dead on the spot, and finished the affair without help of other regiments." This was a piece of puffing pride, with too sensitive a memory of Falkirk. The captain wanted his readers to know that in his opinion Barrell's had been saved by the enfilade fire of Wolfe's, and by the support of Sempill's to the rear. Barrell's had more casualties than Munro's, one hundred and twenty dead or wounded, and although it was on its left that the Royal Army suffered the greatest loss, the figures were nothing against the dead and the dying of Lord George Murray's clans.

"But you may judge the work," wrote this same captain of Munro's, "for I had eighteen men killed and wounded in my platoon. I thank God I escaped free, but my coat has six balls through it. In the midst of this action the officer that led on the Camerons called to me to take quarter, which I refused and bid the rebel scoundrel advance. He did, and fired at me, but providentially missed his mark. I then shot him dead and took his pistol and dirk, which are extremely neat. No one that attacked us escaped alive; for we gave no quarter nor would accept it of any."

In Bligh's, and in the second line, Michael Hughes the volunteer watched this struggle to his front. "It was dreadful to see the enemies' swords circling in the air as they were raised from strokes, and no less to see the officers of the Army, some cutting with their swords, others pushing with their spontoons, the Serjeants running their halberds into the throats of the enemy, while the soldiers mutually defended each other, and pierced the Heart of his Opponent, ramming their bayonets up to the socket. But still more terrible to hear the dying groans of either party."

Wolfe's men fired regular, plunging volleys into the flank of the mob about and before Barrell's, and by doing so they killed many of that battalion. For a moment, and it was a very short moment, it seemed as though the Camerons were to sweep Barrell's away. They broke into and through its centre, striking down four officers there. Ensign Brown lay on the ground, still holding the Regimental Colour and refusing to release it, though broadswords cut at its staff and at his fingers. In this close confusion, where a man had no room to swing a sword or to lunge with the bayonet, the clansmen stabbed and thrust with the dirks in their left hands. Colonel Rich, surrounded by the centre platoons, now had six cuts on his head as well as a missing hand, and his face was masked with blood. Some of Barrell's twelve platoons broke under the pressure, but they did not run: they fell back and reformed on the flank of Sempill's Border Scots, and gave their fire with that regiment's upon the Highlanders between the lines.

"There was scarce a soldier or officer of Barrell's," wrote one of them, "and of that part of Munro's which engaged, who did not kill one or two men each with their bayonets and spontoons. Not a bayonet but was bent or bloody and stained with blood to the muzzles of their muskets."

A man saw only what was to his front, and little of it at that. An army of opponents became a single enemy soldier with whom it was necessary to settle the issue. Robert Nairn had charged as a private soldier with the Athollmen, and when the regiment was halted by the fire of the Campbells and the volleys of Wolfe's, he ran to his left to join the Cameron men. Four years later he told the historian Home what little he could remember of those minutes. He ran through the smoke and climbed over the dead, and there, suddenly before him, were two soldiers. One of these, wrote Home, "poked his bayonet into Mr. Nairn's eye, and he lay all night on the field."

Still more of Barrell's platoons fell back to form on Sempill's, and the ground between the first and second line began to fill with clansmen. John Huske rode up to the Borderers and, said Colonel Yorke in his letter home, reminded them of the charge they had been given earlier. "He bid the men push home with their bayonets, and was so well obeyed that hundreds perished on their points."

Until at last the fury slackened. One by one, and then in twos and threes, and finally in tens, the Stewarts and the Camerons fell back, running, or walking with heads turned in defiance. Though Ardshiel survived, of the three hundred Appin men who had gone forward "with the smoke, the Lowland wind and rain" ninety-two were killed and more than sixty wounded. Eight of Ardshiel's family were among the twenty-two officers dead, including his old uncle, Duncan. The others were the gentlemen and tacksmen of Appin, Fasnacloich and Achnacone, Invernahyle and Ballachulish. The little chiefs and little septs of Appin lay in bloody tartan before Barrell's and Munro's. The standard-bearer of Appin had died beside Ardshiel's uncle, and when the retreat began a common man from Morven, called MacAntle, tore the blue and yellow silk from the staff, wrapped it about his body and, like *Donuil na Braiteach* of Clan Chattan, he took it from the field.*

Lord George Murray, cropped head bald, a fresh broadsword in his hand and a buckler on his arm, was coming up now with support from the second line. He was coming with Glenbucket's men, their rheumatic old commander still riding his pony. Father John Tyrie marched with them, armed for the Lord's battle with prayer and pistol, but it was too late. Neither Glenbucket's, nor other Gordons of Lord Lewis's regiment would or could advance through the retreating Camerons and Stewarts. The Royal guns on the left were once more firing, sweeping the

---

* The saltire standard of the Appin Regiment now hangs in Edinburgh Castle, in the same room with the King's and Regimental Colours of Barrell's (4th) Foot, The King's Own.

heather with grape. The Camerons paused by Lochiel, lifted his lamed body, and carried him with them.

Now was the moment for the Argyll men. They stood up behind the dry-stone wall and fired a volley into the flank of the exhausted, staggering retreat. They loaded calmly and fired three more volleys, and then they drew their broadswords. They yelled "*Cruachan!*". They climbed over the wall and rushed upon the Camerons, but they did not have it all their own way. The half-witted fellow in one of the companies saw his dream realised. "Here we had Ballimore killed," wrote Duncan Campbell to his chief, "with three of his company, and two wounded, and Achnaba wounded who died the Friday after."

Where the fight had been strongest, and where uneasy odds might have been turned in the Rebel's favour, there was now defeat. The clans on the right had expended their one great advantage, the charge. "Nothing could be more furious than their onset," Surgeon Grainger told his brother, "which no troops but these, headed by our magnanimous hero, could have withstood." He meant the Duke of Cumberland. "We had some hundreds of them breathless on the ground. They rallied, and before our left could load came again like lions to the charge, sword in hand, but the claymores could make no impression against the bayonet charged breast high. Our men stood like a wall, shoulder to shoulder."

As for Barrell's, one of them bragged, "the old Tangereers bravely repulsed those boasters with dreadful slaughter, and convinced them that their broadsword and target are unequal to the musket and bayonet when in the hands of veterans who are determined to use them." Which was all very true.

Colonel Charles Whitefoord, of the Fifth Marines, served Cumberland as a volunteer officer, "thinking it his duty to serve His Majesty", and supplying stores and transport at great expense to himself. Riding along the lines and to the rear he saw the great shock on the left. "Nothing could be more desperate than their attack and more properly received. Those in front were spitted with the bayonets; those in flank were tored in pieces by the musquetry and grape shot."

James Wolfe, too, was a witness, seeing the fight from Hawley's staff, and he was particularly proud of Barrell's, for he was a captain of that regiment, and had been since he was sixteen. "They were attacked by the Camerons (the bravest clan amongst them), and twas for some time a dispute between the swords and bayonets; but the latter was found by far the most destructable weapon. The Regiment behaved with uncommon resolution, killing, some say, almost their own number, whereas forty of them were only wounded, and those not mortally and not above ten killed. They were, however, surrounded by superiority, and would have been all destroyed had not Col. Martin with his regiment (the left of the 2nd line of Foot) moved forward to their assistance, prevented mischief, and by a well-timed fire destroyed a great number of them and obliged them to run off."

Writing the day after the battle, Brevet-Major Wolfe under-estimated the casualties in his regiment, but he rightly saw the decisive part played by the men of his father's. All witnesses agreed that if grape were the king of battles the bayonet was the queen of weapons. With it a resolute soldier could kill an enemy two yards from him, and a battalion standing in line with bayonets charged was a match for the most impetuous swords-men.

From where they had been waiting, across the sunken road from Hawley's six squadrons of dragoons, Fitz-James's Horse saw and heard the defeat of the clans. And now the Highlanders came running past them, throwing away their weapons and their plaids. Sir Jean McDonell, the Franco-Scot who was colonel of these sixty rib-bare riders, took them forward against the dragoons. Hawley's five hundred, also seeing how the fight was going, had now found the courage and the skill to plunge down into the sunken road and ride along it toward the rear of the Rebels. There was no firm ground for a charge, but the Jacobites moved in close enough to halt the dragoons and to exchange pistol and carbine fire, from which they suffered more than Cobham's or Lord Mark Kerr's. The Royal cavalry's contribution to the battle, which was to be largely a matter of butchery when it was over, was now more cowardly than anything else, although Trooper Enoch Bradshaw did not think so. "The regiment," he said, speaking of Cobham's, "will be welcome to England now, for (it) had always been in front upon all occasions where hard and dangerous duty was to be done. . . ."

The hard and dangerous duty here was for half a thousand sabres to scatter sixty wretched men, and to ride down the Foot which Harry Gordon of Avochie still held on the ridge to their front. It was not done, the dragoons preferred to advance slowly, with a jingle of scabbard and chain, with squadron guidons snapping, while McDonell and Avochie retreated slowly, protecting the routed clans.

John William O'Sullivan had lost his head. He came riding from the left wing, crying to Captain Robert O'Shea of Fitz-James's, "*All is going to pot . . .*"

"Have the clansmen of my name deserted me?"

THE MACDONALDS, SAID the Chevalier de Johnstone who advanced
with them on the left wing, were fifteen or twenty paces from
Pulteney's and the Royal Scots when the right of the Rebel
Army fell back. "If the right could only have maintained its
ground three minutes longer, the English Army, which was
very much shaken, would have been still more so by the shock
of our left. . . . And if our centre, which had pierced the first
line, had been properly supported, it is highly probable that the
English would have been soon put to flight." But these were ifs
and might-have-beens, written down years later at the Chevalier's
lodgings in Paris, and he was no different from other soldiers
who cosset their pride with the thought that defeat has been a
matter of minutes only from victory. The fact was that the
Macdonalds never came to the shock, nor could have done so with
any great effect, for they had six hundred yards or more to cross
before they reached the infantry, and this under fire from grape
and musketry.

When they heard Clan Chattan's slogan, and felt the forward
surge of Roy Stewart's and the mixed clans on their right, they
advanced also, in sullen anger. There was some hesitation at first,
for the slope of the moor was steep, the heather wet and the
ground uncertain. Alexander Macdonald of Keppoch, the matriculated student of Glasgow University, looked over his shoulder
and saw that his rent-roll was hanging back. He called to them
angrily, *"Mo Dhia, an do threig Clann mo chinnidhmi?"* My God,
he cried, have the clansmen of my name deserted me? They
came on at that appeal to their blood and pride, and came on so
furiously that Keppoch's brother, Donald, outran his own
company by several paces, his sword raised, dirk and target held

before his face in a rush to be the first Macdonald to fall upon Colonel Cockayne's men in the ranks of Pulteney's, or upon the Lowland Scots of the Royals.

All the Macdonalds, running over the heather in the three regiments of Clanranald, Keppoch and Glengarry, were striking at the right of Cumberland's first line. It was ready to receive them, muskets charged, and the word passing along the platoons. *Make ready . . . Present . . . FIRE!* The musketry rolled and the battalion guns jerked back from the fling of grape. A third or more of the Macdonalds never came within a hundred yards of the infantry. Nor was their charge an unbroken run from where they had stood to where the enemy was formed. They ran forward and they halted. They ran forward and halted again to fire their pistols and firelocks. They ran forward once more, this time almost to the bayonets, with their broadswords and axes lifted, their plaids rolled about their left arms. They fell back a few paces, and there they stood, snarling at the infantry like animals encaged. "They came down three several times within a hundred yards," said Cumberland, "firing their pistols and brandishing their swords, but the Royals and Pulteney's hardly took their firelocks from their shoulders." These three rushes, and the short withdrawals, were feints, desperate and hopeless attempts to tempt the British infantry forward in disorder.

The Chevalier de Johnstone, a tartan sash across his Lowland coat, and a Highland buckler on his arm, charged with his friend Scotus of Glengarry's, and he came close enough to Pulteney's to see their red coats and primrose facings, and to remember years later*: "As far as I could distinguish, at the distance of twenty paces, the English appeared to be drawn up in six ranks, the three first being on their knees, and keeping up a terrible running fire on us." This fire chopped down the Macdonalds by scores, but still they stood. "My unfortunate friend Scothouse was killed by my side, but I was not so deeply affected at the moment of his fall as I have been ever since. It would almost seem as if the Power that presides over the lives of men in battles marks out the most

---

* Not altogether accurately: the British battalions were formed in three ranks, not six. But Johnstone can be forgiven the mistake, it was scarcely the moment for dispassionate addition.

deserving for destruction and spares those who are most un-worthy." It was a trite enough observation, but one that comes sincerely from most fighting soldiers. "Military men, susceptible of friendship," thought Johnstone, "are much to be pitied. . . ."

The manner in which the Macdonalds stood before the Royal infantry, and were shot down with no cost at all to the ranks of Pulteney's, amused the delighted English officers. It appeared to demonstrate both the savage nature of the tribesmen and their lack of soldierly intelligence. But, said Johnstone, "as the High-landers were completely exhausted with hunger, fatigue and the want of sleep, our defeat did not at all surprise me; I was only astonished to see them behave so well."

And a sergeant of the Buffs, who had stood behind the Royals, wrote to his wife and expressed the respect which the ranks of one army will often feel for another: "The Rebels, I must own, behaved with the greatest resolution."

Kingston's Horse were coming up on the flank of Clan Donald. The clansmen could not break the infantry, or even close with it through the musketry, and they had a simple and desperate fear of mounted men. Forlorn and useless sacrifice was not a part of Highland warfare when a battle was patently lost. A man quickly ran from the field, for how could he defend his family and his land if he were dead? So the Macdonalds of Keppoch and Glengarry, of Clanranald and of the little septs of Scotus, Glencoe and Glenaladale, all went back, running in panic. "What a spectacle of horror!" said Johnstone. "The same Highlanders who had advanced to the charge like lions, with bold and deter-mined countenance, were in an instant seen flying like trembling cowards in the greatest disorder." He went back with them.

The men of Keppoch, running, passed by the body of their chief where he lay in his tartan of red and black. He had advanced with them up to the fire of Pulteney's, and kept them in line all the way, sending away his servant, Angus Ferguson, with a testy order for his brother Donald to keep in line, and not bound ahead of his company like a fool. Back from Pulteney's in a feint went Keppoch's, and then came the grape and musketry that killed Scotus and twenty of his company, killed Donald the brother, and struck Keppoch in the arm, paralysing it and bringing him to his knees. The Macdonalds fell back about him, but he was recognised by Donald Roy Macdonald from the Isle of Uist, who had once been a lieutenant with Keppoch's but was now a captain of Clanranald's. He stopped and entreated Keppoch to leave, saying that he might thus reform his regiment. But the old man would not listen, and told Donald Roy to save himself. "Oh, God, have mercy upon me . . ." he said.

Donald Roy believed the chief already dying, so he ran on alone. He was hit in the foot with grape, and began to limp, but paused again by the body of Ranald Macdonald of Bellfinlay, a "tall, strapping, beautiful young man", both of whose legs had been broken by grape. He had wrapped his plaid about him and prepared himself to die. When he saw this, and that there was nothing he could do to help, Donald Roy spoke words of pity and once more ran on alone.

James Macdonell of Kilachonat was the next to find Keppoch. He picked the old man up and began to drag him to the rear, and at this moment another bullet struck Keppoch in the back, throwing him to the ground again. Kilachonat ran from the field, crying to every man with a Macdonald badge in his bonnet that Keppoch was dead of an English ball. He ran well, this James Macdonell of Kilachonat, as far as Keppoch's country, carrying the news to the chief's lady, still in bed with her new-born. "He told her of her husband's being killed, for which he was reproved by several of Keppoch's friends, considering the situation the Lady was then in *causa scientia*."

But Keppoch was not yet dead when Kilachonat left him, though he seemed so to Angus Ferguson, returning from his errand. He, too, bent over his chief, and then ran weeping. Other men of Keppoch's passed, without recognising this tartan hump as their lord, master and father, until John MacKenzie, a private soldier of Tulloch's company, bent low beneath the musket fire and lifted the old man's head. As much as six years later he could remember, and depose before a court, what he saw. He saw the chief's broken arm, the blood on his ash-white face, and a hole in his body "about the right pap" where the ball had found an exit. John MacKenzie, too, thought Keppoch dead.

But he was still alive when one of his sons, Angus Ban, found him. He could speak a little, though his tongue was partially paralysed. Angus Ban called for help and gathered enough of his father's people to lift Keppoch in his plaid and carry him away. They passed a wounded Macdonald who was leaning on the shoulder of a young son, and this Macdonald told the boy to leave him and to go to Keppoch, for his first duty was to his chief and not his father. They carried Keppoch to a little bothy some distance away, and Angus Ban told the clansmen to put the old man there so that his wounds might be dressed. The hut was full of wounded Macdonalds, and there were also some beggars who had come to loot the dead but who had now gathered in terror behind the protection of the sod and the stones. When Angus Ban lifted his father's head he saw that this time the old chief was truly dead. Outside the bothy there were yells and the roll of hooves as Kingston's Horse rode down on the rout of Clan Donald. Angus Ban took his father's sword and dirk, and he ran towards his home country. The weapons were heavy, however, and they made it difficult for him to run, and he stopped by marshy ground, plunging them into it.

Not only were Keppoch's broken, but Glengarry's and Clanranald's too. Those who were left of Glencoe's men were running, with MacIan their chief, the great wit and poet who had no humour and no verse in him at this moment. All the Macdonalds were running, sullenly ignoring the Duke of Perth's weak and desperate cry of "*Claymore!*". They ran past the second line where the exiles of the Scots Royal and the Irish Picquets let them through, closing ranks again under Walter Stapleton. Here was the crisis gloomily forecast by the old mercenary, and if the Highland Scots were retreating from it, as he had expected they would, he was determined that his command should stand and protect them. He took his place among the red and blue ranks, in King Louis's uniform and with his sword in his hand, directing volleys that kept back the Nottingham volunteers of Kingston's. The Irish of Dillon's, Ruth's and Lally's held the flank where the dock-tailed horses and curved sabres were thickest. Kingston's fired pistols and carbines, hacked with their sabres in a brief and excited flurry that lasted a few moments only, during which Stapleton was terribly wounded and many others killed. Then the exiles began their retreat, still keeping between the troopers and the running Macdonalds, facing about several times and standing their ground, until Kingston's let them go and went off yelling in pursuit of other fugitives.

The tartan tide was ebbing back all over the moor, and when it passed beyond the three score yards at which a musket was effective, the Royal line stopped its volleying, although Belford's gunners kept up the grape. The east wind was still blowing strongly, but the rain and the sleet had long since stopped, and the sky which had been steel-grey was now a sulphurous yellow from the smoke. Along the ranks the subalterns and sergeants cried "*Rest on your Arms!*", and the men of Pulteney's and the Royals, of Cholmondeley's, Price's and the Fusiliers, the bloody platoons of Munro's and Barrell's, grounded their muskets and stared. The heather before them writhed and heaved, and the air was full of the cries and the groans of the wounded. Where the fallen were thickest the bodies made little pyramids, from which naked arms or legs jerked in agony, and the red and yellow of the tartans were mixed with the blood and bile of the clans. Not only Fusilier Linn, but other veterans of the dead ground at Fontenoy thought that they had never seen a field so heavy with dead and dying. Beyond, some Rebel units still kept their formation, too confused to advance or retreat, played upon with grape and harried on the flank by Cobham's and Lord Mark Kerr's Dragoons who had now broken through Fitz-James's and Avochie's men.

Lord George Murray, dismounted and still without wig or hat, stood in the rout of the army he might have commanded in victory, had he been given the chance. He was to be one of the last to leave. The Prince had gone. When O'Sullivan came crying to O'Shea that everything had gone "to pot", he and other Irish galloped to Charles. They begged him to leave, but the young man, unable to understand what had happened, or perhaps understanding it too well, was as irresolute as ever, staring forward to where his clans were running back. For a moment it seemed as if he were about to spur his horse forward and ride into Cumberland's lines, but O'Sullivan seized his bridle and turned him about. And so he was taken away, his face wet with tears. Lord Elcho, the rancorous and bitter young man who commanded the Prince's Life Guards, lost his love, respect and some of his loyalty for Charles at that moment, yelling (so he claimed later), "Run, you cowardly Italian!"

The red dragoons were riding all along the ground that had been the rear of the Rebel Army, doing their best "for our dear Bill", as Trooper Bradshaw put it. Some of them rode down on Father John Tyrie where he was kneeling by the dying of Glenbucket's, and they cut him twice upon the head with their swords, from which terrible wounds he miraculously survived. Lord Strathallan gathered a few Jacobite Horse, not more than forty, and tried to hold the dragoons, but they were of no more value than a handful of gravel thrown against a wall, and their saddles were quickly emptied. Strathallan spurred into Cobham's with furious desperation, and was cut through the waist by a sabre. He was the only Lowland leader to die at Culloden. John Daniel the Englishman was in this charge, too, "coming to the place I was on before, and seeing it covered with the dead bodies of many of the Hussars who at the time of our leaving had occupied it, I pressed on, resolving to kill or be killed. Some few accompanied my standard, but soon left it."

Dazed by a wound in his left arm, he found himself alone, and he rode along the field with his standard until he met Lord John Drummond, commander of the Rebel centre. This "jolly lord", who had walked far to the front of his command before the action began in an effort to tempt Cumberland into an advance, was now unnerved and defeated. He yelled to Daniel to fly with him, "shewing me his regiment, just by him, surrounded. We left the field of battle in a body, though pursued and fired upon for some time."

The four Camerons who had carried away Lochiel had not gone far. Their chief was heavy and they were exhausted. Toward Balvraid they found a little barn into which they took him, and "as they were taking off his cloaths to disguise him the barn was surrounded by a party of dragoons". They prepared themselves to die with him, but the troopers were called away for easier work elsewhere, and the Camerons hurriedly threw Lochiel across a stray horse and took him away.

Old Balmerino, John Daniel's commander, did not run, though Elcho urged him to ride away. Balmerino shook his head calmly. He was too old for flight, and too wise not to see that this was the end of the Cause. He was not afraid of death, by muskets there or the axe later. He left the field, then turned about and rode to surrender with his back straight. The Earl of Kilmarnock, looking for his regiment, was captured when he mistook Royal horsemen for his own. They surrounded him in the smoke and yelled for his sword. He was an iron, proud man, to whom this was disaster. There were tears on his face as he rode by the thistle and saltire colours of the Royal Scots Fusiliers. A tall Fusilier officer met him, and held a hat before the tears and shame on the earl's face. He was James, Lord Boyd, a handsome young man who was to remind Dr. Johnson of the Homeric Sarpedon, and he was also Kilmarnock's son.

The Royal cavalry was now moving in red swirls all over the ground the Rebels had held. Squadrons of Cobham's and Kerr's were hallooing down the moor toward the Ruthven road and the valley of the Nairn. Kingston's Horse, on the right, advanced on loose rein through the policies of Culloden House, chasing the Macdonalds and exiles who had taken the Inverness road. With them rode James Ray of Whitehaven, who seems to have gone where he liked "as I had the honour of being a volunteer under His Royal Highness and at liberty to chuse my own station". He was a provincial snob and a great name-dropper, who had joined Cumberland's army to protect His Majesty, or so he said, but proved his interests to be largely murder and plunder. Early in the day he had ridden with Cobham's where, by his own telling, he exchanged gentlemanly politenesses with the young Lord Ancrum. When the rout began his lordship asked Trooper Ray whether it was his pleasure to charge with Cobham's, but the Whitehaven man thought he would rather have a sally with Kingston's this time, so "his lordship then wished me good success". Ancrum was a chivalrous and compassionate man, and it is unlikely that he would have approved of the manner in which Ray carried out these good wishes.

Now the cannon had stopped, and Belford's men wiped the powder and sweat from their faces, leant on their ramrods and looked at what their guns had done. One of Cumberland's young aides was already away down the brae with a message for the captain of H.M.S. *Gibraltar*, who had brought his ship past Fort George into the inner haven of the firth and was now off Alturlie Point to the north-west of the moor. His Royal Highness's compliments, and he wanted rum and brandy, biscuits and cheese immediately for his brave boys. And although the cannon on the field were silent, the guns of all the ships and all the transports were firing courteous salutes, the noise bouncing against the hills of the Black Isle, and the smoke rolling low on the water.

No order was yet given to the infantry for a general advance along the line, to take customary and victorious possession of the ground deserted by the enemy. His Royal Highness rode up and down, fat stomach extended against buff vest, and the light livid on his white wig, white stock and white cuffs. From regiment to regiment he rode, calling out to each. "Wolfe's boys, I thank you," he said. "You have done the business!" And "Brave Sempill's!" he said, bowing to the Scots Borderers. When the Argyll men came by him, carrying the body of Ballimore, he lifted his hat again and called them his "brave Campbells". To Pulteney's and Munro's he also spoke kindly, letting them understand that he thought they had more than redeemed their scoundrelly behaviour at Falkirk. The soldiers put their black hats or their mitre caps on the points of their bayonets, and raised them in the air. They shouted "Billy! Billy!", and then, all along the line, "Flanders! Flanders!". They meant him to understand that now they had finished this business for their Billy, they would be happy to return with him to more conventional warfare in the Low Countries.

The last of the Rebels were running, darting, dodging before the dragoons. The Duke of Cumberland, who had ridden back to the right of the line, put on his hat and pulled it down over his nose in his characteristic fashion. "They run!" he said. "Rise up Pulteney's and shoulder!" The subalterns and captains cried the orders. *Shoulder your firelocks. . . . Rear ranks close. . . . MARCH!* The Army went forward with bayonets advanced, to the tap of swinging drums, white gaiters lifted above the heather, and ammunition boots coming down on the dead and the dying. They marched to where the Rebels had stood, and there they halted and grounded their muskets. They cheered, the short huzzas, the barking triumph of British infantry. Two thousand yards away by Balvraid, where he had halted beneath a tree, Prince Charles heard them. He was surrounded by what was left of his Army, the wrack of the left wing, and he made two divisions of it, wildly telling them to seek what safety they could before he rode away along the Ruthven road. "Do as you wish," he said, "only for God's sake let us go now."

Surgeon Grainger rode forward behind Pulteney's, much pleased, he told his brother, that they had regained their character in this battle. For a medical man and a non-combatant he was curiously exhilarated by what he saw. "You may be sure it gave me infinite joy to see those who threatened ruin to our glorious Constitution of Church and State dead on the field. . . . The whole field on their side was one continued scene of slaughter and dismay."

"'Tis mine and everybody's opinion," said Enoch Bradshaw, "no history can brag of so singular a victory." This was an ordinary soldier's judgment, and ordinary soldiers, who are asked to do most of the dying, count great victories in terms of loss to themselves. Of nearly nine thousand Horse and Foot who had advanced from Nairn, fifty only were dead, and two hundred and fifty-nine wounded, or such were the figures published by the Government. Since an army defeated and routed is in no position to determine its casualties, and since an army victorious may be inclined to exaggerate those it inflicts, the Rebel losses are hard to assess. Some reports put the dead at two thousand, which would be nearly half the numbers engaged. The figure was certainly not less than twelve hundred, which is the most modest figure. A Presbyterian minister, living close to the moor, was told later by one of the Duke's surgeons, "a very sedate, grave man", that he had counted all the bodies that lay on the field of battle as exactly as he could, and had made the number about seven hundred and fifty. These were bodies lying where the fight had been fiercest, and did not include those who crawled away to die in the hills, the fugitives ridden down on the roads,

the wounded who were to be slaughtered on the moor during the
next two or three days. Even while the surgeon counted, the
infantry were stabbing and thrusting at any movement in the
bodies before their stationary line.

"Would to God the enemy had been worthy enough of our
troops," Cumberland was to write to his old commander, Sir
John Ligonier. "Sure never were soldiers in such a temper.
Silence and obedience the whole time, and all our manoeuvres
were performed without the least confusion. I must owe that
you have hit my weak side when you say that the honour of our
troops is restored; that pleases me beyond all honours due to me."

Due or not, the honours would come in plenty, and there
was no doubt in most of his brave boys' minds that the Duke
deserved them, "he beeing the darling of mankind" in Enoch
Bradshaw's opinion. "Down on your knees all England," Enoch
apostrophised his stay-at-home brother in Cirencester, "and
after praise to God who gives victory, pray for the young British
hero!"

Surgeon Grainger, in his ride across the field, found an overturned coach which he assumed had once belonged to Prince
Charles. It had the Welsh arms painted upon it, he said, by
which he presumably meant the Prince of Wales's feathers, and
there were the words *Prince Charles* in letters of gold. The surgeon
climbed upon it to watch the scarlet skirmish line of Kingston's
Horse galloping toward Inverness. The Nottingham men had
already flushed the truant schoolboys from the heather, and
ridden with bloody sabres among the exhausted clansmen still
asleep in the parks. Now they rode towards the town, cutting
down the men, women and children who had come to see the
battle, firing their pistols or carbines at any face staring from a
window. James Ray the volunteer was the first rider to enter
Inverness. He came rattling down the street past the Tolbooth,
and he stopped by the well-house in which he had seen two men
taking shelter. He yelled to Margaret Grant, a servant-girl,
ordering her to hold his bridle. She did so, and stood there while
Volunteer Ray went inside, but, when she heard screams from the
two men whose throats James Ray was cutting, she ran away
and hid behind a corner.

She saw him come out at last, with blood upon him. He walked up the street, pulling his horse, and he hammered the hilt of his sabre on the door of the minister's house declaring that he was a volunteer come from the County of Cumberland to fight for his religion and liberty. He demanded lodgings and food, "for ministers," he shouted, "always have good things".

"Lord, what am I when so many brave men lie dead"

THE INFANTRY HELD the field and rested, eating the biscuits and cheese brought to them from the bread-wagons. The tension of battle was over, releasing in many of them an animal brutality and a macabre sense of fun. They laughed at the comic stupidity of death, and because they had recently been in fear of it they had to humble it. Their officers watched without protest, although one of them wrote with faint nausea of what he saw. "The moor was covered with blood," he said, "and our men, what with killing the enemy, dabbling their feet in the blood, and splashing it about one another, looked like so many butchers rather than Christian soldiers." There is no record of where the chaplains of brigades were at this moment of victory for which they had prayed. Some of the soldiers, their cheese eaten, rose to bayonet or shoot any clansman trying to struggle from the heaps of dead. And the men still eating watched with professional detachment. To the indignity of death the soldiers added profaner, obscener humiliations, unconsciously revenging themselves on the fear they had recently felt.

There were clansmen who still fought. Gillies MacBean, the major of Clan Chattan, was not yet dead. Although he had gone down under bayonet thrust and butt stroke on the second line, he had been able to rise and, with broadsword in his hand, follow his retreating clan. They soon outstripped him, and by a wall, six hundred yards from the field toward Balvraid, he was overtaken by dragoons and infantrymen. He put his back to the stones and faced the horsemen, and fought with such fury and determination that Lord Ancrum cried out, "Save the brave fellow!" But the dragoons were maddened by his defiance and they rode in upon him together, trampling him down under the hooves. Still he was not dead. When the dragoons had gone he crawled to a barn, where an old woman covered him with straw, and under this he finally died. The farm-folk buried him beside their house, covering the hole with a lathe-stone so that it might not be seen.

Robert Mor MacGillivray, a young man from Dalziel of Petty, was overtaken in a corner of the Culwhiniac enclosure, and he was without sword or dirk or any weapon. He picked up the tram of a peat-car, swinging it about his head and knocking down seven soldiers before he was shot. The soldiers who killed him remembered his bravery with a grudging admiration for its stupidity. Later that afternoon when they called at a cottage for water they were still talking about Robert Mor, and although he had been one man against many they thought enough of his courage to boast of having overcome it. The woman of the house, Mrs. Alexander MacGillivray, listened to them, and knew from the way they described the Highlander that they were talking of her brother-in-law.

Mrs. Macdonald, the cottager, continued with her desperate bread-making all through the battle, and even when the running clansmen began to pass her door. She had freshly made up the fire when "a poor Highlander who had lost his hand rushed in, and staunched the bleeding stump by thrusting it on the hot stones of the fireplace". The women in the hamlets and the houses westward of the moor were Clan Chattan women, with men in the battle. Half a century later, the son of one of them remembered, "Oftentimes I heard my mother speak of the anxiety she felt, how she strained her eyes from the door of the bothy where I now dwell. Exhausted with fatigue, as clansmen passed the bothy, they exclaimed to my mother '*A bhean, a bhean, thoir dhuinn deoch!*' Woman, woman, give us a drink! My mother busily employed herself in handing basins of water to the men from the bothy." And at length she saw her brothers come with the remnants of the Mackintosh regiment, and she fed them and helped them on their way.

On the field, John and James Chisholm had found the body of their young brother, surrounded by the dead of almost all their clansmen, and they cleaned the boy's face, straightened his limbs, and stood by the body to protect it from mutilation. Elsewhere General Henry Hawley was riding with his staff, urging soldiers to kill any man still alive, and that if there were any doubt, to plunge with the bayonet just the same. He shouted oaths and orders from a red and impassioned face. He was an old man, his commission dated from 1694, and his men hated him and called him "The Hangman", and they would have been surprised to hear that he believed he stood no higher in the estimation of the Almighty than did they, and that his will, already written, asked that he be buried with "no more expense or ridiculous show than a poor soldier (who is as good a man)". He rode by the ground in the middle of the field where the Frasers lay thickly, among them their commander, young Charles Fraser of Inverallochie. He was still alive, and he stared up from the blood at Hawley's face. The General turned to one of his staff, who is thought to have been James Wolfe, and told him to pistol the Rebel dog. The officer refused, offering his commission instead, and Hawley found a soldier who killed Inverallochie without scruple.*

There were some among the infantry and the dragoons who refused to join in the murder and the obscene atrocities. But they were few. Even the gentle Michael Hughes seemed to think the brutality justified. "This rebel host had been most deeply in debt to the publick for all the rapine, murder and cruelty; and since the time was now come to pay off the score, our people were all glad to clear the reckoning, and heartily determined to give them receipt in full." However, Lachlan Shaw, Quartermaster to Sempill's regiment, was sickened by what he saw and did his best to save some of his fellow-Scots, though he did think them traitorous rebels and papists most likely to boot. He was mounted that day, and he left his regiment where it had grounded its muskets and he rode about the field. He put his horse between a soldier and a maimed clansman, telling the cripple to take hold of the stirrup, and in this fashion he carried the man out of danger. Coming back he saw another wounded clansman, staggering and crying for mercy. Shaw stood by the fellow, protecting

* This story is often told with Cumberland as the principal, but it fits Hawley's character better, particularly if Wolfe were the officer concerned. He was on Hawley's staff, not the Duke's.

him from the troopers until Hawley rode up. "Damn you, Shaw!" yelled the General. "Do you mean to preserve the life of a Rebel?" Shaw rode on reluctantly and, turning his head, he saw the dragoons stabbing and slashing at the wounded man.

The Horse, "Cobham's heroes" according to Enoch Bradshaw, did most of the murdering. They went hurrahing after every human being between Drummossie Moor and Inverness. Close by Barnhill, outside the town, some of them came up with "a very honest old gentlemen of the name of MacLeod" who had nothing to do with wars in general and the Rebels in particular. He had come to see the battle. He ran before the horsemen until he could run no further, and then he turned, going down on his knees with a cry for mercy. The dragoons swore at him and pistolled him through the head.

The Rev. James Hay, at whose door Trooper Ray had hammered, kept a very careful account of what he saw that day, and added to it first-hand accounts from other eye-witnesses, sending the whole to his good friend the Reverend Robert Forbes of Leith, who was collecting such stories of the Rebellion. Among them was a copy of a letter "in the handwriting of some unknown person". He was unknown, perhaps, because in the climate of the times he had no wish to have his name associated with this sort of thing, but his letter said that he had found himself caught up in the rout and pursuit outside Inverness that Wednesday afternoon. He saw what the dragoons were doing and had done. He saw "a woman stript and laid in a very indecent posture, and some of the other sex with their privites placed in their hands". Further along the Inverness road he found twelve or fourteen bodies, not all of them Rebel soldiers, and they too had been stripped and treated in the same manner. By a corner at King's Milns, close to Inverness, he saw a boy of twelve lying, "his head cloven to his teeth".

This was not a day for innocent bystanders, and one of them, Alexander Munro, counted himself lucky to have escaped, though he had to kill before he did. He was thirty years of age and the keeper of the ferry at Bona. On Tuesday evening he and his neighbour decided to go out to watch the battle promised for the next morning. They left at seven o'clock, walking excitedly toward the moor. The first interesting thing they found was a sword, lying on the earth by the quarry. They tossed a coin, by which Munro became the winner and placed the weapon beneath his coat as they walked on. It was a long walk, and the battle was over before they got to Drummossie Moor. First there were the clansmen running about them, a picture of war which Munro and his neighbour had not imagined. They decided that they would be wiser to go to Inverness instead, but before they reached the town the dragoons were upon them. Munro ran for shelter on the braes west of Craigmore House, pursued by a yelling trooper who finally cornered the ferryman against a dyke. Munro took the sword in both hands and brought it down on the head of the dragoon's horse. The animal fell, bringing its rider down beneath it, and, while the dragoon lay there the now-maddened Munro slashed at him and killed him.

Being a powerful man, he dragged both horse and soldier into the bushes, threw away the sword and ran for his home. Arriving there he found that his neighbour was busily looting the house, having told Mrs. Munro that her man was dead.

Cumberland's soldiers had little sympathy and no regret for the civilians killed on the roads. They were wrong, but their distaste was for men who had come to watch them die, and in that perhaps their attitude is understandable. Later in the day, as he marched with Bligh's into Inverness, Michael Hughes saw the road "covered with dead bodies, and many of the inhabitants, not doubting of success, who came out of curiosity to see the action, or perhaps to get plunder, never went home to tell the story, for being mixt with their own people we could not know one from the other".

But there were many killed by the dragoons who had not been drawn to the battle by morbid curiosity or cupidity. Two miles from the moor, at Inshes where the bare moor falls steeply, Alexander Young did not know that there had been a battle. The break of the hill above his home, or perhaps the fall of the wind, had brought him no sound, and he was at work in his small field. At two o'clock, when he was behind his plough, he saw the first clansmen come running down the brae. This was no concern of his, he thought, but he took shelter in his house just the same, and there some of the dragoons found him at the door. They shot him in the leg, and then followed him inside, killing him with their swords. They killed his younger son, a boy of eight or nine, and would have killed the other son, too, had he not escaped from them through a hole in the crude earth wall.

At the Mains of Gask, six miles from the battlefield and south-westward where the moor ends in a knot of craggy hills, Elspeth McPhail saw the dragoons coming. She took up her new-born child and ran with it into the fields to find her husband. Four horsemen galloped after her, and cut at her until she had seven wounds. One of these riders took her child by the thigh and twirled it in his hand before releasing it. Elspeth McPhail's husband, who had watched this helplessly, was then chased into the moss below Creag Shoilleir.

Most people in Inverness, who had recently been the enthusias-tic hosts of the Jacobites, hurriedly reorganised their loyalties that afternoon. Their streets were full of Kingston's Horse, among whom were two robust butchers from Nottingham, each swinging his sword and boasting that he had killed fourteen men on the road to the town. Before these horsemen ran fugitive Rebels, calling for help, and knocking on doors for shelter. "There were vast numbers of them," said an English officer, "some crying, some mourning. Some stood astonished and did not know whither to turn themselves."

The bodies of fourteen sabred men lay by the roadside at one spot between Inverness and Moy, among them a woman who had been left for dead "after receiving many cuts of the sword on the face, and many stabs of the bayonet". The Duke of King-ston's Horse, said Michael Hughes, "pursued vigorously, and killed great numbers without distinction; for being new raised men they were more willing to exert themselves". And the exertion, no doubt, was all the more zealous because it carried none of the risks of battle.

On the field, now, the infantry finished their dinner, shouldered their arms and fell into ranks by columns. The bat-wagons had come up to take the wounded, and the women to find their men. They walked through the heather with their skirts lifted and the blood splashed on their calves. The drums were beating, and the voices of the directing-sergeants were hoarser still from the smoke and the strain of the battle. The King's fat and young son was dismounted, sitting on a large stone and staring at the field. After some minutes of deep meditation he rose and walked among the dead. He laid his hand upon his breast and lifted his face to look at the sky, and he said, or he was reported to have said,

"Lord, what am I, that I should be spared when so many brave men lie dead upon this spot?"

"Pleased to take lodgings where Charley kept court"

CUMBERLAND ENTERED INVERNESS at four o'clock in the afternoon. After-orders of the day, issued briefly from the saddle on Drummossie Moor, said all that was necessary at the moment: "Field of Battle near Culloden Park, 16 April 1746. The Surgeons to take immediate Care of the wounded. The Army and Artillery to form in Columns and march through Inverness to Camp. The Q.Mrs and 6 men per Company to go back for the tent poles and bring them up with the Battn Horses. Lord Sempills Regt to March forward to Inverness and take Charge of the Town and the Prisoners there. The Cavalry to pursue the Enemy as fast as they can." So the Army formed its columns and marched down the brae to the firthside road where- it formed again in column of route. Sempill's Borderers, with grenadier drums beating and yellow colours advanced, set off for the town in quick time.

Cumberland paused a while at Culloden House. His young officers wandered curiously through the rooms and corridors, and found them littered with the debris of the Jacobites' hurried evacuation that morning. The empty hogsheads were a disappointment, but there was still the table with its roast side of lamb and two fowls, albeit cold now. At Culloden House Cumberland is said to have written a detailed dispatch to the King, telling his father of the great victory secured by his arms. Well before sunset, he was in Inverness.

He rode in at the head of a captain's guard of dragoons, his sword bare in his hand as befitted a victor, his chubby face wet with sweat, and his fine scarlet coat spattered with mud. Behind him came his army which, according to his servile biographer, was "all huzzaing and seemed prodigiously pleased". On the outskirts of the town he was met by a Rebel drummer in the uniform of the Scots Royal, his sticks beating a sad and slow request for parley. With him was a dragoon officer from General Bland's staff who told Cumberland that the General held the French units prisoner and that their commander, Brigadier Stapleton, was asking for quarter. Still in the saddle, Cumberland asked Colonel Yorke to dismount and pencil a note, telling Stapleton that his men, being French or in the French service, were assured of fair quarter and honourable treatment. That little punctilio concluded, with its nostalgic reminders of more chivalrous affrays in Flanders, the Army marched on, down the slope and into the town where the Scots Royal and the Irish Picquets stood behind their surrendered arms and within a guarding square of Borderers and Horse. Brigadier Stapleton was still alive, but would die of his wounds before a week was over.

The bells began to ring. The churches of Inverness, which weeks before had given Prince Charles the same iron clang of welcome, now gave out for the Duke, the ringers pulling so heartily and so desperately in their new loyalty that nothing else could be heard until Cumberland held up his hand for silence. He appeared to be quite moved by the ovation.

He halted his horse beside the Tolbooth and called for the keys, and also for the keys of other prisons in which the Rebels had kept his soldiers prisoner. When the pale-faced men came out, blinking in the strong light, the Duke was there on foot to greet them, moving among them and putting his arm about their shoulders in great emotion. He called "Brother soldiers, you are free!". Most of them were very glad to be free. A week before, a Rebel officer (who was probably John Roy Stewart) had stripped them almost naked in order to clothe his own men, and they had shivered for some days until Lord George Murray heard of the incident and ordered the clothes returned. But they remembered this barbarous treatment with indignation. The Duke, hearing of their hardship, ordered that each of them should receive a guinea. He also told his secretary, the London silk merchant Sir Everard Fawkener, that twelve guineas from the ducal purse should also be given to every man wounded that afternoon. The old man made a note of the order, by the clear mercer's handwriting in which he corresponded with his friend Voltaire.

The released prisoners could count themselves fortunate. Whether a man remained a brother soldier or became a traitorous deserter often depended less on conscience than on an empty belly or a confused mind. A soldier was just a soldier in the eighteenth century, with no particular stake in the political brawls that required his services. Many of the men held prisoner by the Rebels had switched their allegiance, forty-five of Guise's regiment alone, arguing, perhaps, that service in an army where there was little or no flogging was infinitely preferable to one in which there was too much. And for such men, when they were found among the Rebels taken, there were no guineas, no fraternal embraces from the Duke. They went straight into the Tolbooth and the gaols recently vacated by their comrades, and Major Chambre of Blakeney's, Major Colvile of the Fusiliers and Major Forrester of the Royals were ordered to prepare three General Courts-Martial to try the scoundrels immediately. Carpenters and wrights from the Train were set to building gibbets to carry out the sentences of such courts.

Files of grenadiers, under their subalterns, also left Inverness that sunset to arrest several gentlemen of the neighbourhood who were supposed to be disaffected. Meanwhile the Army had marched through the town, rounded the foot of the ruined castle, and climbed to the high ground of the Crown. There, when the battalion horses arrived with the tent-poles, they set up their company streets. Before Tattoo, Sergeant Joe Napper of Cholmondeley's, and all the other Orderly Sergeants of the battalions who could be relied upon to write a fair hand, paraded at headquarters for the next day's orders. They dipped their pens in their ink-horns and wrote down their young commander's pleasure. "His Royal Highness thanks all ye officers and men for their gallant behaviour this day. . . . His Royal Highness releases all ye Military prisoners who were this day in custody of the Provost." So the men awaiting flogging, stoppages of pay, even hanging perhaps, found that the bloody business upon the moor had won them an unexpected amnesty.

"The Colours and the Standards taken from the Rebells to be

brought in this afternoon, the persons who took them will receive 16 guineas for each. The Artillery to receive all fire-locks and broadswords that are brought in to them, and to pay half a crown for each. A Return to be given in to each Regiment of the names of the Officers and men taken prisoner by them. . . . The Commanding Officers to take care that there be no firing of pieces in the Camp." Whatever His Grace's pleasure and delight in victory, there would be no drunken *feu de joie* from the other ranks.

At sunset, squad-fires glowed on the Crown, and they glowed, too, far back on Drummossie Moor, where sentinels ringed the field and called to each other's loneliness during the night. Among the wounded clansmen lying there, were some who tried to pass through the sentries and were coldly bayoneted. Alexander Mackintosh of Issich, who had charged and fallen with Clan Chattan, was more fortunate. Badly wounded, he crawled on hands and knees along the Culwhiniac wall until he was stopped by two sentinels. From his sporran he took two shillings sterling, and offered them in exchange for his life. The soldiers took the money and let him go, saying they preferred the money to his life, though they could easily have taken both.

"The Duke," said Michael Hughes, "was very pleased to take his lodgings where young Charly had just before kept his Court." Cumberland was always very pleased to take over the house and bed vacated by his cousin, be it at Holyrood Palace in Edinburgh, or a red sandstone building here in Inverness. This last acquisition was the home of the Dowager Lady Mackintosh, whose son served King George, and whose daughter-in-law had raised the clan for the Prince. Because of this confusing relationship, and the fact that she had been hostess to Charles, the Duke decided that she would be best held behind a locked door. So off to the common guard-room the old lady was taken, with a pound of meal a day for subsistence, and a few days later she was heard to make a sharp declaration of neutrality. "I've had two king's bairns living under my roof in my time, and to tell you the truth I wish I may never have another."

Her house, in Church Street opposite St. John's Chapel, was the best there was in the bleak Highland capital. It contained one room that was not encumbered by a bed, a most unusual distinction. This room, in which Charles had once dined on his favourite dish of oysters, blazed with scarlet and gold and blue that Wednesday evening. Young men and grizzled veterans like Hawley and Bland surrounded their royal commander, drinking in the candlelight, and playing piquet in pairs. For the Duke it was an evening of immense satisfaction and triumph. At the age of twenty-five he had saved his father's kingdom and redeemed the reputation of the Army. He had a country at his feet, and permission from the King's First Minister to do what he thought fit for its proper subjugation. His red-haired cousin who, until to-day, had been the heroic Alexander of the hills, was a wretched fugitive in the heather. At dusk the Duke had heard his soldiers calling "Billy!" from the Crown, and now, at his table, old men who had fought under King William or with Marlborough at Blenheim and Malplaquet, were declaring him to be one of the greatest captains of the age. Few young men, even kings' sons, can have had such an evening.

While he enjoyed himself with his staff and his general officers of division, his clerks and quartermasters were drawing up the formidable list of booty captured: 30 pieces of ordnance with swivel guns, 2,320 firelocks and 190 broadswords, 37 barrels of gunpowder, and 1,019 balls, 22 ammunition carts and a food train. There were 14 stands of colours, 1,500 musket cartridges and 500 hundredweight of musket shot. There were tents, canteens, pouches, cartouches, boxes, pistols, holsters, flints, saddles and harness. There were also, in the gaols of Inverness that night, 222 French and 326 Rebel prisoners, including a frightened boy of thirteen, Thomas Gillespie from Linlithgow, servant to an officer of the Duke of Perth's.

For two days the dead, the dying and the wounded of the clans lay unattended on Drummossie Moor, watched by the sentinels of the guard. General Orders for Thursday evening advised all soldiers that the only water fit to be drunk was to be found at the well-house in the town. They were told that Duncan Forbes's estate at Culloden was not to be pillaged or damaged, and that a loyal (or circumspect) gentleman of the neighbourhood, Mr. Dundas, had given a barrel of pork to every corps. The Commanding Officer of the Royals was told to send a sergeant and twelve men with six bread carts to fetch the Rebels' bedding from Fraserfield so that it might be "used for our wounded, and deliver them to the Hospital at the Charity School". Soldiers and soldiers' women were told that any watches, rings, gold and silver plate, horse furniture, "or anything of that kind" coming into their possession since the battle should be taken to Ensign Bryce, "who wants to look at them and will fully satisfy them for anything he purchases". The looting was being properly organised.

And the orders further said that the commanding officers of all battalions should see that their ammunition was completed to twenty-four rounds for musket or carbine, and eight for pistol. All letters, orders, maps or other papers picked up on the field or elsewhere were to be handed to Sir Everard Fawkener. A sergeant-major from each battalion was to go directly to the Tolbooth and other gaols, and there make a careful return of all deserters from his regiment whom he found among the Rebel prisoners.

And there was one final and important order on which a great deal was to depend, and which was to finish the agony of those not yet dead upon the Moor: "A Captain and 50 Foot to march directly and visit all the cottages in the neighbourhood of the field of battle, and to search for rebels. The officers and men will take notice that the Public orders of the rebels yesterday was to give us no quarter."

This order, oblique and ambiguous, is the only one on record by which Cumberland seems to have authorised murder and brutality. He could have been instructing his soldiers to dispatch any Rebel found alive, which is what they were to do, or he could have been warning them against savage and desperate acts of resistance. But the "Public orders of the rebels" to which he referred did not exist. It was generally believed in the Army that such an order from Lord George Murray had been found in the pocket of a Highland officer. Certainly Lord George's orders of the day had been found, but the phrase about no quarter was a crude forgery added afterwards. Cumberland must surely have known this, and whether he did or not, whether he cared or not, he was, as commander of the Army, responsible for its behaviour.

And if nothing was put to orders, to be read before the battalions, what passed across the table with the claret and the port when he sat with his general officers was probably far more positive. Cumberland, in his letters to London, made no secret of his contempt for Scots in general and Highlanders in particular. He had a young man's hasty emotions, and a prince's touchy sense of insecurity. Behind him, too, during those days in Scotland was Henry Hawley, the brutal professional soldier who had the manners of a medieval baron. He was always ready with advice for a young man whose noble nature might betray him into too much clemency. Three months before Culloden Hawley had set up gibbets in the Grassmarket at Edinburgh, and refused the citizens' plea that they be removed once the Rebels hanged upon them were dead. The sight of a gallows, he thought, was t he best physic for a sick kingdom, next to a regiment of dragoons. Cumberland occasionally made faint protest against Hawley's methods, but he never took strong steps to restrain the rough man. He did not think much of Hawley as a general, but he seems to have recognised his value as a policeman, and it is always comforting to have someone ready to do necessary work of an unpleasant character.

Yet, it was with cries of "Billy!" that the execution squads of the Royals marched for Drummossie Moor on Friday, followed later by thirty-six men and two drummers of Cholmondeley's under Captain Trapaud, and by detachments from other battalions.

The nights of Wednesday and Thursday had been intensely cold, and many of the wounded clansmen had been stripped of their clothes by the beggars who came out of the hills. Throughout the hours of darkness the people of Culwhiniac, Urchil and Leanach heard the crying and the moaning from the field. On Thursday the women and children of Clan Chattan came looking for their men, and were either driven away by the sentinels, or allowed to proceed upon payment. Elizabeth Campbell of Clunas found the body of the red-haired Dunmaglass by the spring where he had died, at the corner of the Culwhiniac enclosure. Many wounded of Clan Chattan had crawled there, too, and bled to death in the water. A woman of the district had tied a handkerchief about the arm of Dunmaglass, so that Elizabeth

Campbell might recognise him among so much uniform death. By one story she took MacGillivray's body to the churchyard of Petty down the brae, a small green hill overlooking the firth, and there he was buried. But by another enduring story the sentinels drove her away, and Dunmaglass's body was later thrown into a pit with fifty others of his clan. Only six weeks later, when the grave was opened and "ankers of whisky poured into it", was it possible to take MacGillivray from thence to Petty.

On Thursday, too, detachments of soldiers buried the British dead inside the enclosure, and so fierce did they look, their gaiters as red with blood as their coats, that few men or women of the district had the courage to approach them. A small boy, driving his father's cattle westward from Lochend, heard the clink of metal upon stone, and, seeing nothing, he left the black cows, climbed over the heather and came upon a trench with soldiers standing in it. He stood there watching them, until one looked up and saw him. The soldier swore, lifted a severed arm from the trench and struck the boy on the cheek with it, shouting at him to go away.

It was these burial parties who reported that there were many clansmen still alive on the moor, in the heather or taking shelter in the bothies. And it was to deal with this situation that the men of the Royals, and of Cholmondeley's and of other battalions, marched out on Friday. Among those they found was John Fraser, commonly called MacIver. An officer of the Lovat regiment, he had fallen with a ball through the knee when his clan charged. After the advancing infantry had passed over him he was then robbed and stripped by the rejoicing Campbells. He lay on the field all night and, at dawn, managed to crawl to a small wood down the brae toward Culloden House, where eighteen other wounded officers had also taken shelter. On Thursday the burial parties found them, took them down to the policies of Culloden House and threw them against a wall.

They were kept alive by Thomas Stewart, secretary to the Lord President, who brought them what food and water he could, but on Friday they were discovered by the Royal Scots. They were tied with ropes, thrown into a tumbril, and carried to a park wall near Balloch eastward of the House. There the Royal

Scots officer curtly told them to prepare for death, and, while some were bowing their heads in prayer, the soldiers moved to within six feet of them and shot them. John Reid, a soldier of the Royals, saw this done by his comrades, but always, he said afterwards, thanked God that he had nothing to do "with the black wark". Although MacIver had been one of these shot down he was still not dead. Naked and bloody, he crawled from the bodies of the others until he was found by Lord Boyd. The young man was riding with orders, and was sick with the sight of the slaughter that was going on in the warm spring air. He dismounted beside MacIver and asked if there was anything he could do, even offering money, which, however crazily worthless, was well meant. MacIver asked only that Boyd shoot him. Instead he was carried to a corn-kiln some distance away, and there Boyd hid him. MacIver was to live for another fifty years, mangled and crouching on crutches.

The remorseless executions went on through Friday and Saturday. About the field were several small hovels, byres of sod and stones in which some of the wounded took shelter during the night. Three of these huts were burned on Friday, with the clansmen still inside. One was the hut in which Keppoch's son had left his father's body, and in which the frightened beggars had hidden. Chief's body, wounded and beggars were all burned. The soldiers surrounded the hut and fastened the door, and set light to the roof, yelling back at the cries from within. In another hut eighteen clansmen were burned. Mrs. David Taylor, wife to a wright in Inverness, saw this hut. She had come to the moor in search of her brother-in-law, and "she saw in the rubish the bodies of severals of those that had been scorched to death in a most miserable, mangled way".

Twelve wounded men had taken shelter in the house of William Rose, grieve to Lord President Forbes. On Friday there came a party of soldiers, headed by an officer who spoke civilly to Mrs. Rose, saying that the Rebel officers should get up, for he and his men had come to take them to a surgeon. "Upon which," said Mr. Francis Stewart, who heard the story from Mrs. Rose, "the poor men made a shift to get up and went along with the party with an air of chearfulness and joy, being full of the thought that their wounds were to be dressed." Some minutes later Mrs. Rose heard a volley, and she picked up her skirts and ran to the sound of it. She found the twelve men dead, and the soldiers marching away.

After Donald Roy left him, running with the wrack of Clan Donald, young Macdonald of Bellfinlay lay in the heather with his broken legs and watched the men of Pulteney's marching toward him. They passed over him and "gave him knocks upon the head and shoulders with the club ends of their muskets." That Wednesday night he was stripped by beggars, and he lay naked all night in the rain that fell again, and in the frost that came before dawn. He was eighteen, and perhaps his youth and his strength helped him to survive. When day came he crawled as far as he could, the rimed earth taking the skin from his legs. He lay for a while in the heather, watching the sentinels who were clubbing or bayoneting the clansmen near them, and he waited to be killed too. But when this was about to happen he was saved by a compassionate officer called Hamilton, and was sent to Inverness as a prisoner.

There were others who had compassion. Lachlan Grant, a writer of Edinburgh, was travelling to Inverness that Friday, and his way took him across the moor and into the shambles. By the farm at Culwhiniac he found a Badenoch man called Shaw lying against the wall, wounded and without clothes. Grant gave him a shirt and some money and rode on until he came to another wounded man, with head so cloven that his tongue hung from his mouth and he could not withdraw it. Lachlan Grant gently replaced the man's tongue and tied up his head with a handkerchief. And there were others who wished to show compassion but who had not the courage when it came to the matter, like Angus Shaw the Presbyterian preacher of Petty. He went to the field on Friday, it being not far from his house, and he arrived there when the man Shaw, whom Lachlan Grant had helped, was about to be killed. The preacher wished to stop the soldiers but, when they threatened to shoot him too, he was frightened and ran away.

As well as to the field, detachments of infantry and files of dragoons were sent to the farms and estates beyond Inverness and the moor, to search for hidden Rebels. They came, for example, to the house of Lees at Inshes. This was the home of the truant boy who had watched the battle with his friends Fraser and Mackintosh. His father, Robertson the Laird of Inshes, had died in Inverness that week, and was being lowered into his grave just as the guns began on the moor. On Friday Mrs. Robertson thought it safe to return to Lees from the town, but the journey was more horrifying than she had expected. The road to Inshes was the south road toward Moy, climbing the brae right to the top of Drummossie Moor. All along it Mrs. Robertson saw heaps of bodies, stripped of their clothes, and when she arrived at Lees she found sixteen dead men lying before her door. She called her terrified servants and ordered them to bury the clansmen.

The graves were being dug when some soldiers came down from the Moor, with their muskets slung and unaccompanied by an officer. Their sergeant, or corporal, swore at Mrs. Robertson for a Rebel bitch which, he argued, she must be, otherwise the dead men would not have tried to take shelter in her house. They were angered by her calmness, and they took her by the arms, dragging her to the back of the house and saying that they had a rare sight for her. In the garden lay two more bodies with a curtain over them. They were uncovered, and Mrs. Robertson was held close to them, so that she might see the dead and mangled bodies. The soldiers laughed, they said that the dragoons who had ridden here after the battle had wounded these two men but not killed them, and they, the soldiers, had rectified that. We dragged them out, they said, and gave them "a fire to their hinder-end".

"For," they said, "we roasted and smoked them to death, and have cast this curtain, taken down from the side of one of your rooms, over them to keep us from seeing the nauseous sight."

In the Orders of the Day published on Wednesday evening there was this final instruction: "A detachment of 2 Captains, 6 Subs. and 200 Volunteers to parade immediately at Poultney's Regt. and take their orders from Col. Cockayne." Lieutenant-Colonel Thomas Cockayne, the commander of Pulteney's, was a Flanders veteran, and in what little record there is left of him he is described as "a most discreet, civil man". He found no difficulty in getting his two hundred volunteers, for the purpose of the detail was widely known in camp. He was to march upon Moy House, the home of the Laird of Mackintosh, fifteen miles to the south of Inverness, and to bring back the Lady Anne as prisoner. Any soldier in the battalion streets would have been a fool if he did not scent booty in that duty.

The detachment marched from the Crown on Thursday, passing the long line of wagons which were bringing in hay from Inshes for the cavalry. They took Marshal Wade's military road where it climbed eight hundred feet to the top of Drummossie Moor at its south-westerly end. There the land was bleak, treeless and brown, with a wide and beautiful view of the firth and the mountains. The loneliness of the land dwarfed the soldiers, and they marched like scarlet toys, and their drums were scarcely heard above the wind. They came down to Strathnairn by the Bridge of Faillie, crossed the water and marched up again, this time a thousand feet to the saddle between two hills known as The Great Knob and The Old Woman. It took them a day to reach Loch Moy. However discreet and civil Thomas Cockayne may have been, he does not appear to have been much of a disciplinarian. "He found it impossible to restrain the barbarity of many of his party," said Mr. Francis Stewart, "who, straggling before, spared neither sex nor age they met with." Or perhaps the colonel did not care, thinking his men had earned their pleasure, and that the people of this country deserved to receive it. Harsh and unrewarding though the hills were, they were the land of the MacGillivrays, of whom the soldiers killed more than a dozen, men, women and children, before they came down to the green fields about Loch Moy.

There Cockayne divided his party into two divisions, the first to drive off all the Laird's sheep, cattle and horses, the second to accompany him as an escort for Colonel Anne. An officer of Pulteney's hammered on the door of Moy House with his sword-hilt, demanding "that bloody rebel Lady Mackintosh". When she came, young and beautiful, Cockayne and his officers would not at first believe that she was the Amazon who had raised her husband's clan, and who, they believed, had led it in the battle. She greeted them calmly, and invited them into her house.

The soldiers ranged through the rooms, breaking open

cupboards with their musket-butts, pulling down curtains and overturning chests. The minister of Moy, Mr. Lesly, followed them, hoping to keep a business-like account of all that was stolen or destroyed. Taking out his watch to mark the time of each deplorable vandalism, he had it snatched from him by the soldiers. He was even more distressed by this, since he was loyal to the Government, and he was made no happier when the Laird's wife, offering a soldier fifty guineas for the return of the watch, had purse and guineas taken from her. The officers of Pulteney's, charmed though they were by her beauty, made no attempt to retrieve her money.

The detachment spent the night in Moy House, and Colonel Cockayne and his staff made the stay endurable by free use of the Laird's kitchen and cellars. The next day Colonel Anne was mounted on her horse, and the soldiers fell in about her, their pockets full and their backs loaded with plunder. The cattle party drove the great herd of stock toward Inverness, and the mocking drummers of the other party played the dead-beat, the funeral slow march. Lady Mackintosh did not speak on the ride, even when the detachment passed the dead of her clan. An officer rode beside her, and once he spoke with admiration of the way Clan Chattan had fought on the moor, saying that they had fallen three and four deep before the front of the battalions. The Army, he said, had great respect for their valour.

Retreat was beating on the Crown when Colonel Cockayne rode in with his prisoner, and at the sound of the drums Colonel Anne's horse pricked up its ears and quickened its step. The soldiers behind her saw this, and nodded, saying "this is surely the horse she charged upon at the battle". Colonel Cockayne, who would seem to have recovered some of his discretion and civility, dismissed his detachment on the Crown and took the lady alone into the town, offering her his arm so that she might not appear the prisoner she was. She walked beside him proudly in her blue bonnet and tartan riding-habit. Sir Everard Fawkener was waiting at Cumberland's quarters like an aged crow, and he took her before the commander-in-chief who was sitting in the Dowager Lady Mackintosh's best room (without the bed). Nothing that the Duke said has been recorded, and nothing that she replied, but there could have been little grace on both sides, for she was that night committed to the common guard-room where her mother-in-law already was. Colonel Anne spent six weeks there, and the stay was not too unpleasant. It was, in fact, extremely comfortable when compared with what the imprisoned clansmen were enduring. Her bright charm, her fresh beauty, and her spirited defiance of Cumberland attracted to her the company of young officers. They paid calls which were a pleasant break in the routine of the Army, and which were almost like the dalliances of London society, particularly since the lady could not be said to have a loyal attachment to her husband. Mention of her was made in most letters home.

Thus Captain Alexander Stuart of Dunearn, an officer of Lord Mark Kerr's Dragoons, wrote of her more than once to his brother. After speaking nostalgically of his sweetheart "Miss Willie" he added this, "I drank tea yesterday with Lady Mackintosh. She is really a very pretty woman, pity she is a Rebel." General Hawley was less charmed with her. At Cumberland's table, when there was talk of the honour due to her, he leant across the board and shouted, "Damn the woman, I'll honour her with a mahogany gallows and a silk cord!"

Hawley was always talking about the gallows.

"What's become of my son? Then all's well with me"

GEORGE KEPPEL, LORD BURY, took ship for London on Wednesday afternoon, when the drums were beating the battalions up to the Crown. He was still wearing the uniform he had put on for the battle, the blue and scarlet frock-coat of a major in the Coldstream Guards, and it was now stained with mud and blood. He was not well, the fever for which the Duke's surgeon had bled him twice on Tuesday had returned with the sweat and the excitement of the day, but Cumberland had chosen him to carry dispatches to the King, and this was not something a young man would cry off.

After five wretched days that did nothing to improve Bury's health, the transport anchored off North Berwick. There Bury and his escort set out for London, riding at an unbroken gallop, changing horses at every post, and scarcely taking time to sleep at night. On the morning of Thursday, April 24, they came down the Great North Road into London. The Duke of Newcastle embraced Bury affectionately, although the King's First Minister had already received news of the battle. A messenger from Lord Milton, the Lord Justice Clerk of Scotland, had outraced Bury somewhere along the road, and arrived in London the previous night. But a hired messenger from a lawyer was not an Earl's son, and was not one who had seen the battle, fought in it, and brought messages from the Duke. So Newcastle hurried Bury ("who was much mortified to have been tossed about so long") to the Palace at once. In St. James's Street the crowd was so great, with more men and women coming from Pall Mall and Piccadilly, that the coach was halted for five minutes while outriders cleared a way.

The whole Royal Family then present in London was gathered

in the morning-room at St. James's Palace, and George II, waiting for no introductions or courtesies, asked abruptly, "What's become of my son?" He was not unfamiliar with battles, having stood at Dettingen waving a useless sword, and he knew what could happen to a man, even a general. Bury assured him that the Duke was very well indeed and the admiration of his soldiers. The King nodded and said, "Then all's well with me." He retired to the other end of the room, "unable to speak for joy", while the rest of the Family asked question after question of the fevered young Guardsman. Then the King came back, a dull, comic little figure with cheeks wet. He patted Bury on the shoulder and told Newcastle to see that he was given one thousand guineas as soon as possible. His Majesty was left with Prince Charles's dispatch-case, the contents of which he found so morbidly fascinating that he locked himself up for a whole day to read them.

"Poor Bury," said Newcastle, when he wrote to Cumberland that night, "behaved like a *Hero* and a Politician." Which may have meant that he possessed a combination of all the talents.

At noon, when Bury was making his aching way to bed, the great guns in Green Park and at the Tower of London began to fire salutes. They were answered by ships on the river from the Pool to Tilbury. All companies of the Household Brigade were drawn up in the Park, and they fired volleys of joy by platoons. The bells of every church from Mile End to Mayfair were ringing, stirring music like *Britons Strike Home!*. London thought it had reason for its relief. Throughout the whole Rebellion it had been uneasy, and the uneasiness had come close to panic in December when the clans marched south to Derby. The ladies of the Royal Family had packed their bags for a rapid departure to Hanover, which most of them considered to be their real home, anyway. Only the King refused to be dislodged, saying "Pooh!" when anybody talked of disaster. Orders were issued against the day when the rapacious tribesmen fell upon the capital. Seven guns would fire an alarm from the Tower, upon which every soldier was to proceed to a pre-set rendezvous and await orders, and every citizen would be advised to lock his doors, hide his women, and retire to some upstairs room.

But now the Tower guns were firing salutes to victory, the streets were crowded with yelling mobs, and every man in scarlet, though he may have been no closer to the Rebels than Hounslow Heath, was chaired and made drunk enough with free ale for him to believe that he had truly stood in the line at Culloden. The news of victory, however, was not in itself enough to keep a mob entertained. London, a city of diversions, did not disappoint them. Yelling lies and rumours about the battle, the mob gathered at Tyburn to watch the hanging of a handsome young footman. He had been found guilty of murdering his mistress, Lady Dalrymple, and his turning off promised to be an elegant social event. The stands were full of ladies and gentlemen who had known Lady Dalrymple very well, and some of the ladies had also known the footman. The young fellow, despite his audience, did not enter into the spirit of the glorious day. He whimpered, struggled with the hangman, and made no bold and brave dying statement. The mob was so upset by this that they would have overturned the executioner's cart and torn down the gallows had there not been a sudden accident. A moment after the unco-operative footman had been turned off, the stand collapsed, and with it the ladies and gentlemen.

Much entertained by this, and after shouting loyal cheers to the King and Duke Billy, the mob moved southwards down Tyburn Lane to Hyde Park Corner, and from there to St. James's Park where more was promised. The King's Guards were drawn up in line, their drummers striking the dead-beat. Five sergeants were to be shot for desertion, or rather for attempted desertion since none of them had got very far in an effort to transfer their military services from King George to King James. These men died very well indeed, and so well that they silenced the mob for a minute or two, but when their bodies had been removed on carts, and the Guards had shouldered arms and marched away, the mob yelled once more and moved eastward, much larger now.

At Charing Cross they found a fellow sitting in the pillory for some unspecified misdemeanour, and he was accordingly pelted with stones and filth and vegetables from Covent Garden, until word came that a man was to be publicly whipped in the City.

Sitting in his house in Arlington Street, that evening, Horace

Walpole wrote to a friend. "The town is blazing around me as
I write, with fireworks and illuminations. I have some inclination
to wrap up half a dozen sky-rockets and make you drink the
duke's health. Mr. Doddington, on first report, came out with a
very pretty illumination, so pretty that I believe he had it by him,
ready for any occasion." Mr. Doddington was suspected of being
too broadminded a man, likely to welcome Prince or Duke.
Walpole was delighted that Bury should have been the one to
bring the news from Scotland, and, as soon as possible that day,
he had hurried to his young friend for news of the battle. The
news he probably wanted was gossip rather than stories of Homeric
valour, and Bury does not seem to have disappointed him. "The
Duke gave Brigadier Mordaunt the Pretender's coach," wrote
Walpole, "on condition he rode to London in it. 'That I will,
sir,' said he, 'and drive it till it stops of its own accord at the
Cocoa Tree.'" The Cocoa Tree was a Jacobite coffee-house in
St. James's Street.

This was the sort of story people were telling about the young
Duke and his gallant commanders. Hastily drawn and rough-cut
portraits of Cumberland were sold on the streets within hours of
the news reaching London. In them his round, pudgy face, pointed
nose and pop-eyes underwent a curious transformation so that
while a recognisable likeness was retained the profile also resembled
noble Caesar's. The Duke was the Saviour of the Nation and the
Reformation, everybody said. "The soldiers adore him," wrote
Walpole, evidently quoting Bury, "and with reason, he has a
lion's courage, and, I am told, military genius." No one remarked
that while the military genius of His Royal Highness had undoubtedly scattered the Rebels in the north, it had yet to inflict
a resounding defeat on the more professional soldiers of the
King's enemies in Europe.

As London society prepared that week for Sunday's court of
thanksgiving, expected to be the most magnificent since the
days of Charles II, London's theatres missed no opportunity
offered by the victory. At Drury Lane somebody dragged out of
a chest a play that had not been performed for thirty years. It
was called *The Honours of the Army*, and had been written to
celebrate the successful conclusion of the War of the Spanish

Succession. Mistress Woffington appeared as "a female officer new dressed" with handsome calves displayed, and she spoke a dashing prologue, an achievement which, considering the length of the piece and the fact that it had been resurrected only the day before, was a remarkable victory in itself.

To compete with the Lane's presentation there were other performances. "At the New Wells, the bottom of Lemon Street, Goodman's Fields, this present Evening will be several new Exercises of Rope-dancing, Tumbling, Singing, and dancing, with several new scenes in Grotesque Characters called Harlequin, a Captive in France, or the Frenchman trapt at last. The whole to conclude with an exact view of our Gallant Army under the Command of their Glorious Hero passing the River Spey, giving the Rebels battle, and gaining a complete Victory near Culloden House, with the horse in pursuit of the Pretender."

With the horse in pursuit of the Pretender. . . .

The news-sheets published the text of the King's message to his son: "I desire you may give my hearty thanks to those brave officers and soldiers who fought so gloriously at the late battle, and assure them no less of my real esteem than of my constant favour and protection." It was thought to be a noble expression of sincere emotion. There was, for a while that spring, a surge of genuine affection for the King and his quarrelsome family, and people forgot that for most of his reign they had considered George II an object of fun. Now, for a few weeks, he was an *English* King, and his third son William Augustus was "the young British hero". Both embodied all the virtues of the race: courage, sobriety, compassion and adherence to the Great Revolution and the Reformed Religion. Loyalty, gratitude, sentiment, self-interest and opportunism were so well mixed in public feeling that when a Veterans' Scheme was set up to reward the Army in Scotland more than £6,000 was subscribed within a few days. Nothing makes a man more willing to part with a penny than the feeling that he has narrowly escaped being robbed of a pound.

But soon, behind the flood of loyal addresses to the Throne, the thankful messages from both Houses of Parliament, from the clergy of the Established Church, the two Universities and various corporations and dissenting bodies, there was a savage and revengeful spirit. No Scot in London was safe, and no suspected Catholic either. Most Londoners had already visited the Tower, and seen there the quantities of arms captured at Carlisle: broadswords, dirks and Lochaber axes, dags, muskets and targets. They had deplored the murderous nature of these weapons, although there was nothing on exhibition to show them what a discharge of grape can do to a man at ten yards, or what a woman looks like when she has received seven cuts from a trooper's sabre. Joy and relief turned rapidly to a desire for revenge. This was so, even on the night the news reached London.

On that evening, Tobias Smollett and Alexander Carlyle were at the Golden Ball coffee-house in Cockspur Street. Both were young men and both were Scots. "London," wrote Carlyle, "was in a perfect uproar of joy. About nine o'clock I asked Smollett if he was ready to go, as he lived in May Fair. He said he was and would conduct me. The mob were so riotous and the squibs so numerous and incessant that we were glad to go into a narrow entry to put our wigs into our pockets and to take our swords from our belts and walk with them in our hands." Smollett warned Carlyle that neither of them should speak a word, even when addressed, for their voices were unmistakably Scots, and in this manner the two writers made their uncomfortable way home.

A few days later the mob turned from jostling or stoning any Scot they saw in the street, to the vindictive persecution of Catholics. On Tuesday a crowd of carpenters, shipwrights and sailors from the wharves stormed through the City crying death to all Papists. They found a Catholic chapel north of Newgate and they set it on fire, beating away anybody who tried to stop the flames from spreading. The chapel and four houses were destroyed. Later that week another mob sprang up from the dark streets on Thameside, rushed to the house of a widow who was believed to have a private chapel, and tore it to pieces, not forgetting in their religious zeal to take what was valuable in the house. The mob could have claimed, if justification was thought necessary, that the country's Glorious Hero had set a good example. His Army had burnt Catholic and Non-Jurant meeting-houses wherever found, one in Inverness on the evening of the battle. Until this moment Catholics had lived unmolested if uneasy lives, but now "many very peaceable Catholicks," said the *London Magazine*, "are selling off their effects and quitting the town".

Much the same rejoicing and persecution went on all over the kingdom. Edinburgh's first news of the battle was of victory for the Prince. When the clans charged down on Cumberland's left, a courier appears to have left the Rebel Army and ridden post-haste for the south, believing that the Royal troops would stand the onslaught no better than they had at Prestonpans and Falkirk. He arrived in Edinburgh on April 19, circulating among the Stuart sympathisers there. There was great delight and celebration. "Balls and dances were held by the disaffected ladies," said the *Caledonian Mercury*, not itself unsympathetic toward the Jacobites, "whose mirth was interrupted about One in the Sunday morning by a round of great guns from the Castle."

The Governor had also received news from the north, and it was much more reliable. He fired off his guns in salute, the smoke rolling down from the rock and along the Royal Mile, and the salvoes were answered by warships in Leith Roads. To drive home the fact that victory had, in fact, gone to the Protector of the Reformation, the Governor had a gunner publicly flogged for drinking the Young Pretender's health. The man was still able to walk after three hundred lashes, and he was drummed out of the Garrison and through the streets.

The point was taken. The Jacobites of Edinburgh locked themselves in their houses and turned from triumph to mourning. Now the Whigs began to rejoice, and all those who did not care who won so long as there was commercial stability. A day was set for public thanksgiving, and "next Thursday was observed with the utmost gaiety, as a day of rejoicing for the victory obtained: the most ingenious devices capable of striking the nicest taste were continued". These included window illuminations, candles arranged in the Royal Cipher and in the initials WDC. There were also cut-out illustrations of "Victory trampling Rebellion underfoot, and Justice plunging her naked sword into its bowels." The Edinburgh mob behaved as riotously as that in London, searching the wynds for suspected Jacobites and Papists, hanging effigies of the Pope, the Pretender and any unpopular baillie. They "set on bonfires, brought on liquor, and celebrated the area of their freedom". The Non-Jurant ministers of the city locked their meeting-house doors and fled to the country as quickly as they could, while the Whig gentry held balls and routs and decided to christen some of their newborn sons with the illustrious names of Cumberland William.

Hawley's gibbets still stood in the city.

3

INVERNESS

"Laws? I'll make a brigade give them!"

FOR THE FIRST time in its history the town of Inverness had its streets cleaned at public expense. This was by order of the Duke of Cumberland. Until then the dust, refuse, garbage and emptied chamber-pots had been disposed of economically and naturally. When Edward Burt asked a baillie why some effort was not made to keep the streets pure and clean, he was told "Why? There will soon be a shower." And in that country, Edward Burt discovered, there soon was. This, however, was far too fortuitous a system for the Duke, and while the people of Inverness may have thought him a fool, and certainly too prodigal with their money, the soldiers of the Grand Guard and the Town Picquet, who had stumbled at night among the filth, were once more grateful to their Billy. The British soldiers were very disappointed with Inverness. They were accustomed to Low Country towns that had had seven centuries of experience of armed men, and knew what to expect from them and what to offer to them. Inverness neither wanted their presence nor knew what to do to make it endurable.

Field and staff officers of the Army established their mess in the principal inn opposite the Tolbooth, thereby making it unavailable for use by private soldiers. Any resentment this may have caused was shortly made unimportant by an order that placed the town out of bounds to other ranks, unless they were on duty. After one or two visits, it is doubtful whether any soldier thought the place a great loss, and may have considered it good riddance. Inverness was small, insignificant, and, to men with memories of Bruges and Ghent and Brussels, sadly laughable. It had four principal streets only, of which three met at the Cross. The Town House was a plain building of rubble, with one main room in

which the Magistrates met. This building, thought Burt, "would
be tolerably handsome, but the walls are rough, not white-
washed, or so much as plastered, and no furniture in it but a table,
some bad chairs, and altogether immoderately dirty". The dirt
of the Highland capital was something most officers complained
of when writing home, and since London, with which they
made comparisons, had no public cleansing service either, Inverness must indeed have been dirty.

Business was conducted daily at the market-cross, where the
merchants once more gathered every morning after the expected
rape and sack did not occur. "There they stand in the middle of
the dirty street, and are frequently interrupted in their negotiations by horses and carts which often separate them one from
another in the midst of their bargains." But such roadside haggling
was important to the Highlands, Inverness being their only gate-
way to the world. Until Admiral Byng's fleet filled the firth, more
ships from Boulogne and Bordeaux called there than vessels from
London. There were four or five regular sailings to Rotterdam
each week. The merchantmen brought the Highland chiefs their
claret and books, their broadsword steel, Mechlin lace, Spanish
silver, velvet, silk, shot, powder, spices and spies. Through the
town's merchants they sold their malt and meal, beef and wool.
Inverness had less than five hundred houses and no more than
three thousand inhabitants, but it was vital to the bleak economy
of the hills. It was also of strategic importance, as Cromwell had
seen. He had built a castle there, and later men had built another
on the hill, which Prince Charles had blown up.

Most of the chiefs of the eastward clans had town-houses in
Inverness, like the Laird of Mackintosh, but its social life was
stark. God and the Kirk ruled with Bible and bye-law. There
were two main churches, "one for the English and the other for
the Irish tongue" and there were also Non-Jurant meeting-houses
which were soon attended to when the Army marched in. Apart
from the inn opposite the Tolbooth there was only one other
worthwhile social centre. This was a coffee-house where, Burt
said, "the furniture, utensils, the room appear as if never cleaned
since the building of the house, and in frost and snow you might
cover the peat-fire with your hands". Jokes about the mean

Sawney began with the eighteenth-century Englishman's contempt for the Scots. The real forum of the burgh (and its palladium) was the *clach-na-cuddain*, a great blue lozenge of stone half-buried in the earth by the Cross. On this women rested their wash-tubs after climbing the hill from the Ness, and on this men hammered out the price of meal, the genealogy of their families, and the interpretation of the Law.

To the Highlanders, coming rarely to Inverness from their glens, the town was a wondrous place, and even to British officers, where they were reflective enough, it had a certain crude charm. The red sandstone houses, with their stepped gables and turnpike stairs, were quaintly un-English. Some had upper galleries that hung over the narrow streets, so low that the dragoons of the Duke's Grand Guard had to bend to their horses' manes when riding by. Most of the houses were marked on the outside with the owner's initials, and those of his wife, chipped into the stone. Others had long and didactic texts painted on the walls, the words of the prophets, the pessimism of the psalms. Something of the old fortress character of the town persisted, few houses having windows of any size on the ground floor. There was good reason for this. "In their clan quarrels," said Burt, "several had been shot from the other side of the way, but I believe the real reason is the expense of glass." Like other Englishmen, he found the townsfolk perverse in their terminology. "They call a floor a house, the whole building is called a land, an alley is a wynde, a little court is a close, a round staircase is a turnpike, and a square one is a skale stair."

Outside the town, beyond the Crown or across the River Ness, were groups of dirty hovels, windowless and faced with turf, and a bottomless basket in the roof for a chimney. In these lived the flotsam of the hills, clanless men and women, fragments of the tribal system which the existence of Inverness had broken from the whole. They wore the Highland plaid and bonnet, as did almost everyone in the town (five men only had hats, the provost, sheriff and three ministers), and brogues of rough bull-hide, the leather slashed to allow rain and water to drain through. The women went without shoes or stockings. They washed their clothes and scrubbed their vegetables every morning in the river, watched by British soldiers who flipped stones at them and shouted invitations.

In the months of April and May that year Inverness was crowded, with officers, soldiers, sailors from the ships, speculators from the south who had sharp eyes on the loot of the Highland estates. The kirkyards were full of cattle, the fierce-looking but timorous beasts lowing mournfully and slipping on the stones. There were lawyers from England and writers from Edinburgh, and couriers riding out every day with dispatches for London. The emotional centre of the town was the Tolbooth, the tall court-house and gaol at the corner of Bridge Street and Kirk Street, below Castle Wynd. At street-level were two shops, but up the outside stairs was a large room, now crowded with prisoners. The disposal of these was the immediate concern of the Provost Marshal, and first under consideration were those held as deserters. Thirty-six had been discovered when the regimental sergeant-majors went round the gaols on the evening of the battle, and twenty-nine of them were hanged before a month was over. Day after day Orders contained the names and sentences passed upon men brought before the General Courts-Martial. The trial of each man was a miserably brief affair, held in the open before a tent on the Crown, with the wind snapping at the papers laid on the drum-heads. It had only to be proved that the accused had been a soldier of the King and that he had been found in arms, or seen in arms among the Rebels. Nor does it appear that any of the twenty-nine attempted to justify their desertion, or put pleas for mercy except to the Almighty. Theirs was a brutal profession in a brutal age. Soldiers regarded death as a gambler's risk, and if the dice fell against them there seemed to be no point in disputing the fall.

They were hanged at eight o'clock in the morning, walking to the gallows a mile from the town, each man bearing a card on his breast stating who he was, and what he was. The Picquet on duty formed the dead-man's guard, making square about the gallows, and the chattering sticks of the Picquet drums were the last sound heard by the blindfolded men before they were turned off. The bodies of the deserters hung from the gibbets until the trees were needed for other men. The Order Books contain their names: Thomas Water of Sackville's, William Chisholm of the Scots Fusiliers, John Sudden of Battereau's, John Morice of Conway's and many more. Just their names and a cold valediction, "condemned for deserting their Master's service and Inlisting with the Rebels". And the last to be hanged remained there until the Army went away from Inverness. This was perhaps Hawley's order again, since he held to the belief that a deserter left hanging meant half a dozen less in the ranks.

The hangings were watched by the comrades of the condemned, it was almost the only entertainment available, for the Duke had ordered that no man was to go above a quarter of a mile from the camp without orders, "several outrages and disorders having been committed which he will not permit on any account". Some of the deserters hanged in Inverness that April were not men who had abandoned their units in England or Scotland. They had deserted in Flanders, and, for want of an occupation or bread to eat, or from Jacobite sympathies, joined the French companies leaving for the Rebellion. One of these was Alexander Douglas, who must have been a foolish man. He deserted in Holland, joined Drummond's regiment and came to Scotland. He got left behind in the northward retreat, having decided to rob a minister's house near Perth, and during this escapade he was caught. Other deserters were Scots who felt the pull of family loyalties, and one of these must have been William Chisholm of the Scots Fusiliers. There is no record of why he deserted, but his name hints at his probable confusion. Two sons of The Chisholm were officers in his regiment, and the clan of his name was in rebellion. Whatever his reasons, he was hanged.

Understandably, desertion was a serious crime in that army, at the least punished savagely by the lash, at the worst by the halter if the crime included enlistment with the enemy. There was no room for debate, and, within the arbitrary rules of the profession, trial and sentence were logically necessary. Marching through Britain in pursuit of the enemy, Cumberland's general officers fretted and fussed about desertion. General Roger Handasyde reported bitterly and uneasily about his men: "The Foot with me will I think do well; but the dragoons I am jealous of, not without reason, five having deserted since yesterday. Added to this a damned rebellious spirit, and a disposition to rob everywhere. I only wait to take some of them, and the decree of their fate shall be put into execution after the court-martial."

Officers of the same mind as Handasyde got their wish at Inverness. From April 20, onwards to May, the drums rolled below the scaffolds, and men became bored by the hangings. Now and then the circumstances of a deserter's departure from the cart were sufficiently out of the ordinary to be talked of and remembered awhile. There was a sergeant of Sowle's regiment called Ninian Dunbar, who had joined the Rebels early in the Rising, becoming a lieutenant and adjutant among them. At the battle of Falkirk, where he charged with the clans, he had stripped the fine clothes from Major Lockhart of Cholmondeley's regiment, there taken prisoner, and put them upon his own back. This fiery and choleric Scot, Lockhart, was to make a reputation for himself in the campaign, and its beginning was with the affair of Ninian Dunbar.

When the sergeant was brought from the Tolbooth to his court-martial he was still wearing the Major's uniform. Lockhart wanted it back, just as he wanted back his horse, which had been stolen from his battalion lines by some scoundrel in another regiment. But Cumberland, or Hawley, amused by the thought of a deserter masquerading as an officer, ordered that Ninian Dunbar be hanged in Major Lockhart's scarlet and gold since he set so much store by them. Dunbar appears to have been a young man of some education, and a follower of Henry Whitfield, the nonconformist divine. He walked to the gallows with his head held up, and his strong voice joining in the hymns sung by the dozen Methodist soldiers who kept him company. He behaved, said Michael Hughes who watched the hanging, "with decency and courage, and though he talked much of Jesus Christ, yet he died without acknowledging his Treason and the Justice of his Punishment".

The hanging of another Scots deserter, a man called Forbes who was a relative of the Lord President, provoked a fight between the English and the Scots of the Royal Army. Suspicion and distaste were never far below the skin of their alliance. It was the custom among some officers and men to amuse themselves after a hanging by mutilating the bodies of the dead, and on this occasion an officer of an English regiment thrust his sword several times into Forbes's body, saying that "all his countrymen were traitors and Rebels like himself". This windy generalisation offended an officer of Sempill's or the Royal Scots, and he drew his own hanger, inviting the Englishman to test both his weapon and his political theories in a duel. The offer was immediately accepted, and the quarrel joined by private soldiers of both regiments. They were stabbing and thrusting at each other with bayonet and sword when Cumberland rode up and stopped the fight. He soothed the Scots' pride with soft compliments about their bravery on the Moor.

With the exception of Ninian Dunbar, the deserters hung naked on the gallows, for their clothes were by custom the property of their executioner. According to Henderson, the Duke's first and contemporary biographer, Cumberland remonstrated with Hawley for putting so many deserters to death. "You may try an officer for surrendering up a fort when under no necessity to do it, but let not the blood of the poor be spilt profusely." But when that was written, twenty years after Culloden, Cumberland had become known as The Bloody Butcher and his military career had been undistinguished and dull. Perhaps Henderson felt his reputation needed polishing with a little fiction, or perhaps Cumberland really did make such a protest, albeit more colloquially. Certainly records show, without explanation, that eleven deserters from Guise's regiment were released and returned to duty after the intercession of Alexander MacBean, a minister of Inverness.

Daily the Tolbooth and the other gaols, the cellars, kirkyards and houses taken over by the Provost Guard were filled with more prisoners brought in by the patrols. On the evening of the battle three hundred and more had been driven into the town before the lowered sabres of the dragoons and the advanced bayonets of the infantry. The people of Inverness, for the most part, turned their backs on the wretched and half-naked men, afraid lest it should be thought they were in sympathy with the Rebel cause. There was not enough room in the tiny, suffocating prisons for kindness, even had the Army wished to show it, and the suffering of the prisoners was bitter and prolonged. One of them was John Farquharson of Allargue, a captain of the Clan Farquharson regiment, and a farmer from Ellich in Banff.* He was also a "Highland blooder", an unqualified doctor who ministered to the sick by letting blood, and he always carried a lancet in his pocket for that purpose. When the Rebellion was long over he wrote an account of his imprisonment and that of his comrades, and sent it to the Reverend Robert Forbes. Because he had escaped under sentence of death, and still feared discovery, he took the melodramatic evasion of writing as if he were an English officer, a pose that contradicts itself as his account swings from "they" to "we" and back again to "they".

"To begin," he wrote, "when we had filled all the gaols, kirks and ships at Inverness with these rebel prisoners, wounded and naked as they were, we ordered that non should have any access to them either with meat or drink for two days. By means no doubt we thought at least the wounded woud starve either for want of food or cloaths, the weather being then very cold." When the two days were past, a number of officers came to the prisons to make a list of all captured, by name and rank. Farquharson pretended that he had been one of these. "But, oh Heavens! what a scene open to my eyes and nose all at once; the wounded feltering in their gore and blood; some dead bodies covered quite over with pish and dirt, the living standing to the middle in it, their groans woud have pirsed a heart of stone, but our corrupt hearts was not in the least touched, but on the contrary we began to upbraid them the moment we entred their prisons. Doctor Lauder's case of instruments was taken from him for fear he shoud end any of the wounded, and on, John Farqrson of Aldlerg, who was, I believe, a kind of Highlander blooder, his lancet was taken out of his pocket for fear he should begin to blood them, after his Highland way, to save some few of the wound(ed) to have fallen in fevers."

* Forbes says that Farquharson was commonly known as "John Anderson my jo". Burns's poems of that name was founded on an eighteenth century ballad which was, in its turn, a parody of a sixteenth century anti-Catholic song. So the reason for Farquharson's nickname is interesting, if not at all clear.

When the bodies of those who had died in the prisons were carried away, it was not by detachments of soldiers, nor by the citizens of the town, but by beggars rounded up for the work at bayonet point. The dead were always naked, their clothes taken by their comrades or by the beggars, and they were dragged by their heels through the streets to the kirkyards or to open ground for burial. As Farquharson indicates, there were doctors among the prisoners. John Rattray and George Lauder, both surgeons of Edinburgh, had served with the Rebel Army. Neither was in the battle. Rattray had been on the night-march to Nairn and had been so exhausted by it that he went back to Inverness and threw himself upon his bed. The cannon awoke him and he got up and stumbled toward the moor, but the wash of fleeing men carried him back into the town, and he was standing in the street when the Royal Army entered. There he was seen and recognised by Lord Cathcart, Cumberland's eye-patched aide. Cathcart dismounted and stood by the surgeon, shaking his head. "I'm sorry to see you here, Mr. Rattray, I'm afraid it'll go hard with you." Other officers crowded round the two men, and were less sympathetic. They shouted "By God, sir!" and "Damn you, sir!" and "We know you! If anyone hangs, you will!"

Rattray was imprisoned in one of the churches where he found Lauder, also taken in the street. They asked for permission to treat the wounded about them, but got no permission, and, as Farquharson saw, their instruments and medicines were taken from them as legitimate booty. Although they did their best with their unaided hands, they were unable to halt the pain and the daily deaths. A few days later both men were removed to the Tolbooth where, because of the confined space, the agony of the sick and wounded was worse, and although they asked again for instruments and medicines they were again refused.

The smell from the gaols and the churches, the moaning of the wounded at night, the white faces at the high windows, were enough to inform the people of Inverness of what was going on. Two men made an effort to get fair treatment for the prisoners, Provost John Fraser, and his predecessor John Hossack. Both were Whigs and loyal supporters of the Government, and both, as officials of the town, may have thought that they would be listened to with respect. They went to the Town House where Hawley and General Huske were, according to one report, "making out orders about the slaying of the wounded on the field of battle". Hossack bowed, and began a cautious little speech. "As His Majesty's troops have happily been successful against the Rebels, I hope your excellencies will be so good as to mingle mercy with . . ." And at that Hawley looked up from his papers in astonishment.

"Damn the puppy!" he yelled. "Does he pretend to dictate here?"

Someone else cried "Kick him out!", and, willing to oblige, Sir Robert Adair of the staff spun Mr. Hossack about, kicked him from the room, and kicked him down the stairs to the street. Provost Fraser departed quickly, before the same thing happened to him, but Hawley had not forgotten him. That evening a file of grenadiers called at the Provost's house and escorted him to the General's stable, which he was ordered to sweep and clean. Mr. Fraser could be a Highland gentleman with the best, and he said that since he never cleaned his own stables he certainly would not clean the General's. This stout affirmation of class privilege was admired by the grenadier captain, and the Provost was permitted to hire three or four "common fellows" to do the work for him, but he was ordered to stand by and watch. Although the civic pride of Inverness was hurt by this insult to its dignitaries, a pawky sense of humour saw the comedy in it also, and from then on Mr. Hossack and Mr. Fraser were known as Provost Kick and Provost Muck.

If most reputable people of the town pretended that conditions in the prisons were not their concern, and were probably no worse than the rebel rascals deserved, some ordinary folk were moved to help the prisoners. "It was," said Minister Hay, "reckoned highly criminal and very dangerous to give them anything, even water. The servant maids had more than common courage. They did all that was possible, though they were sure of maltreatment." One of these courageous women was Anne M'Kay. She was, said Hay, a "poor Isle of Skye woman," a member of Clan MacLeod, and she lived in a wretched cellar in one of the wynds. Into this were put two prisoners, Robert Nairn

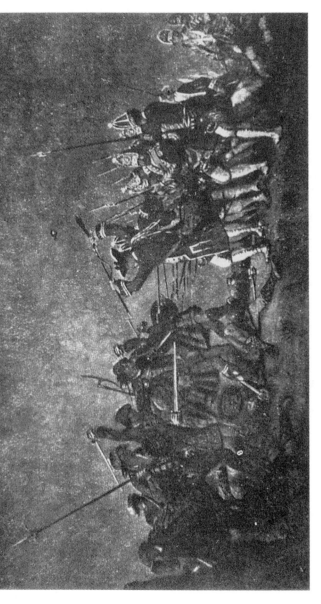

I. "RUN YE DOGS!"

At the extreme left of the Hanoverian line Barrell's Foot receive the onslaught of the Camerons, Stewarts and Athollmen. David Morier, the artist, was a Swiss military painter who worked under the patronage of the Duke of Cumberland. He is believed to have used Jacobite prisoners as models for his Highlanders.

(From a copy, in the possession of The King's Own Royal Regiment Museum, of Morier's painting in Windsor Castle.)

2. A KING IN HIS OWN GLENS

A model for all, this Highland chief is Donald Cameron the younger of Lochiel. The portrait was painted some years after his death by George Chalmers. Although known as "Gentle Lochiel", he was ready to burn the cottage and hough the cattle of those of his clan who were reluctant to join him in the Rebellion.

(From a painting in the possession of Mrs. L. St. John Secker of Callart.)

3. "BILLY THE MARTIAL BOY"

A caricature of the Duke of Cumberland, drawn some years after
Culloden by his A.D.C. George, 4th Viscount and 1st Marquess
Townshend.

(From the original in the possession of R. W. Ketton-Cremer of Felbrigg Hall.)

4. "THE GARB OF OLD GAUL"

The central figure is believed to be Lord George Murray in his campaign dress. By a contemporary artist, it is perhaps a more accurate representation of Highland dress than the romantic figure in Plate 8.

(From a painting at Blair Castle.)

5. A TOWN OF FOUR STREETS

Inverness early in the eighteenth century and seen from the west. The River Ness and the old bridge are in the foreground. The Castle was destroyed by the Jacobites before Culloden.

6. ORDERS OF THE DAY

A page from the Duke of Cumberland's Order Book, written the day after the battle of Culloden. The book, beautifully penned and stoutly bound, is in the possession of the Scottish Record Office.

7. "TAKE CARE WITH THAT DAMNED AXE!"

Lord Balmerino dies well in London, declaring that had he a thousand lives he would lay them all down in the same cause. A contemporary illustration of his execution.

(*Radio Times* Hulton Picture Library.)

8. ROMANCE IMPROVES ON FACT

This was how the early Victorians liked to imagine the Highlander. The print, by Robert M'Ian the historical painter, claims to show a Clanranald Macdonald, but the tartan would have been unknown to any Clan Donald man at Culloden, and the sporran is a fanciful Victorian absurdity. From such popular illustrations, however, grew an indestructible legend.

and Ranald Macdonald of Bellfinlay. Nairn was the Deputy Paymaster of the Duke of Perth's Regiment, and his arm had been almost severed by a dragoon's sabre. The boy Bellfinlay was the "strapping, beautiful" captain of Clanranald's whose legs had been broken by grape.

They lay in Anne M'Kay's cellar for many weeks and many months, and she brought them food and medicines which Jacobite ladies of the neighbourhood gave her for them. For no other reason than common sympathy she agreed to help when those ladies proposed a plan for the escape of both men. "Of this plot," said James Hay, "the poor Highland woman was made the principal manager, and indeed she managed wonderfully. For after equipping Nairn in warmest manner he cou'd then be cloathed in, she decoyed the century of the door of the cellar into a back close just by it, by which means Nairn slip't out and made his escape." So it was not a very elaborate plan. Nairn got away successfully, but Bellfinlay was still too lame to move from the cellar, and he stayed a prisoner until the Indemnity, and died not long afterwards, before his twenty-first birthday.

Once Nairn's escape was discovered, "all were in an uproar". Anne M'Kay was brought before Colonel Leighton of Blakeney's regiment, then garrisoning the town. He asked first who had given Anne M'Kay food for the prisoners, and she said that she did not know, a man it was but "he no be a M'Leod or M'Donald or any Mack at all". Leighton offered her five guineas, but she would not take money. He then threatened to put her in the Bridge Hole, and although she pleaded tearfully against it, there she was sent. This was a coffin-shaped cell in the middle of the bridge, a narrow slot with no more room than enough for a man or woman to stand. There Anne M'Kay remained, while her legs swelled and her head ached with the endless noise of hooves and feet and wheels just above it. "There was an Irish woman," said Hay, "a soldier's wife, sent to her with some strong liquors in order to intoxicate her that she might confess. The wife came to her accordingly and offered her a hot pot or some possat, and said she wou'd drink Prince Charles his health."

Anne M'Kay had been some days in the Bridge Hole by then, and was in great agony, but her stubborn pride was unweakened.

If she would not betray the Jacobites she had helped, neither would she betray the loyalties of her clan. "I like the Duke," she called up from the Hole, "for I be a MacLeod, and MacLeods do not like Charley." What was more, she said, she was drinking no strong liquors, no posset, her drink was milk and whey. Her obstinacy and courage won in the end, and she was taken from the Hole to the Tolbooth. When Leighton proposed to drub and drum her through the town, Provost Fraser persuaded him to let her go. But the sentry, whose dalliance had allowed Nairn to escape, was given five hundred lashes.

There were many women in the prisons, sharing the same foetid rooms with the men. "I saw enough of tyranny and oppression," a prisoner wrote to Hay, "a part of which was acted against a widow gentlewoman, and a young lady sent from the country to her education and boarder with the woman, and the servant maid, all three lying in the common guard-room for 12 or 14 days, exposed to all the rudeness these polite people inclined to show, for they had not as much as the benefit of a place for the ordinary private conveniency."

Forty-eight hours after the battle it was decided that the prisoners, many of whom had eaten no more than a biscuit since Monday, might now be given half a pound of meal a day. Hawley thought that this was too much for the scoundrels, but for once he was overruled. "I could not help laughing in the time of distribution," said John Farquharson, still posing as a flint-hearted Englishman, "when the poor things had nothing left them to hold their meal but the foreskirt of their shirts, rather exposing their nakedness to the world than want of their meal. They made very odd figures, every one with his half pound of meal tied up in his shirt lap, and all below naked."

Some prisoners, from whom the guards expected violence or escape, were manacled, and were not released to eat, sleep or relieve themselves. Two officers of the Duke of Perth's regiment, Major James Stewart and Major Alexander Mac-Lachlan, were handcuffed for ten days, and MacLachlan so tightly that "his hands swell'd so that the irons could not be seen". Their daily and dignified request for larger irons was daily and obscenely refused. In the same prison, the Tolbooth, Farquharson said that he tended a dying Frenchman who lay to his waist in excreta. There was little the Highland blooder could do but put a stone beneath the man's head for a pillow. The dead were not taken from the prisons immediately, they were left until there were a dozen or more, enough to make the employment of the beggars worth the few pence paid. Until then, the living endured the rotting company of the corpses.

In such an atmosphere the possibly innocent as well as the patently guilty went to prison. David Taylor, the workman of Inverness whose wife had seen the burnt clansmen on the Moor, was arrested on suspicion late in April. Five officers of Blakeney's had already taken possession of his house, and their servants stole or sold his meagre furniture. When a garrulous neighbour, informed against Taylor (saying he had heard the wright wish the Pretender well), soldiers came and took the fellow to the Tolbooth. It was said against him that he had worked for the Rebel Army, but what counted most was probably the fact that he regularly attended the Non-Jurant meeting-house. This was no time and no place for vagaries of worship. Taylor was held in a small room known as the Justice of Peace Loft, with twenty-five other men, most of them wounded. "And no person," he said, "durst come to give any support to these wounded for nine days." There were also a number of dead in the loft.

What embittered many Rebels, when later they wrote their stumbling stories, was the relentless cruelty of the King's officers. From the soldiers, perhaps, the prisoners expected brutality (though they frequently received kindness), but from the gentlemen of England and the Lowlands, from Highland officers in the Crown's service, they hoped for some human mercy. They rarely received it. "All the officers of Blakeney's regiment except three," said Farquharson, "were extremely cruel, but none exceeded Captain Dunlop." Dunlop, a Scot, was an interrogation officer, and any prisoner who thought that his part under interrogation meant saying anything more than Yes or No soon found himself gagged by a drum-stick. Late in the year, when the prisons of Inverness were still full and the Highlands were rimed with frost, Dunlop ordered that no fires and no candles were to be lit in the gaols. Major Lockhart of Cholmondeley's, Captain Caroline

Scott of Guise's, and Captain John Fergusson of the Royal Navy, three more Lowland Scots, also earned reputations that would not have been out of place in a mess of the *Schutzstaffeln* two centuries later. Here and there were officers with compassion. Joseph Ward of Battereau's and Hugh Fraser of Blakeney's, both lieutenants, were cashiered and imprisoned for allowing two women into the Tolbooth to attend their wounded husbands. Such mistaken mercy was carefully avoided by other officers. Zeal in the persecution of the King's enemies was admired by men like Hawley, and was a step to advancement. If Cumberland put nothing on paper that was an authorisation of brutality, he knew what was being done, and believed that what was being done was necessary. When Lord President Forbes suggested that the young man temper the laws of the country with princely mercy, the Duke gave him a gauleiter's answer. "Laws? I'll make a brigade give the laws!"

When the gaols and the churches, the cellars and the lofts could contain no more prisoners, and when the stench of their suffering hung remorselessly in the wynds, some of the Rebels were transferred to the transports in the firth. John Farquharson was one. "I saw everyone in the most deplorable condition, particularly the commonality who amounted to about four score or a hundred, all confined to the hold, lying and sitting on the bare stones that were ballast, all of them in a most sickly condition, and some dying every day." A sentry stood above the hatch, and any prisoner who attempted to climb to the deck without permission, "to discharge nature in the common way that's used aboard", was beaten back with a musket butt. Aboard Farquharson's ship, this greatly amused the skipper, and he yelled "Well done, by God! Do your duty, sentry!" On the other hand, the master of the sloop to which Taylor was sent, was Thomas Nicol, and "he was very good to the prisoners in generall, and as their was no officer on board but a serjeant's command, I gott the favour of a dozen of prisoners on dake att once till they came all up by turns from morning till eaven, for they were in a most miserable condition in the hold". Nicol also gave the prisoners a pound of meal a day, though he had been told to give them eight ounces only.

The transports anchored in the firth or moored to Citadel Quay were awaiting orders for the disposal of the Rebels, and, while they waited, the prisoners died on the small white stones of the ballast. They died of gangrenous wounds, disease and despair. And all the living saw of each day was a square of blue above the hatch, the white gaiters and scarlet breeches of the sentry. In May some of them, including Taylor, were brought ashore to the Tolbooth again for examination. Then, said Taylor, came his greatest hardship and misery, and Captain Dunlop was his principal persecutor. He was kept in a small room with two young men who had served with the Prince's cavalry. Both were wounded and both died of their wounds in that room while Taylor watched. He remained in prison for eleven more months, and he did not see his family, though his two children were taken sick in a fever and died. General William Blakeney was commanding in Inverness at this time, a tough, scarred Irishman of 75 whose thoughts, and philosophy were all inspired by Orders of the Day. Taylor petitioned Blakeney for permission to see his wife after his children died, "but his cruell heart would not allow me". A minister of Inverness, who may have been Alexander MacBean, offered to go to prison and stand in David Taylor's place if the General would give the wright leave to visit his wife on promise of return. Blakeney ordered Taylor from prison and brought to him for a decision "If you had a hundred wives I would not allow you to see them without orders from the Earl of Albemarle."

There was one last hanging, after the deserters had been disposed of, and the victim was Murdoch McRaw who was a common Highlandman by general opinion, but the kinsman of a chief by his own. He came from Kintail to the west, from the MacRae country which was a blue mountain peninsula between Loch Duich and Loch Hourn, and where The Five Sisters watch the Pass of Glen Shiel. There had been MacRaes or MacRaws or MacGraths in some of the Clan Donald units, although Clan MacRae had not come out as a regiment for the Prince, so Murdoch McRaw had his name against him when he was arrested at the house of Macdonald of Leek near Fort Augustus. He was accused of spying, though he protested that he was about his own affairs only. He was taken to Inverness, arriving there at eight o'clock in the morning, and by ten o'clock he was hanged. He was taken to an apple-tree by the Cross and the tub-stone, a famous tree that grew fine fruit known as Jenny Sinclairs. He did not believe that the soldiers intended to hang him, even when the halter was placed about his neck, for he said "You have gone far enough, if this be jest." But it was not a jest. He hung on the tree for two days and a night, and, said Minister Hay, he appeared to be sleeping. Occasionally soldiers whipped the naked body. After the two days and a night the beggars cut down Murdoch McRaw and buried him somewhere. The leaves of the tree withered, and no apples grew on it again, thus proving the innocence of Murdoch McRaw. Or such was the legend.

All this, the deserters hanged, the gaols filled, and men waiting on the transports, was the beginning of things after Culloden. No word was given to the prisoners of what might happen to them, of what more they might expect than another day, another week or month of bitter suffering. In the tiny hold of the *James and Mary*, by Citadel Quay, were one hundred and twenty-five men at one time, and "numbers of them died every day, and were thrown overboard like so many dogs; and several of them before they were really dead". The rest dug holes into the earth and stones of the ballast and kept themselves alive as best they could. "From such another sight, good Lord deliver me!" wrote William Jack, a soldier of Strathallan's and a merchant of Elgin. This he wrote a year later when he was still a prisoner, and now on a Thames hulk. "For it's impossible to describe the condition we was all unto," he said, "for you should thought we hade no interalls within us, and all our jointes of our bodies as perceptele as if we were cute out in wood or stone."

"A little blown up by such a success"

PRINCE CHARLES WAS hiding in the West, passing by night in an eight-oared boat from one lone isle to another. His red beard was growing and his bonny tartan tattered, and the contents of a little bottle in his pouch were beginning their long life as the solace for all his troubles. He was playing out the last act of a lost cause as if the part had been written for him. "Come, come," he said, "give me one of the bottles and a piece of the bread, for I was never so hungry since I was born!" He was to live another forty-two years, and none of them would have the sweet bitterness of these few weeks when he was hiding in the heather. Soon he was to draw up his letter to the chiefs: "But, alas, I see with grief I can at present do little for you on this side of the water, for the only thing that can now be done is to defend yourselves till the French assist you . . . My departure should be kept as long private and concealed as possible on one pretext or other which you will fall upon. May the Almighty bless and direct you."

The last body of Rebels to retain anything like military formation had disbanded themselves as a field force by the beginning of May. These were the MacGregors, the turbulent men from Glenstrae, Glenlyon and Glengyle. 'S Roigmal mo dhream! they said, Royal is my race, but to the rest of Scotland they were a tribe of rebellious thieves and as a punishment for their behaviour the name of their clan had been proscribed long ago. Many of them had come out for the Prince because thereby, at least, a man might call himself MacGregor again. They had been in Sutherland when the battle was fought, chasing Campbells, but they would not take to the hills yet. They marched home to the Braes with their pipes playing, their broadswords drawn, and the pine-sprig badge of Clan Gregor in their bonnets. They marched by Stratherrick to Ruthven, by Garvamore, Rannoch and Glenlyon, past Finlarig Castle where John Campbell of Glenorchy, having twelve men only, thought it wiser not to dispute their passage. And thus they came to their homes. Or what had once been their homes, for the Royal troops had been there with the torch. "Every man to his own house," lamented their bard, "and did not know where it was."

Lord Glenorchy, the anglicised Christ Church Highlander, wished he could have stopped the MacGregors, as he wished he could have stopped the MacLarens, when they went by earlier with their wounded chief. In his correspondence with Colonel Joseph Yorke he expressed sour mortification that MacGregors should still cock a snoot at God, King and the Campbells. "They ought to be extirpated from thence, being the most pernicious race of mankind in being." Nobody liked Clan Gregor, least of all the Campbells at this time, for the MacGregors were boasting that when they passed Finlarig Castle the Argyll men "durst no more move than pussies". Having no roof-poles under which to bide, they lived in corries on the Braes of Balquhidder, raiding and robbing as their fathers had done under Rob Roy. "They continue still in a martial appearance," complained Glenorchy, "carrying arms wherever they go and wearing white cockades. They don't keep in a body, but can assemble 2 and 300 men in a very little time and talk of going to Lochaber."

There was much talk among the scattered clans of a great gathering in Lochaber when the Prince's standard would once more be raised. This was a dream to some chiefs, Lochiel principally, and part of the dream was that a French fleet would be seen one day soon in a western sea-loch, bringing gold, arms and regiments of soldiers. Cumberland and the King's ministers took this possibility seriously, for, however treasonable the Rebellion, it had also been an extension of the war with King Louis, and Cumberland knew that all resistance and all thought of resistance must be stamped out until the French no longer saw Scotland as a second front against England. "All the good we have done is a little blood-letting," the Duke wrote to Newcastle, "which has only weakened the madness, not cured it.

I tremble for fear that this vile spot may still be the ruin of this island and our family."

At the end of April some of the skulking chiefs, led by Lochiel and Macdonalds, talked about a bond, a solemn oath by each to raise "as many able-bodied men as they could on their respective properties", and to meet later in Badenoch from whence they would march once more behind the pipes. But when Lochiel and Coll Macdonald, younger of Barisdale, came to the rendezvous they had few men with them, and these soon dispersed when soldiers were seen in the glen. On April 29 two French frigates, the *Bellona* and the *Mars*, had run in to Loch nan Uamh, landing stores, arms and money and hoping to pick up fugitive Jacobite leaders. Bo' : had left after a spirited fight with H.M.S. *Greyhound* and *Terror*, and when the loch was clear of sails the Macdonalds of Barisdale fell upon stores and treasure. They carried off 240 casks of brandy and 800 *louis d'or*. The Macleans of Mull, getting wind of the landing, sent men over, too, who helped themselves to more brandy. The rest of the treasure was buried somewhere along Loch Arkaig, and there it still may be.

Real resistance, another rising in the summer, was something the chiefs talked about as they hid in holes above the gutted ruins of their homes, but the clansmen were dispirited and exhausted, and the ancient bonds of their society were rotting rapidly. Chiefs began to betray men of their own name. The Laird of Grant had taken no part in the Rising and was known for his dislike of the Stuarts, but he was still chief of the clan, and when sixty-nine men of Glenmoriston, and twelve more of Glen Urquhart who had been out with the Prince, asked him for guidance, he told them to march to Inverness, lay down their arms, and take his word that no harm would come to them. So they marched to the town from their homes in the northern wall of Loch Ness, and by the church they formed the line in which they had stood at Culloden, and they laid their broadswords at their feet. Cumberland surrounded them with a regiment, asking who they were and to whom they surrendered. "To me," said the Laird of Grant, "and to none but me would they have submitted."

"I'll let them know they're my father's subjects," said the

Duke, "and they must likewise submit to me." Instead of being
allowed to return to Glenmoriston and Glen Urquhart as they
had expected, the Grants were marched down to Citadel Quay
and the transports. From thence they went to prisons in England,
and further still to the plantations in the Barbadoes. Three years
later eighteen only of the eighty-one were still alive.

Cumberland's duty as dictator of Scotland was simple, the
suppression of all rebellious spirit and the capture of the Prince if
possible. This duty he discussed with his father's First Minister,
and their correspondence was sometimes an amiable exchange
between friends, and at others a pat-ball game of unctuous
flattery. Before Culloden, Newcastle had softly advised the young
Duke on his task: "I know YRH's zeal for the King, Devotion
to his service and Detestation of this Rebellion, will not suffer
you to omit anything that may be necessary for putting a speedy
end to it." At the same time he added a warning against giving
"any just Cause of Complaint to a Country so ill-disposed to the
King and so willing to find Fault with everything that is done for
His Majesty's service". Cumberland's reply was that usually given
by the man-on-the-spot. "Don't imagine that threatening military
execution and many other such things are pleasing to me, but
nothing will go down without it in this part of the world."

By April 30 he was telling Newcastle that all military operations,
such as the engagement of armies, were over, "but Jacobite
rebellious spirit is so rooted in the nation's mind that this generation must be pretty well wore out before this country will be
quiet". He trusted no Scotsman, but could accept them with
apparent good humour so long as he needed them. "Lord President has just joined me, and as yet we are vastly fond of one another, but I fear it won't last, as he is as arrant Highland mad as
Lord Stair or Crawford. He wishes for lenity if it can be with
safety, which he thinks, but I don't, for they really think that
when once they are dispersed it is of no worse consequence than a
London mob, and but yesterday a Sir William Gordon wrote
to one of the officers to complain that his house has been plundered
while he was out *following his duty* (as he is pleased to call the
Rebellion). They are now dispersed all over the kingdom at their
own homes, and nobody meddles with them except I send a

military force after them ... One half of the magistracy have been either aiders or abettors to the Rebellion, and the others dare not act through fear of offending the Chiefs or hanging their own cousins."

Yet he was feeling very pleased with himself that spring. He was twenty-five, the commander of a victorious army, and he could bully grey-heads into silent submission. The First Minister wrote him flattering letters, or gravely asked his advice on how best to deal with this rebellious kingdom. The company of military men, to whom he was a hero, was intoxicating, and it all went to his head a little. "You must allow the Vanity of a young man to be a little blown up by such a success," he told Newcastle. He was full of enthusiasm and confidence. "I thank God most heartily that I was an instrument in the affair ... I really believe that a month or six weeks will enable me to do all that will be necessary for the Military." And, to give him more reason for thanking the Almighty, a letter from Newcastle, dated April 30, informed him that his annual income was now to be increased from £15,000 to £40,000. As a matter of balance alone, this seemed only just. The Government's reward for the person of the Prince he had recently defeated was £30,000.

He circulated the country with orders and proclamations that were nailed to Town House doors or read from Kirk pulpits. These orders were backed by twenty battalions of Foot, three regiments of Horse, six thousand Hessians, Admiral Byng's sloops-of-war, and the eager clansmen of the Whig lairds. On May 1, Cumberland repeated his order of February requiring all "sheriffs, stewards and their deputies, magistrates of boroughs, Justices of the Peace, and other officers of the Law whatsoever to make diligent search for all persons of what rank soever who have been at any time in arms against His Majesty". Orders demanding the co-operation of the clergy in this witch-hunt were read before the General Assembly of the Church of Scotland, and from every pulpit in the kingdom. Ministers were asked for the names of all men and boys who had been away from their parishes too long for innocent explanation, and they were asked for the names and hiding-places of any Rebels believed to be lurking in their neighbourhood.

All this came as a great shock to the reverend gentlemen. Happy as they had been to see the idolatrous Prince humbled and his schismatic followers scattered, and extreme though their praise had been for the letting of blood at Culloden, they did not think of themselves as informers. Officers of the Law obeyed Cumberland with considerable zeal, committing guilty and innocent alike to gaol and Tolbooth, but the General Assembly of the Church immediately began to haver. Its members carried on a tortuous correspondence with Sir Everard Fawkener, not saying yes they would, and not saying no they would not, in fact not saying anything at all which that old gentleman could rightly understand. He answered them with suave ambiguities, now and then warning them tartly of the Duke his Master's displeasure, but the ministers would make no promises, and they should be remembered for this.

Gentlemen in England less immediately concerned, not having Rebels on their doorsteps, as it were, or sitting in their pews on Sunday, were full of bloody indignation. Lord Chesterfield, in a moment between the teaching of civilised manners to his bastard son, offered Newcastle advice on how to treat the Highlands: "Starve the country by your ships, put a price on the heads of the Chiefs, and let the Duke put all to the fire and sword." And the Duke of Richmond, who was the grandson* of one Royal Stuart, also knew what should be done to the followers of another. "I own I had always much rather the Duke should destroy the rebels than that they should lay down their arms," he said. "The dread example of a great many of them being put to the sword, and I hope a great many hanged, may strike a terror in them and keep them quiet, but depend on it nothing but force can do it, for 'tis vain to think that any Government can root out Jacobitism there."

Cumberland's power to do what Chesterfield and Richmond suggested had been established before Culloden. "I shall," he had told Newcastle, "take upon myself more than I should care to do, and shall not wait for orders when anything of this kind shall appear to be absolutely necessary for the King's service.

---

* His father was Charles Lennox, the son of Charles II by his mistress Louise de Keroualle, Duchess of Portsmouth.

I don't expect very explicit orders upon this head, but should be glad to know His Majesty's thoughts and determinations." And Newcastle had quickly reassured him, the responsibility and the power were his. "His Majesty had commanded me to acquaint YRH that as General of His Majesty's army YRH has his authority to do whatever is necessary for the suppressing of this unnatural rebellion." And, should peculiar circumstances raise particular doubts, he added this rider: "No general rule can be given . . . that must depend on the circumstances."

So Cumberland set about bringing the Highlands to heel in the manner he thought best. In every town at tuck of drum his orders were read, demanding the submission of all arms under penalty of hanging, demanding the laying of information against hidden Rebels under penalty of hanging, demanding the surrender of the Young Pretender under penalty of hanging. For the moment he kept his headquarters at Inverness, and from there he sent detachments of Foot to harrow the nearby glens, to burn Rebel dwellings and Non-Jurant meeting-houses, to drive in Rebel cattle, to kill all men resisting or running with arms. He proposed, when the weather improved, to march his Army down the Great Glen to Fort Augustus, from which he could control the Highlands as the hub of a wheel controls the spokes and rim. His Horse, having been let loose after Culloden so that they might (as the Duke put it) have "some sweets with all their fatigue", were now sent to guard the Lowland passes and to garrison the east coast.

From Dundee and Perth, Aberdeen and Stonehaven there had been desperate attempts at escape by the small gentry and merchants directly or indirectly concerned in the Rising. There were shipmasters sympathetic enough, or ready enough to be bribed to carry such men to Scandinavia, and some of these masters were later to find themselves in the plantations because of it. The *James Wemyss*, out of Dundee for Bergen, made Norway in a few days, and thirteen rebel gentlemen came up on her decks to thank God for their safe delivery. But the King of Denmark, as a courtesy to his cousin of England and with the solidarity of all reigning monarchs, had agreed to place such escaping rascals in prison. Thus the unlucky thirteen went to the dungeons below the Castle of Bergen.

The riders of Cobham's, Kingston's and Lord Mark Kerr's were sent to the coasts and the Lowlands to see that such escapes, successful or not, did not become too common. They carried out their work with relish. The rule of the dragoon was nothing new in the history of the northern burghs, but that did not make it any more endurable. The Horse filled the gaols of Perth, Dundee, Aberdeen and Stirling with prisoners, and they made free with the stock, furniture, cellars and women of whatever house they occupied for the night or the month. From their talk it was plain that they thought they had won the late battle by themselves, and they were anxious to know what their grateful country thought of them. "I should be glad to hear," wrote Enoch Bradshaw to Cirencester, "what the caracter of Cobham's is in England." He and his fellows were stationed at Stonehaven, with posts along the Aberdeenshire shore. "We are guarding the coast that Charles may not get off. I pray God I had him in this room, and he the last of the Stuart race; it wou'd be my glory to stab the villain to the heart. Beside, it wou'd look well in history for him to fall by the hand of a Bradshaw."

In the Highlands the Whig clans were enjoying themselves as much as the dragoons below the hills. They came down on the Chisholm country in Strathglass, driving Father Farquharson high into the hills and burning his meeting-house. In the west, eight hundred Campbells, with seventeen hundred other Highland militia, were preparing for a great raid into Lochaber. Four regular battalions of infantry came by sea from London to reinforce the Army and to allow the Hessians, who had not been engaged in the campaign, to return to Europe. The new battalions brought with them something more than the common desire to share the plunder. They brought a malignant fever. When Houghton's battalion landed at Nairn the fever flared up suddenly like an ember in a draught, and the doctor called from Inverness to treat the sick officers died of it as well. Dr. John Pringle, Chief Physician to the Army (and also a professor of metaphysics and moral philosophy), went to Nairn to get the fever in hand, and seems to have done this extremely well.

Since Simon Fraser, eleventh Baron Lovat and hereditary chief of the Frasers, had thoroughly compromised himself this time after a life of prevarication and plot, earlier orders to leave his estates in peace, his cattle at their grazing and his salmon in their run were now countermanded. MacShimi was the King's enemy and the King's subject in Rebellion, and his land, along with his seventy-nine-year-old head, was forfeit. He was a lapsed Catholic, a man of fine taste, and a barbaric Highland chief all in one, and at this moment he was in hiding somewhere to the west, his obese and pain-wracked body being carried from one hole to another by his devoted clansmen. His land, the Fraser country, stretched from Inverness into the hills along the River Beauly. There he had many homes, the chief of which was Castle Dounie, a black and ancient keep of crenel-lated stone surrounded by rich, soft meadowland. There was a more civilised house at Kirkhill, and this and Castle Dounie and all the old fox's holes came now under the displeasure of His Royal Highness the Duke of Cumberland.

Four hundred men of Cholmondeley's and the Royal Scots marched out of Inverness, commanded by Brigadier John Mordaunt. They crossed the Old Bridge over the Ness and took the road along the tidal waters of the Beauly Firth, where the sea-fowl keened on the sand-banks. Since the battle men had talked of the great plunder to be taken from the Fraser lands, should the Duke ever permit it, and now, on a sweet, hot day at the end of April, the rape was to begin. Cholmondeley's and the Royals marched in good heart, for even though a man might not be able to pick up a watch, a piece of silver, or a bolt of cloth for himself (once his officers' backs were turned) his share of the plunder when sold would amount to a good handful of guineas. Mordaunt's orders were to bring off all that was movable from Lord Lovat's lands, and to burn that which was not, to pull stone from stone, and to lay the glen waste from the firth to the hills.

"All this," said Michael Hughes, "was very cheerfully under-taken and performed. One thousand bottles of wine, three hundred bows of oatmeal, with a large quantity of malt, and a library of books to the value of four hundred pounds, was all brought to

Inverness. His fine salmon weirs were destroyed; and salmon in abundance brought into the camp and divided among the soldiers."

The smoke of burning roofs and smouldering peat hung along the Beauly River, and Castle Dounie became a black rubble of stone. The Fraser men, who had returned to the glen from the battle, now ran higher into the central Highlands until Mordaunt's men marched back to Inverness. Battalion horses and wagons followed them with the plunder, and the town was now full of rich food such as the British infantryman rarely enjoyed. Simon Fraser's goods joined the stores of meal, the hogsheads of beef and pork, the barrels of ale which had been taken from other estates, or had been sent by the neighbourhood gentry in an effort to buy off the sack of their own lands. Some of the food was sold direct to the Army (officers bought Lord Lovat's wine, Madeira at two shillings a bottle, claret at one shilling and eightpence) and the rest to merchants, but, however it was sold, the money received was divided among the men who had brought in the plunder. That spring all the soldiers in Inverness became hucksters, and their commercial transactions were those familiar to any occupying army. What they took from the country they sold back to the country, therein making a profit without the initial disadvantage of outlay.

"The traffic on the Rialto Bridge," said Hughes, "is nothing in comparison to the business that was done by our military merchants in Inverness; here being great sortments of all manner of plaids, broadswords, dirks and pistols, plaid waistcoats, officers laced waistcoats, hats, bonnets, blankets and oatmeal bags; for in the field near Culloden House there was a magazine or granary of oatmeal that lay scattered about anyhow. And while our highland fair lasted, if a soldier was seen in the streets of Inverness the good wives and lassies would certainly run after him to buy a plaid. As we sold them very good pennyworths we had customers in plenty, so that our chap-women would hardly give us time to sleep in our tents."

Nobody has ever succeeded in preventing a victorious army from looting. Victory under arms gives a man the stature of a giant, and occupation the temptations to match it. Licence to kill cheapens the value of life, and respect for property falls in proportion. The less a soldier is paid for the killing (and the dying), the more indifferent society is to his hardships, then the greater will be his greed. The British battalions in Scotland were old soldiers. They expected Cumberland's repeated orders against free-lance looting, and they did not complain overmuch when the lash fell upon those who were caught. But neither orders nor the whip stopped them from plundering. Every day that Cumberland spent in Scotland after Culloden his drummers were flogging men for marauding, and although no other General ever used the whip so much on his own men he was never successful in curbing the lust of the Army. His Orders of the Day did not help the soldiers to understand. "No Plundering on any account," they said, "except by order and in presence of an officer." Plundering was not the sin, doing so without permission was the crime, and a soldier, if he were sharp enough, knew what to do about that.

His officers set him no example. Ensign Fawlie of Fleming's led a volunteer party to plunder the house of Oliphant of Gask without orders from his commanding officer. Ensign Daniel Hart of Munro's extorted money from a merchant's wife in return for "protection". Both ensigns were cashiered for this, of course, but the lesson for the soldiers was plain: do not get caught. They ran greater risks than their officers, to lose one's commission was not so bad as losing the skin from one's back. The flogging of a condemned man was carried out with grave and ritual ceremony, and all the men of his battalion were called on parade to watch it so that they, as much as he, might learn from it. The regiment formed a hollow square, facing inwards to the whipping-post, a triangle made from the halberds of four sergeants, three making the legs and the fourth a steadying cross-bar. Two ensigns stood with the battalion, the King's and Regimental colours displayed. The offender was marched to the square under escort from the Provost Guard, and once there his sentence was read to him by the Adjutant. He was stripped to the waist, examined by the Surgeon, and then strapped to the halberds by the Drum-Major. Drum-Major, Adjutant and Surgeon were always present. The first to see that the halberds were properly fixed, the cat-of-nine-tails in order, and the drummers correctly instructed. The second to read the sentence and to declare the punishment fully administered. The third to assure himself that the prisoner was able to endure the flogging without danger to life. The strokes were given by relays of drummers, each with his sleeves rolled up, and each giving no more than twenty-five at a time. The cat fell to the tap of drum and, as a general rule, not more than three hundred strokes were laid on in one morning. If the man's sentence was for more he was paraded every morning until it had been completed.

Every morning the sound of the lash was heard on the Crown, the tap of the drum and the yells of the victim, but the lesson was never learned. Every night men crept away from their tents, slipped past the sentinels on individual forays. Three days after Cumberland's order that no man should go beyond a quarter of a mile of the camp, three men of Pulteney's and a Campbell of the Argyll militia were tried for looting and brutally flogged. At the beginning of May Roger Weigh of Wolfe's received one thousand two hundred lashes "for morauding and steeling", two hundred and forty a day for five days. On the first day of his punishment two men of Sackville's received five hundred strokes each for stealing meal. Later, Samuel Kelsell, also of Wolfe's, was sentence to two thousand strokes in groups of two hundred for the stealing of fifteen sheep. He was also ordered to pay 3s. 9d. for the sheep he and his comrades had eaten before discovery.

No man seems to have died from a flogging while the Army was at Inverness, and most were on duty, with pack and musket slung, two days or less after the punishment.

With the correction of the lash went discipline of the spirit. The whole Army attended compulsory church parade on the Sunday following the battle, so that the soldiers might admit that however strong had been the arm that thrust the bayonet it would have been less powerful without the help of the Lord. Cumberland allowed his chaplains of brigade no privilege of their cloth, and he considered them to be the servants of his men. "The Commanding Officers of Regiments to give in the names of their absent Chaplains with ye reasons why or by whose leave they are absent." And then, two days later: "The

Chaplains to take their Turns in visiting the Hospitals and attending ye Condemned prisoners, & will be more diligent in doing their duty for the Future, otherwise they shall be tryd by General Court Martial."

Similarly he badgered his surgeons, many of whom had come north with the Army for some excitement and a little experience, but were now wishing themselves at home in practice. At headquarters Dr. John Pringle was seriously alarmed by the rise in fever cases. Whatever his fanciful notions of metaphysics and moral philosophy, he was a good and sensible general practitioner, and that the Army did not suffer more from sickness was largely due to his care and devotion, though his professional services did not extend to the rotting prisoners in the gaols. He established an adequate hospital in the old Charity School and Almshouse, to which each regiment sent three of its worst cases (the Artillery sent Sergeant Bristow, who was a long time dying from a broadsword cut). Again and again Pringle asked for orders to be published against the drinking of water from the Ness, which, he told the battalion surgeons, would give their men the flux. He recommended "timely bleedings in ye feverish and Pleuretick disorders, and if for the future such patients are sent to ye hospital without bleeding, complaint will be made of ye Surgeon".

As well as the fever and pleural disorders there was also, of course, the disease that marches with all armies. An After-order of May 4 demanded "An immediate return to be given in to the Major of Brigade of the Day of the Pox'd men of each regiment who the Surgeons think necessary to be sent to Edinburgh in order to be salivated, this return is to be given in as soon as possible that they may be sent aboard to-morrow morning." And accordingly, the next day, Sergeant Willey of Blakeney's sailed for the south as escort to a party of fourteen afflicted men.

Confined to the camp, except for foraging parties, punitive detachments, or occasional journeys to the Moor to gather fresh heather for their tent-floors, the soldiers on the Crown became bored and restless. They turned naturally to gambling, but although their officers freely passed the time with whist, piquet and dice, they discovered that the Duke was having no

such behaviour from them. "His Royal Highness expects that all
Officers take care to prevent gameing among the men, for which
they will be answerable to him without any further orders on
that head."

But further orders were necessary, nobody having taken
the Duke seriously. "Whereas Officers were seen yesterday
going by and neglecting to take notice of soldiers who were
Gameing; the first officer that shall be found neglecting the
orders shall be confined and brought to a General Court Martial
and all officers are to observe that orders once given are not to be
repeated to them again." The Duke had a princely temper, and
his officers saw the warning. That night and every other night
they went round the tents at sunset, taking the names of all men
found with dice or cards in their hands. "All those men·which
are or shall be taken up for gameing to be tryd immediately
by Regimental Courts Martial, at ye head of ye Colours, & if
found guilty to be punished by 400 lashes." So the halberds were
set up, the drummers rolled their sleeves, and the Drum-Majors
counted the strokes. This did not stop gambling, of course, but it
did make it more circumspect, and a man took his turn at the
cards and his turn as look-out by rotation.

Looting went on, though perhaps less profitably now that
the larger estates in the neighbourhood had been officially raped.
A man took what he could get when he went out for forage or
heather. "The Batmen and officers servants of every regiment
that foraged yesterday to be searched immediately, and if any
Bedding, Bedclothes, wearing apparel or anything else that has the
appearance of Plunder to be found on any of them they are to be
confined and a report to be made of it to General Hawley."
The risks added excitement to the profit, and to outwit Hangman Hawley was something of which a man might justly boast.

In such a cunning assembly of freebooters as the Army rapidly
became, no one man's property was safe from his comrades, and
no officers' possessions inviolate. When John Mordaunt brought
his command back from the sack of Lovat's land he discovered
that MacShimi had not been the only man robbed. Corporal
William Edwards, standing at headquarters with his Order Book,
took down an order of special application to his comrades in

Cholmondeley's: "Whereas, by mistake, some soldiers took away a blue greatcoat with gilt buttons belonging to Brigadier Mordaunt in the plundering of Lord Lovat's house, that soldier is required to bring it to the Brigadier's Quarters and he shall receive a crown reward." There is no record of whether this subtle appeal produced the greatcoat.

And Major Lockhart of Cholmondeley's was still hoping that his horse would be returned. He had seen it in the camp, among a number of mounts taken from the Rebels, and he put a sharp request for its return in Regimental Orders: "A large, bright bay horse, 15 hands high, much chafed with carrying a cloak-bag. The person who has him to return him to the owner."

As they waited for the day when they would march down the Great Glen, indiscipline, thieving and petty plundering increased among the bored soldiers, and the Orders of the Day were heavy with the punishments given. Samuel Johnson of the Royals, five hundred lashes . . . Ralph Nisson of Conway's, three hundred lashes . . . William Page of Cholmondeley's, one thousand lashes . . . Thomas Webb and Caleb Shaw of Sackville's, five hundred lashes for stealing of meal . . . Alexander Campbell and Walter Anderson of Sempill's, one thousand lashes each at five different times for picking the pockets of Robert Knox. Desertion and absence without leave increased, and Cumberland ordered that regimental rolls should be called four times a day, and that the Town Patrol (three hundred men) should range between the streets and the camp, taking up stragglers. When Retreat was beaten every evening the flying picquets formed, and marched about the town until eight in the morning.

For a while, a group of soldiers in one regiment went into the horse-coping business, acquiring a number of animals which had been running stray since the battle or had been lifted from the stock brought in from the estates. This herd they kept some distance from the camp, helped by the battalion women, and they were trading them at handsome profit to southern graziers until Cumberland threatened to hang any man or woman found engaged in the business. Even this did not entirely stop matters. Weeks later, when the Army had gone to Fort Augustus, Orders of the Day still snarled threats at the horse-copers.

But the Army's principal answer to indiscipline, boredom and low morale, was what it has always been. On the flat ground by the Crown there were endless parades, company, regimental, brigade and army, with the red lines wheeling, retiring and advancing. The slap of hands on musket stocks, and the clouds of powdering pipe-clay, went on all day from dawn to Retreat, until it was hoped that the men were too exhausted to think of anything else but sleep. Some evenings, as the blue darkness came down from the mountains, the regiments paraded for a ceremonial Camp Beating. They stood in line with their colours, corporals to the flanks of the platoons, sergeants a pace to the front, and field officers advanced well before the captains. The drums beat the passing of the day, beginning on the right of the regimental line and rolling down to the left. And the light passed and the last to be seen of the Army was the white wall of gaiters standing steady.

4

FORT AUGUSTUS

"People must perish by sword or famine"

BY THE MIDDLE of May the dead hills had come to life, and the sun lay upon them and warmed them. The grass of the Crown, where it had not been crushed by ammunition boots or cropped by horses, was fresh and green, and the winds from the mountains brought the scent of young leaf and flowers. It was the weather for rebel-hunting. The Prince was still in hiding, living in a forester's cottage on South Uist, on the outer buckler of the Hebrides. He killed time and boredom by fishing for cod with a hand-line, and once he shot a deer that started from the heather before him. He was eating collops of this when a crofter's boy came by and watched. The Prince's followers would have whipped the boy away, but Charles stopped them, saying "I cannot see a Christian perish for want of food and raiments." And he gave the boy some of the meat. On May 16, when the Prince was thus charitably occupied, three battalions of the King's Foot marched from Inverness for Fort Augustus to make sure that all Christian clansmen still in rebellion wanted for both food and raiment. They were Howard's Buffs, Cholmondeley's and Price's, and with them marched eight companies of the Earl of Loudoun's kilted militia. They were the advance party which His Royal Highness intended to follow later in the month with the rest of the Army. Fort Augustus, on the green meadows between Loch Ness and Loch Lochy halfway down the Great Glen, was to be the middle link of Cumberland's Chain by which he hoped to shackle the Highlands. To the north of it was Inverness, and to its south was Fort William on Loch Linnhe. From all three points would depart detachments of soldiers, by platoon, company or battalion, to harry the lands of the Jacobites, and to crush all sign or suspicion of resistance.

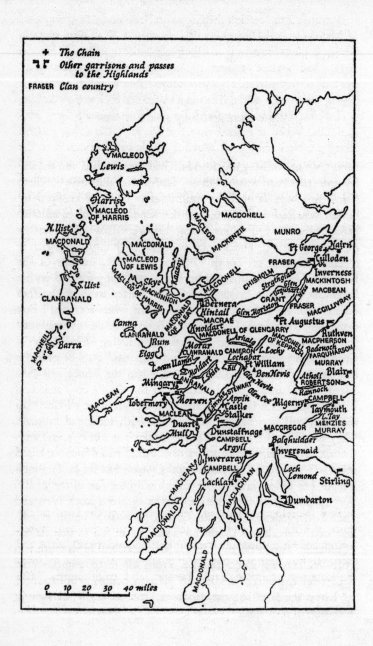

+   The Chain

꒭ ꒭   Other garrisons and passes
       to the Highlands

FRASER   Clan country

MACLEOD
Lewis

Harris
MACLEOD
OF HARRIS

N. Uist
MACDONALD

MACDONALD
MACLEOD
OF LEWIS

S. Uist

CLANRANALD

MACNEILL

Barra

Skye
MACKINNON
MACLEOD OF HARRIS
MACDONALD
OF SLEAT

Canna

CLANRANALD
Rum

Eigg

Loan Uamh

Moidart
CLANRANALD

Mingary

Tobermory

MACLEAN

MACLEAN

Duart
Mull

Morven

CAMPBELL

MACLEAN

MACDONALD

MACLEOD

MACKENZIE

MUNRO

Ft George Nairn
Culloden

FRASER

CHISHOLM
Strathglass
Glen
Urquhart

Inverness
MACKINTOSH
MACBEAN

MACDONELL

Abernera
Kintail
MACRAE
Knoidart
MACDONELL OF GLENGARRY

GRANT
Glen Moriston

FRASER
MACGILLIVRAY

Ft Augustus

MACDONELL
OF KEPPOCH
Arkaig
CAMERON
Lochaber

L. Lochy

Badenoch

Ruthven
MACPHERSON

FARQUHARSON

Moidart
CLANRANALD

Ft William
Ben Nevis
Glen Nevis

MURRAY

Athol
ROBERTSON
Rannock

Blair

JAMES STEWART
Appin
Castle
Stalker

Glen Coe   Migerny

CAMPBELL

Taymouth
L. Tay
MENZIES
MURRAY

Dunstaffnage

MACGREGOR

Balghuidder

CAMPBELL
Argyll
Inveraray
CAMPBELL
Lachlan
MACLACHLAN

Inversnaid

Loch
Lomond

Stirling

Dumbarton

MACLEAN

MACDONALD

MACDONALD

0   10   20   30   40 miles

Howard's Brigade* left the Crown at noon under the command of Major-General Humphrey Bland, an old Yorkshire dragoon whose copious writings on discipline were text-books for the Army, and because of them he had the ear of the Duke on all matters of regulation and procedure. The night before their departure the men of the Brigade had cleaned their copper kettles, paid their debts, and drawn bread and cheese to sustain them until the 20th. When they had marched through the town and on along the Ness, they took Marshal Wade's military road to the south-west. The grenadier drums struck up the beat at the head of each battalion, and behind the grenadier companies marched the Pioneers, with hatchets ready to clear any obstacle placed in the path of the Brigade. The Campbells acted as scouts and skirmishers, sent ahead to discover possible ambush or resistance. There was none. And they saw nothing but the red deer on the brae and the eagle on the mountain wall. On the first day the Brigade marched twenty-three miles, and by dusk it was in the craggy passes of Boleskine. It lay the night in the open, with picquets formed and sentries placed. The parole was "Culloden", which each man called upon relief, and at three in the morning, when the mountains boiled with mist, the battalions arose from the stony ground. They marched before dawn. They marched until nine o'clock, when they came down the fall of Borlum brae to the lochside ruins of Fort Augustus.

A week later they were followed by the rest of the Army, which left Inverness in a great thunderstorm of drums; eight fine battalions in scarlet and white: Barrell's, Bligh's, Skelton's and Wolfe's, Houghton's, Munro's, Conway's and the Royal Scots Fusiliers. Vedettes of Kingston's Horse, drawn from the Duke's mounted guard, rode in the van and at the rear, and the Duke himself led the forward battalion. The Army marched no further than Dores that day, ten miles down the road to the shore of Loch Ness, and there the soldiers saw the wide water. It stretched far to the south-west in its mountain trench, black and silent. It was beautiful but its grandeur unnerved the soldiers; the country promised hard marches and cold nights. "The

* A brigade took its title from the senior regiment serving in it. Howard's, third regiment of the line, had been in existence longer than either of the others.

mountains," said Michael Hughes, "are as high and frightful as the Alps in Spain, so we had nothing pleasant to behold but the sky. 'Tis rainy, cold and sharp weather. . . ."

The bivouac fires were lit that night by the Loch at Dores, and Barrell's men provided the outlying picquets. At ten o'clock in the morning the General was beat, with the Assembly half an hour later, and by two o'clock the Army was marching again, in column by the right, with Skelton's bringing up the train in the rear. When the ground on either side of the road permitted it, the battalion-horses moved on the flanks of the regiment. A captain and a hundred men marched as an advance guard, and another captain and a hundred men to the rear. Thus they moved along the southern side of Loch Ness, with the mountain rise steep and bare above them, and the beat of their drums rolling across the water to strike again on the sandstone cliffs. They marched to Foyers, and passed the walled graveyard where the Fraser tacksmen buried their dead. They climbed away from the water high into the hills, passing through ravines of black and scarlet stone. The voices of the soldiers were stilled by the hostile loneliness of the land, and only the regular urging of the drums kept their feet moving. They marched through the chill and narrow Glen of the Birds, into which the sun could fall at noon only, and came out of it to see the pretty meadows below, and the tents and welcome fires of Howard's Brigade. There, where Loch Ness was fed by the curl of the River Oich, was the spot which Cumberland was to call "this diamond in the midst of hell".

The hell was not yet, it was something the Army was itself to create, though this was not what the Duke meant. The battalions were stationed at Fort Augustus for six weeks, the six weeks which Cumberland had said would be necessary, and in that time the whole of Lochaber and most of Badenoch rotted from the poison they brought. "For the space of Fifty Miles," said Michael Hughes, "neither House, Man nor Beast was to be seen."

When Cumberland arrived, toward dusk, the sun was setting at the end of the Great Glen and filling it with prophetic crimson. The Highlanders of Loudoun's companies had prepared a bower for him, cutting branches of pine and oak with their broadswords. "They made a pretty place for the Duke to reside in," said Hughes, "with handsome green walls. They built a fine hut with doors and glass windows, covered at the top with green sods and boughs, so that His Royal Highness resembled a Shepherd's life more than that of a courtier." The Duke accepted the gift with expressions of pleasure, and he lived in the hut to the delight of the Campbells and to the possible discomfort of himself. The fort and barracks that had once stood by the loch had been destroyed by the Rebels, and in a country where so many buildings were being destroyed this was the only one over which His Royal Highness grieved. "He expressed some concern at seeing vast tracts of uncultivated ground," said Henderson, "and at the blindness of those who had blown up the beautiful and commodious barracks that had so lately been an ornament to that unfortunate district."

The tented streets of the eleven battalions were laid on the fields beside the River Oich, and all day and all night men heard the water's spirited quarrel with the stones. The camp was, within its own context, a happy camp. The fever rate fell and morale rose in the pure air. Voices rang from wall to wall of the mountains, and soon the loch was filled with white sails as the galleys came down from Inverness with stores. Although the Rebels had used nineteen barrels of powder to demolish the fort and the barracks, it was found that there were still some rooms, cellars and stables that could be used as kitchens to prepare fitting dinners for the Ducal Shepherd and his staff. The curious soldiers, picking over the stones, found something else. In a well or cistern to the back of the barracks were the bodies of nine soldiers, their white gaiters green with slime, and their red coats rotting. An officer, writing home to London of this discovery, said "that they were drowned by the Rebels after having been made prisoner; that the bodies were then floating, and that Rebel prisoners brought in by Howard's that day were set down by the well to view their own cruelty".

Whatever had happened to the drowned men, how they had got into the cistern and why, was never clear, but the discovery of them put the Army into the necessary mood for the work its commander proposed. From his green bower, in which he sat plump, pop-eyed and dressed in fine lace and soft scarlet, the Duke planned to direct all military operations in the Highlands.

The back of all serious resistance, he thought, could be broken within those six weeks or less, after which his successor could attend to the business and he could depart for a gentleman's war against the French in the Low Countries. The bulk of his Army was with him at Fort Augustus, including the bloodied battalions of Barrell's and Munro's. There were large garrisons at Fort George, in Inverness, and at Fort William to the south-west of the Great Glen. He visited Fort William soon after his arrival at Fort Augustus, riding there at the gallop by the islands of Loch Oich and the black water of Loch Lochy. He rode with a hundred clattering troopers of Kingston's as his escort, and when he arrived he extended a podgy hand to Captain Caroline Scott and other officers, allowing them to kiss it so that they might understand his pleasure at the way they had held the Fort against the Rebels.

Brigadier John Mordaunt, with the Royals, Pulteney's and Sempill's, was sent down to Aberdeenshire and Perth to hold the towns there and to sweep all suspected Rebels into the gaols. Major-General Blakeney held Inverness with Handasyde's, Mordaunt's, Battereau's and Blakeney's. Away to the west in Appin and Argyll two thousand Campbells and MacLeods under John Campbell of Mamore were already on the march with broadsword and torch. In the grey waters that broke on the Western Isles the Royal Navy's small sloops and bombs were on constant patrol, ready to engage any French ship and to arrest any attempt at escape by the Young Pretender.

Daily the orders at Fort Augustus instructed a hundred men of this battalion, or two hundred of that, to draw bread, cheese, powder and ball for a week's march into the glens. There were great days of burning and murder and plunder, and reprisals by the scattered Highlanders were rare, and, when they did happen, they were curiously directed against their own people. Thus, one night, the rich timber plantations of the Laird of Grant were set on fire by somebody who remembered, perhaps, his betrayal of the men of Glenmoriston and Glen Urquhart. When Mamore's men were let loose in Lochaber, the bond which Lochiel and the Macdonalds had signed became worthless. The Camerons faded away before the march of the Argyll men, and all the Campbells saw of the Rebels was now and then the bare thighs of a lone man leaping for shelter in the heather. The Earl of Loudoun's command scoured Badenoch and brought the Macphersons to submission, though their chief, Cluny, took to a cave on his mountains. Chief after chief surrendered, handing in the arms of their clans, sometimes worthwhile weapons that had been blooded at Falkirk and Culloden, and sometimes a token surrender of rusty blades and useless firelocks. Even MacIan of Glencoe, his land within a morning's walk of Fort William, came in and submitted, uneasily aware of what had happened to his clan fifty-four years before when it failed to surrender on time. But all this did not stop the harrying of the glens.

The King's Army in Scotland recovered from the boredom that had afflicted it in Inverness during the last days there. Although the soldiers hated the beautiful mountains, their wits and appetites were sharpened by their surroundings. A foot-soldier's desires on campaign may in time be reduced to the simple dream of a good pair of boots, and by now most of the men were lamentably ill-shod. Duke Billy did not disappoint them. Up from Glasgow by pack-horse, and down the loch by boat, came one thousand pairs, which were sold to the battalions at four and six shillings a pair. They had been made by Robert Finlay who, in his tender, boasted that he "kept 80 shoemakers in a Manufactory continually making shoes". The Army was grateful to Mr. Finlay, but probably thought the fellow a profiteering scoundrel when, some months later, he complained that he was still owed £178 14s. 11d. for the boots.

Writing home in June, Lieutenant-Colonel Whitefoord said: "We have by now pretty well cleared our neighbourhood about this place. Private Rebels who come in and surrender their arms receive certificates and return unmolested to their homes until His Majesty's further pleasure is known." This was a generalisation and needs qualifying. Whether a surrendering Rebel was permitted to return to his home or not depended on the whim and the liver of the officer to whom he surrendered. And whether or not he had a home at all now depended on how thorough had been the work of the battalions. Coming in with arms to surrender was also risky. A clansman who had nothing but the Irish tongue was not always able to convince a Suffolk infantryman that he wished to abandon his broadsword. "Those who are found in arms," said Whitefoord, "are ordered to be immediately put to death, and the houses of those who abscond are plundered and burnt, their cattle drove, their ploughs and other tackle destroyed."

An officer wrote anonymously to the *London Magazine* to say that his men were "carrying fire and destruction as they passed, shooting the vagrant Highlanders they met in the mountains and driving off the cattle". Such letters gave people in the south their first inkling of what was happening in the Highlands, although for the time being the Duke's harsh methods had general approval. It was believed that he had been driven to this by the obstinacy and intransigence of the clans, and that in the beginning, as another officer explained, he had treated the Rebels "in a gentle, paternal way, with soft admonitions and a gracious promise of pardon and protection to all the common people". Thomas Lobster was, in the public eye, a peace-loving, amiable fellow reluctantly administering punishment on wilful savages. He was also the national hero, and any account of his heroism and artful cunning was eagerly read. He was, said one of his officers, becoming remarkably well-adapted to this mountain campaign, to the astonishment of the hillmen. "They are greatly surprised to find our soldiers climb over their rocks and mountains full as nimble as they can themselves, and to bring cattle from places which they deemed inaccessible to us. In short we have detachments at present in all parts of the highlands, and the people are deservedly in a most deplorable way, and must perish either by sword or famine, a just reward for traitors." And when the raiding parties came upon empty or abandoned houses (regardless of whether their owners had or had not been out with the Prince) "these our soldiers commonly plunder and burn so that many of them grow rich from their share of the spoils."

As May passed into June the green fields about Fort Augustus were blackened by herds of cattle, oxen, horses, sheep and goats. "We bring them to our camp in great quantities," readers of *The Gentleman's Magazine* were told, "sometimes about 200 in a drove." Neither fire nor sword, bayonet nor hangman's hemp, was to have so terrible an effect on the clan system as this vast robbery. His shaggy, timid animals were to the Highlandman what the buffalo was to the North American Indian. He lived on them and by them, they were his wealth and his livelihood, and without them he had nothing. Cumberland knew, as General Sherman was to learn in the American West a century later, that a warlike people may be more easily starved than fought. So every day the cattle came lowing from Glen Tarff, Glen Garry and Glen Doe until the camp, said Michael Hughes, "was like a country fair". News of what was happening reached the dealers and farmers of Galloway and Yorkshire, and from there graziers at once took horse to the Highlands. Cumberland welcomed them. The primary purpose of driving off the cattle was to break and destroy the economy of the Jacobite clans, but he quickly saw a secondary value. The money received from the sale of the stock to Lowland and English dealers was distributed among his soldiers. It kept their morale high, and their rebel-hunting enthusiasm in good fettle. Twice or three times a week the cattle and horses and sheep were set up for auction, and the cry of the bidding and the knock of the hammer were heard in the glen. The stock bought, the graziers drove it southwards, until all roads out of the Highlands were covered by hoof and horn. The animals were bought from the Army at ridiculously low prices, and changed hands several times, and at mounting cost, before they reached their ultimate destination in England or the Lowlands.

One of the greatest reivers in the Army was Major Lockhart of Cholmondeley's, he of the stolen horse and the scarlet coat in which Ninian Dunbar had been hanged. His name, and his exploits appeared often in Orders of the Day:

"Distribution of money made by the Cattle brought in by Major Lockhart's last party:—

	£	s.	d.
To a Captain	28	4	8
Subaltern	14	2	4
Serjeant	2	16	5
Corporal	1	15	3
Private & Drummer	1	8	2½

Major Lockhart gives his share against the whole. Mr. Grant, Volunteer, having distinguished himself on this as well as other occasions is to have the share of Lieutenant Campbell of the Independent Company who, it was expected, would have behaved better than he did."

In time the ordinary cattle-dealers, "the jockies and farmers from Yorkshire", were joined by extraordinary men, for word had gone out from the Highlands that a man with a few guineas in his pocket could make his fortune within a week. "Among the number of those new graziers," wrote Henderson, "were some of those immoral clergymen who, by the viciousness of their lives, had brought religion into contempt and opened the mouths of the disaffected; these double dealers were of the names of Grant and of Monro, and among others was one Rose Macinucater, minister of Nairn, a wretch of such wickedness of heart that such a one ought never to have been born. One Alexander Shaw in Braemurray, who agreed to rear such as Rose had bought through the winter at the rate of £2 10s. for every twenty cows, assured me that most of them died through change of food and other inconveniencies, so that Rose rather hurt than bettered his circumstances; and to complete his ruin he died farmer, grazier, adulterer, smuggler and bankrupt, having left at his death debts behind him to the amount of £2,500 and scarce seven farthings in the pound to discharge them."

But if this were the same Macinucater Rose of Nairn, who interceded for the boy whom Cumberland hanged before leaving that town, there must have been some good in him. Though that, too, Andrew Henderson would no doubt have considered disgraceful.

The homeless, the orphaned and the widowed among the clans of Lochaber, came cautiously to *an gearasdan*, the garrison at Fort Augustus. They came not from curiosity but from hunger. They stood in hollow-eyed groups at the end of the battalion streets until the Provost Guard drove them away. They stood at the edge of the fields and watched the sale or the slaughter of their own cattle. They spoke no English, and nobody spoke to them, except to swear at them and chase them with halberds as if they were scavenging dogs. They begged, some of them, for permission to lick up the blood of the butchered animals, and in the evenings, at dusk, they would catch a soldier's sleeve and offer a few pence or a worn plaid, a cairngorm brooch or a shoe-buckle for a handful of meal. From compassion or cupidity, the two governing emotions of an army of occupation, some soldiers gave or sold them what they asked, until Cumberland issued strict orders against it. "There is no meal to be sold to any person but soldiers, their wives are not allowed to buy it. If any soldier, soldier's wife, or any other person belonging to the Army is known to sell or give any meal to any Highlanders or any person of the Country, they shall be first whipped severely for disobeying this order, & then put on meal and water in the Provost for a fortnight."

There was much flogging in the camp at Fort Augustus, more, perhaps, than there had been at Inverness. General orders against unlicensed plundering were repeated, with harsher penalties, but at night men still slipped away from their tents, coming back in the mist before dawn and the beating of Reveille. Cumberland did his best to stop this. "Patroles to goe instantly from the Picquet during the night and take up and search all Soldiers they find out of camp." This brought a few men under the lash, and the rest became more cunning, offering the soldiers of the Picquet a share in the loot. "Notwithstanding the repeated orders given against moroding and plundering the General has again received complaints that several of them had broken out of Camp last night and plundered the country as far as three and four miles around. It is ordered for ye Future that small guards be posted from ye Picquet round ye camp and suffer no man on any pretence after Tattoo to goe out of Camp and ye General recommends it to the Commanding officers of Regts. to order ye Rolls to be called at such time of the night as they shall Judge most proper for detecting those who make a practice of quitting the Camp."

The risk of being caught by outlying picquets, or of being discovered absent by a sudden roll-call, stopped the looting for a few days, but only until the soldiers evolved schemes that would avoid both risks. He is no soldier at all who gives up the

endless fight against his officers. And so, after a week, the lash was
heard again.

"William Pitt, John Rayner, John Prendergast, James Moor
and John Graham of Dejean's, being condemned to receive 1,500
lashes each with the cat of nine tails, viz 500 at the head of each
Brigade, for plundering under pretended Orders from HRH
the Duke, HRH having confirmed ye Sentence, it is to be put into
execution to-morrow morning accordingly."

And then again . . .

"Alexander Murray of Price's, Peter Bermingham of Dejean's
to receive 900 lashes each at three several times by sentence of a
General Court Martial for plundering Glengarry's son without
orders, and not reporting him when made prisoner."

It was to be more than a century before Government and
people realised that there might be some connection between
the brutal treatment a soldier received and his own brute behaviour. An hour's reading of any Order Book of any eighteenth-
century regiment gives one a picture of a huntsman keeping a
savage pack in check, and at the end of it one's sympathy is
with the hounds.

Toward the end of May the battalions were busy filling
the gaps in their ranks made by sickness, desertion, discharge
or death. Recruiting parties led by officers or senior sergeants
went south to the Lowlands and to England, to take drafts
from garrison battalions, or to drum up likely lads from the
tavern doors. Recruits had already arrived before the Army
left Inverness, from Berwick, Salisbury, Carlisle and Chester,
from Plymouth, Portsmouth, Newcastle and Hull. Cumberland
had his own idea of the type of man he wanted in the Highlands
(and later in Flanders). All recruiters were told to take none
but Englishmen and Welsh, except those sent by the Royal Scots
Fusiliers and Sempill's, "who are supposed to be proper judges
of the Scotch Nation". No recruit was to be under five feet
five inches, unless he were a lad bound to grow, and none was
to be above the age of 30 or below 17. Two guineas and a crown
would be paid to any man who persuaded a friend to come with
him into the King's service.

Officers in charge of recruiting parties were warned against enlisting men suffering from sores, rupture and the pox, and any officer who brought such wretches to Scotland would be financially responsible for sending them back. A high proportion of the fresh drafts for the north came from regiments in England whose men were restless enough, or excited enough by rumours of plunder, to volunteer for service under the Duke. Officers receiving such men were ordered to get clean certificates of behaviour for each before accepting them.

These strict orders indicate Cumberland's jealous pride in his army and his determination that they should bring him the best material obtainable. Even so, he had the most unruly army ever let loose within the United Kingdom. For a few weeks after Culloden the people of Scotland were numbed by the shock of seeing a locust swarm of redcoats descend upon them. But then, being Scots, they began to do something about it. Complaints, petitions and writs to court flooded upon magistrates, garrison commanders and colonels of regiments, frequently from men held in prison on suspicion. Such a petition came from Thomas Ogilvie of Coul, then in gaol at Alloa. He had been there since the previous November when, having come to town to collect some parcels of tobacco consigned to him and sequestrated by the Rebels, he had been taken up by Royal dragoons as a Stuart sympathiser, which he may or may not have been. And now, in June, he wrote to say that since he had been in prison a Captain Charles Hamilton of Cobham's Dragoons (of course) had driven away his cattle from Coul, had grazed horses in his park, reaped and sold his crops, and looted his house together with its offices, yards and lands adjacent. What, Thomas Ogilvie of Coul wanted to know, were the magistrates going to do about this? We do not know what the magistrates did. We do not even know whether Thomas Ogilvie of Coul got out of prison or not.

Hamilton was a looter in the dragoon tradition, later taking his riders (Enoch Bradshaw among them) down on the estate of John Watson at Turin in Forfar, and there informing Mrs. Watson that, in return for sixty guineas, he would take them away again before they did any damage. There was no cash available at Turin, but Captain Hamilton was willing to take a bill for sixty guineas, payable in four weeks.

Hamilton ignored the summons to answer complaints of such behaviour, and a court order was issued to seize him and place him "in the next sure prison to the place where he is apprehended". But the order does not appear to have been executed.

Lieutenant Austin Low, newly come to Scotland with St. George's Dragoons, was as busy as the veterans of Cobham's. He took a troop to the estate of a Mr. James Greig, dispatched this Mr. Greig under escort to Aberbrothock gaol on suspicion of having served with Ogilvy's Regiment, and then stripped his land of horses, cattle, sheep and five cartloads of unthreshed wheat. Quartermaster Cooke, also of St. George's, went with a corporal and five men to the farm of James Sinclair who, said the Quartermaster, was a tacksman of the notorious Rebel Murray of Broughton. Cooke removed everything from the farm that was movable and sold it to nearby tenants, distributing the money among his men. When he was finally brought before the courts to answer for this he said that it was well known that Sinclair was a Rebel, and to make the matter worse he was also a Papist. Such information had been lodged with the Quartermaster by Sinclair's neighbours, and since there had been no officer at the dragoon post Cooke had attended to the matter himself. He produced two red sashes, clotted with blood, which he claimed to have found in Sinclair's house, saying that they had been taken from the bodies of Royal officers. Quartermaster Cooke was acquitted of all charges of marauding and plundering, and was commended for his zeal.

Away to the north in Fort Augustus Cumberland was faintly irritated by the babble of legal protest from baillie, provost and magistrate. He was in no mood to answer them, or to censure his dragoon officers publicly. The brigades were still giving laws, and so long as officers could reasonably claim that the men they robbed were Rebels or Rebel sympathisers, and that the plundering was carried out within the terms of his orders, he was satisfied. Captain Hamilton's demand for sixty guineas from Mrs. Watson was, of course, a different matter, but the Duke was careful not to get too involved with that. He was, in any case, much too busy in the Highlands. Not only had his Army to be kept busy, it had also to be kept content, and by mid-May it was beginning to complain that it was being robbed. Sutlers and merchants from the south, hearing of the Great Plunder and how it was filling soldiers' pockets with guineas, had hurried north to milk their share. The Duke's reaction was one the Army expected of its dear Billy.

Henceforth, he said, best beef and best mutton would be sold at twopence-halfpenny the pound and no more. The price of rum was fixed at eight shillings the gallon, brandy at seven shillings the gallon, and a bottle of porter at sixpence. Cheshire cheese was to be fivepence a pound, butter sixpence, and meal tenpence.

The Army had also to be entertained when not on duty. Women were there, of course, wives and doxies. When he first came to Scotland the Duke ordered that there should not be more than one woman to a tent of six men, but even this meant that there were a great many at Fort Augustus, brawling, fighting, gossiping. Soldiers like Alexander Taylor and Edward Linn had wives at home, but to most soldiers of the battalions the Army was their home, and where it went they and their wives went too. The women of the Army came under the same orders, the same lash and drum-beat, as the men, and if their husbands died in battle, of disease and the pox, they took another from among his bachelor comrades, serving him as faithfully as they knew how.

Such women were soon as restless as the men at Fort Augustus, and the Duke satisfied them all by organising horse-races, giving prizes from his own purse. He was extremely fond of racing, though there was a great difference between his Newmarket tastes and the hoof-flinging scramble of Highland ponies along the River Oich, a difference that may have given him a rough amusement.

"Last Wednesday," an officer wrote, "the Duke gave two prizes to the soldiers to run heats for, on bare-backed galloways taken from the Rebels, when eight started for the first and ten for the second prize. These galloways are little larger than a good tup, and there was excellent sport."

Cumberland also offered a "fine Holland smock" to the winner of a race for women "on these galloways, also bare-backed, and riding with their limbs on each side of the horse like men. Eight started and there were three of the finest heats ever seen. The prize was won, with great difficulty, by one of the Old Buffs ladies."

The races took place almost every evening, toward dusk when the smoke of the fires was blue in the glen. Old Hawley, though he was close to seventy, was excited by the sight of the bare-shanked women riding the saddleless ponies, and he challenged Lieutenant-Colonel Howard to race the stretch with him, for a wager of twenty guineas. With the roaring approval of the whole camp, the two old men galloped down the green, wigs and beaver hats flying behind them. Hawley won, and collected his twenty guineas to a cheer of applause.

But, says Michael Hughes, "the pony races eventually made the Army insubordinate and lazy". Almost every man now had his own horse on which he wagered the guineas he got from plunder, and some of them refused to march on patrol, insisting that their galloways carry them, their white-gaitered legs stuck out on either side of the tiny animals. "I saw a soldier riding on one of these horses," remembered Hughes, "when, being met by a comrade, he asked him 'Tom, what hast thou given for the galloway?' Tom answered 'Half a crown.' To which the other replied with an oath 'He is too dear, I saw better bought for eighteenpence.' "

But horse-racing and horse-dealing soon stopped when the Duke saw that it had got out of hand. The work for which the Army was in the Great Glen was not finished, although much had been done to his pleasure. All the houses of the chiefs that were within a day's march of the camp, were now in ruins. Invergarry and his wife had hidden in the heather on the brae while two platoons of soldiers burned their home, drove away their cattle, and carried off their plate, charter-chest and books on a bread-wagon. Deeper in Lochaber two hundred Campbells, searching for the Prince, found and captured Alexander Macdonald of Kingsburgh, bringing him in irons to Fort Augustus where he was accused of having hidden the Prince for three days. Charles was now known to be on the mainland again, and fifteen hundred men, from the camp and Mamore's command, were sent to find him. They found and captured John MacGinnis, an old servant of Mackinnon of Mackinnon, who had helped to row the Prince across from Skye. He was threatened with death unless he told what he knew, so he told what he knew, though it was of no great help to anyone. He said that when he and the Prince had landed they walked for twenty-four miles over very rough ground before parting. He had carried on his back all that the Prince possessed, which was two shirts. No, he remembered, there had been a bottle of brandy as well, but the Prince had carried that himself.

Old Keppoch was dead, and his body probably burned in that bothy on Drummossie Moor, but the soldiers came down upon his glen too, so suddenly that Lady Keppoch had scarcely had time to escape with her new-born. A few of her clansmen kept the soldiers back, with desultory musket-fire from behind the rocks, until she got away to the high corries of the mountains. Then the soldiers came in and set fire to her house and offices.

Not only houses were burnt in Scotland that June. On the last day of May fourteen Rebel standards, taken on the field at Culloden, or in the rout afterwards, were brought south to Edinburgh and lodged in the Castle. With the exception of the colours of the Appin Stewarts and Clan Chattan, all the flags that had flown over the Highland Army had been captured, and their totem significance, to victor and vanquished, was intense. On Wednesday, June 4, they were carried in procession to the Cross, the Prince's standard at the head being held by John Dalgleish, chief hangman of Edinburgh. The rest were dragged, carried and waved by the chimney-sweeps of the city, grinning men and boys still grimed with soot. A great crowd had gathered, from the Castle to the Cross, and they laughed at the cavorting sweeps and mocked the colours. On either flank of the procession marched an escort of Lee's Foot with arms advanced, and following it were the Sheriffs of the city, with their heralds, pursuivants, trumpets and constables.

At the Cross, while the standards lay in the dust, the Senior Herald made a long and declamatory proclamation, explaining that it was by order of His Royal Highness the Duke of Cumberland that these scraps of silk and braid were to be burned by the

public hangman. The Prince's standard was the first to be put
to the fire, and then, one by one, the leaping sweeps came forward
with theirs. The banners were not thrown on to the faggots
without ceremony. Each was held over the flames while the
Senior Herald gave it proper distinction by naming the clan that
had marched behind it, "the trumpets sounding, and the populace,
of which there were a great number, huzzaing".

Later in the week a fifteenth standard was burnt in the same
way, and later still, on June 25, there was burnt the banner
of the Keppoch Macdonalds. This had been found on the field
by a Scottish officer, beneath the bodies of many Clan Donald
dead, and had been sent to a private house in the Lawn-market.
There it remained until John Dalgleish, escorted by four companies
of Lee's regiment, took it to the Cross and burnt it.

When news of all this burning reached London there was
a spirited protest from the old pensioners at Chelsea Hospital.
Awakened from their dozing memories of Marlborough's wars,
they asked why the standards had not been brought to London
and lodged in their great dining-hall beside the captured colours
of the French regiments they had fought in their youth. Nobody
troubled to give them a reason, if there was one.

"They absolutely refused to kneel"

MAJOR-GENERAL JOHN HUSKE had an idea. He remembered laws that had once been passed for the suppression of intractable tribesmen in Ireland, and he said that £5 should be paid for the head of every Rebel brought into camp at Fort Augustus. The suggestion was not adopted, less from humanitarian reasons, it would seem, than from its obvious impracticability. Who could be sure of the political sympathies of any bloody head which a soldier might lay at the foot of his commanding officer? John Huske, who was a good soldier and an otherwise kindly man, was merely acting in character, a general officer outraged and bewildered by men in rebellion against the simple decencies of God, King, Country and The Flag. His savage proposal was also symptomatic of the Army's general mood and behaviour. The killing was going on, even beyond the mountain ring. From Arbroath, in Angus, Captain Berkeley of St. George's Dragoons wrote to friends in London: "We have been dismounted these past two months and taken a great many rebels, both in the Highlands and Lowlands; numbers refused to surrender which has caused many skirmishes wherein several of the rebels have been killed. We seize and divide all their goods and cattle, which is distributed among the private men by order of His Royal Highness who by his conduct has rendered himself the bravest and best of generals."

The words "burn" and "kill", "hang" and "destroy" were easily written, and as easily obeyed. The young Earl of Ancrum, commanding the east coast for Cumberland, had his master's temper spoken from every pulpit and at every Cross: "That wherever arms of any kind are found that the house and all houses belonging to the proprietors or his tenants shall be immediately

burnt to ashes; and that as some arms have been found under-
ground, that if any shall be discovered for the future the adjacent
houses and fields shall be immediately laid waste and destroyed."
From Fort Augustus an infantry subaltern wrote to a Northum-
brian friend: "We hang or shoot everyone that is known to
conceal (the Pretender), burn their houses and take their cattle, of
which we have got 8,000 head within these few days past." However highly his officers may have thought of the Duke, their
conduct this early summer was earning him the nickname of
"Butcher" and an eternity of contempt. The search for the
Prince was now becoming desperate, and the brutality increased
with the desperation, though no one, Duke or Government, knew
what ought to be done with the young fool should he be caught.
He was in Morar somewhere, by the Sound of Arisaig on the west
coast, and protected for the moment by Catholic Macdonalds.
There were enough men in the Highlands of dubious loyalties*
who would have sold him for that £30,000, but by luck and the
good sense of his friends none of these got close enough to him.
He had discarded the old black kilt he had been wearing, and was
now dressed in a coarse brown coat and breeches, his red beard
scrubby and his face browned by the sun. He always had a musket
in his hand, a pistol and dirk at his waist, and there was always
someone ready to shelter him and guide him and keep him until
a French ship could take him away into legend.

Beyond the mountains the Lowland people were cowed by the
dragoons and regiments of Foot, but in the hills there were
still many isolated clansmen who resisted so long as they had
broadswords in their hands and a rock-cave in which to hide. A
letter from Fort Augustus in June told how an officer had taken
his platoon into a wood near Garvamore, upon information that
a chief and his followers were hiding there. The Rebels were
flushed from the trees toward a shallow burn, the crossing of
which they disputed with musketry. They were finally driven
off, and the soldiers climbed on up the brae to a cottage made

* Part of the creaking romance of Bonnie Prince Charlie is the belief that
no one in the Highlands could be found who would betray him. As will be seen,
the Government had spies among the clansmen who would most certainly
have betrayed him had it been possible.

of turf and saplings. It contained one chair and a table on which was "a lemon cut through, some bottles of different kinds of liquors, a fowling-piece, and a few other trifles".

Information of a less quaint nature appeared in some of the letters home. "There were found last week," wrote an officer in postscript, "two women and four children dead in the hills who perished through want, their huts being burnt." Such discoveries were frequent, and starvation was becoming a problem. Not to the Army, for this, like all occupation forces, existed in a vacuum protected from any feeling of moral responsibility. The poor clergy of the Highlands, to whom the orphaned or abandoned families were turning, did not know what to do. "As the most of this parish is burnt to ashes," wrote one minister to *The Caledonian Mercury*, more concerned with his own troubles than his parishioners', "and all the cattle belonging to the Rebels carried off by His Majesty's forces, there is no such thing as money or a pennyworth to be got in this desolate place. I beg therefore you'll advise me what steps I shall take to recover my stipends. My family is now much increased, by the wives and infants of those in the rebellion in my parish crowding for a mouthful of bread to keep them from starving; which no good Christian can refuse, notwithstanding the villainy of their husbands and fathers to deprive us of our religion, liberty and bread."

No one seems to have given him any advice, but the *Mercury* added its comment. "The calamity is likely to become still more general, by parties of soldiers seizing and publickly auctioning the effects of the rebels without a warrant from a civil court, or waiting till the criminals be legally convicted, to the great disappointment of their lawful creditors; and this even in countries that seem to be in a state of perfect tranquility, the courts of justice sitting, and people at full liberty to put the laws in due execution." Worst of all, thought the *Mercury*, and many good people with it, the soldiers were looting houses on Sundays.

Alone among the Jacobite clans, the MacGregors attempted to strike a balance, following their old reiving ways by stealing the cattle of some Whig land-owners and levying black-mail upon others. Glenorchy's Campbells were unable, or unwilling, to do much to stop this, so Brigadier Mordaunt marched to the

Braes of Balquhidder with seven hundred infantrymen. Clan Gregor faded into the hills before him, but he burnt Glengyle's house and every house of every MacGregor in Craigroyston, and he drove off every four-legged animal that he found.

The soldiers enjoyed these raids, there being little or no danger and much profit. The two hundred men who destroyed the Castle of Glengarry received fifteen shillings each if they were private soldiers, the corporals a pound, and sergeants thirty shillings, and so on upwards to the captains who received £11 5s. each. Sometimes a quixotic compassion, or mere indolence, spared houses that the battalions were sent to burn. At Balquhain Castle in Aberdeen, home of the Leslies, the soldiers set fire to damp straw outside the building so that it might seem that they had obeyed their orders.

The three hundred and twenty men of Bligh's who went to destroy Lochiel's house and lands were less merciful. Michael Hughes was with them, keeping his sharp eyes open as usual. They marched away from Fort Augustus on the late afternoon of a dull and clouded day, in the kind of weather to which they had become mournfully accustomed. Their lieutenant-colonel, Edward Cornwallis, was "a brave officer of great humanity and honour," says Hughes. They took old Wade's road to the south-west, a road that drove its stony path up and over the mountains for twenty miles or more along Loch Lochy. That night the soldiers had two hours of uncertain sleep only, before pushing on to Mucomir where the River Spean and the loch mingled their waters. From there the column turned to the north-east, marching up the other shore toward Achnacarry, the field of the weir, the home of the chiefs of Clan Cameron. In the wet dawn the soldiers passed through rich groves of oak to a clearing on which, ten months before, Lochiel's clan had gathered in response to his summons and his whip.

Bligh's men halted uneasily, the rear files closing up. It was five o'clock, and ahead of them in the mist was a body of Highlanders, their faces covered with their plaids and the early light cold on their broadswords. But Cornwallis saw the red saltires in their bonnets, and recognised them as Highland militia under the command of Munro of Culcairn.

"Here we formed into our platoons and marched directly to Loch Yell*, a fine lake eight mile long, the stately seat of old Esquire Cameron, a principal ringleader of this rebellion. The order was to set fire to his mansion house, but the best of his moveables were carried off before the soldiers came; however his fine chairs, tables, and all his cabinet goods were set afire and burnt with his house. His fine fruit garden, above a mile long, was pulled to pieces and laid waste. A beautiful summer-house that stood in the pleasure-garden was also set on fire, and everything valuable was burnt or destroyed."

Trampled under the hooves and the ammunition boots, the brogues of the militia-men, were some of the beech saplings that Lochiel had been planting in a grand avenue when news of the Prince's landing had called him from home. It is said that, with some of his clan, he lay in hiding above Achnacarry, on a hill called The Arm, and watched the men of Bligh's burn his house. Before they came he had been able to bury his plate and jewellery, and may have been grateful that the bread-wagons of Bligh's had not been able to take them from him. But the King's Army in Scotland was not so easily disappointed, particularly since it believed Lochiel to be one of the richest chiefs in the Highlands. Some time later, two platoons of Munro's regiment arrived at Achnacarry, and picked over the smoke-blackened stones. In a mean hut was found the Chief's gardener, and then Lochiel's cook was also dragged from hiding. They were ordered to tell the soldiers where the gold and the silver and the jewels had been buried, but the frightened old men would not say or did not know, though they were flogged again and again by the drummers. With their backs cruelly flayed, they were finally sent in irons to Inverness.

The black smoke of burning Achnacarry was still coiling down Loch Arkaig when Bligh's went away, swinging toward Moidart with Culcairn's militia, "burning of houses, driving away cattel and shooting those vagrants who were to be found in the Mountains". Much of what they did was not reported in

* Hughes means Loch Eil, but even so his geography is at fault. Achnacarry House was on the isthmus between Loch Lochy and Loch Arkaig. Loch Eil is further down the Great Glen.

Michael Hughes's Narrative, but John Cameron, Presbyterian Minister and Chaplain at Fort William, wrote down an account of it in his Journal. He said that when the party camped for the night on the braes of Loch Arkaig they saw what they thought was a boat on the shore. A party went down to examine it, and found it to be a large black stone, "but that they might not return without some gallant action on meeting a poor old man about sixty, begging, they shot him". They also found an old woman, blind in one eye and not much more than a beggar herself, and when she would not say where Lochiel was hidden (if she knew) she too was shot. "This is certain," said Minister Cameron, "but what is reported to have been done to her before she was dead I incline not to repeat—things shocking to human nature."

Culcairn's Whig Highlanders, according to Cameron, were responsible for these shootings, but the men of Bligh's did their share. They saw two men carrying dung to their bitter fields, and these were ordered to come before Cornwallis. They came, but on their way were foolish or thoughtless enough to look back at their field. The soldiers shot them.

And so it was all the way to Moidart.

Moidart was Macdonald country westward from Fort William, and boat's-crews from the sloops and bombs of the Royal Navy had already landed on its white sand shore, to burn and to pillage. It was a land of dark superstition where ancient Macdonald chiefs had kept huge toads as their familiars, and it was a country where, for a while at least, the Prince had thought himself safe. Now Bligh's were there, among the conical, naked hills. They looked westward across the water to the curiously named isles of Rum, Eigg and Muck, and they did not like what they saw. They did not like the tortured volcanic rocks or the plaintive crying of the sea-fowl. But they had little time for meditation. The days were busy and full. There were many rebel Macdonalds in Moidart, and some with no enthusiasm for surrendering. Hughes and his comrades "did great execution amongst those who were still in arms, obstinately refusing to submit and accept of pardon".

It may be that they did not think Bligh's encouraged surrender or wanted it. "There came," said Hughes, "two rebels toward the camp, pretending to surrender themselves, but as they came with firelocks loaded and shouldered tis plain they were upon mischief bent and belonged to some party. So they were brought to the Quarter Guard of the camp and in half an hour's time were brought out to be shot. But they absolutely refused to kneel, or to have caps over their faces, so that the picquet-guard was obliged to perform the sentence as they stood."

In Moidart, Bligh's were joined for a while by their new colonel, Lord George Sackville, at the head of four hundred and eighty infantrymen, most of them from the regrouped platoons of Barrell's. After a convivial evening with Cornwallis, Sackville marched this command northward through Morar to Knoidart, the home of a surly sept of Glengarry Macdonalds. Knoidart was a dark and mountainous country, lying between Loch Nevis and Loch Hourn, one of those gnarled fingers of land with which Scotland claws at the western sea. There were no roads through it, and Sackville's men marched over the hills or along the tide-freed shore, burning and shooting. In Knoidart they joined another party of soldiers, led by Captain Caroline Scott of Guise's, a man who had skilfully held Fort William against the Rebels but who was now building a black reputation for himself. Throughout the western Highlands large bodies of men were marching and meeting at pre-arranged rendezvous, like those of Cornwallis, Sackville and Scott, and it was by such deep incisions into the heart of the Jacobite country that Cumberland hoped to stop the pulse-beat of rebellion.

Lord George Sackville, third son of the Duke of Dorset, was a thin-nosed young man of harsh and aristocratic contempt. He was brave*, arrogant and proud, and for most of his service in Scotland his temper was exacerbated by the pain of wounds he had received at Fontenoy. There was "the leg that is wounded and considerably shrunk up", and there was the wound in his breast. He was childishly proud of the bullet-holes in his coat,

---

* Fourteen years later he was tried by court-martial for failure to lead his cavalry in pursuit of the French at Minden. He was dismissed the service, and his name was erased from the Privy Council. He later assumed the name of Germain.

a coat which he wore as frequently as possible, fine scarlet broad-cloth looped with gold, the blue lapels turned back to show his snow-white lace. Because he was a London dandy his temper was not improved when a few screaming clansmen came down on his baggage-horses, far to the rear of his column, and made off with his bedding, linen, clothes and provisions. He allowed his men to take his revenge at the next hamlet, where the women were first raped and then held to watch the shooting and bayon-eting of their husbands, fathers, brothers and sons.

On his way to Knoidart Sackville had burnt his way across some of Keppoch's country to the east of the Great Glen, coming at last to Tirnadris, the softly-named land of the briars by a curl of the River Spean. There was the home of Donald Mac-donald of Tirnadris, a cousin to the chief, a major of the Keppoch Regiment, and a prisoner now in Carlisle Castle. The house stood on a brae below Meall nan Luath, the hill of ashes, and it was burned by Sackville. The major's people fled before the soldiers in little bands, each taking one or more of his children and going south to the high glens behind Ben Nevis and Stob Ban. One of Macdonald's sons was Ranald, aged seven, and two years later this boy wrote down as much as he could remember of those days and nights in the hills.

"After the battle of Culloden the cruelty of the soldiers made us fly from our homes; and the first night we went and drove all our cows and sheep about two miles from the house and carried all our provisions upon the horses, our bed-clothes, and all the other goods in the house to the place where we took our night's lodgings, and pulled ling to make a fire and bed of, and we laid beside a little water that was at the bottom of two hills."

The next day the clansmen took him to a house on Loch Treig where he again saw his step-mother, Macdonald's second wife. For a while they all felt safe. Mrs. Macdonald and Ranald went across the loch to visit her sister, a young woman lately taken ill with small-pox. "And when I was coming home I felt a pain in my back and could not walk home. But the maid carried me and they put me to bed and I was very bad of the small-pox. They had no whisky in the house or they would have given me some. I was blind about a week, and one day I began to see the walls, and I got up and was very well."

They were able to stay no longer by Loch Treig, for soldiers and Campbell militia had been seen on its water. So they went south by night again, and with them was someone whom Ranald called "a gentleman", but who may possibly have been his step-mother's brother, the Macdonald of Kilachonat who had brought the news of Keppoch's death to the chief's wife. They went to Rannoch Moor, a bleak plateau of bogs and broken grass high against the sky. "I went along with my step-mother. My eldest sister and a gentleman went along with us; four servants and my two youngest sisters went with the cows, sheep and goats and drove them to Ranach. My step-mother, the gentleman, my eldest sister and me went to Ranach through woods and over mountains, on foot. And we used to lie on the tops of the mountains, and the gentleman used to roll me in his plaid with himself, and sometimes we walked all night when we heard the soldiers were near us. Upon a hill we spied our chief's son and all Keppoch's family, but we had very little time to stay with them for we heard the soldiers were coming that way. Then we parted, and travelled all that night on foot, and the next day till seven o'clock in the evening. Then we took our night's rest under two steep hills, where we had four miles to go for wood to build a little house of sticks and sods, and we had as far to go for water as we had to go for wood."

In this hut the fugitives stayed for three days until they were joined by two Keppoch clansmen, Ronald and Samuel Angus, who said that they would take Ranald to their house and hide him and protect him there. "We set forward at six o'clock in the morning, and they got me a little galloway and they went themselves on foot, and they ran all the way as the galloway trotted; and about eight o'clock we got to our journey's end where we saw a drove of cattle and some gentlemen that had been along with the Prince, flying from their houses. We made little houses where we put our milk and curds, for we made cheese when we were not travelling."

But even here there was no safety, and within two days there were soldiers seen again, marching down from the mountain.

"Then we went to a wood where we built a little house and stayed there about a week; and there was a loch near the wood where Samuel Angus used to fish, and strike fire with his flint to make a fire to broil them."

For a fortnight the two clansmen and the boy skulked in the hills, catching fish and making cheese, and seeing nobody, until someone came and told them that the soldiers had gone from Keppoch's country and there were no Campbells there either. So they went back to Loch Treig, and hid for a while in the wood, near the home of Ronald Angus, until at last it was thought safe to occupy the house itself. Campbell militia came back while they were living there, but these were gentle and compassionate men with no sympathy and no liking for what the soldiers were doing in Lochaber. They bought food from Ronald Angus, and they made a pet of the boy, saying that if the English came they would protect him.

"I went to see them before they went away. The head of them gave me a shilling, and I gave it to Ronald's mother. Then my step-mother came to Terndriech, and when she saw her house was burnt she built a little house of wood and turfs. A little after I heard that I was to come to a gentleman's house in England."

Travelling by night, he was sent to Cumberland for safety, and perhaps to be near his father in Carlisle. He was adopted by John Warwick of Warwick Hall, with the intention that he become a Catholic priest in time. He never saw his father again. "I got English clothes," he said, "and I did not love myself in them." All this he wrote down at the age of nine.

Sackville came back to Fort Augustus from Knoidart with a great herd of cattle. He came by way of Glen Dessary, along an old drover's road from Loch Nevis. It lead to Loch Arkaig, and there, near the ruins of Achnacarry House, he camped for the night, not knowing that the Prince was within a short climb of his soldiers. Charles, with a few Highlanders of mixed names, was hiding in a cave below the hill called The Arm. They had been forty hours without meat, and below them, as they looked, they saw the squad-fires of Sackville's men and the fat cattle he had driven from the Macdonald country. "What would ye think, gentlemen," said the Prince, "of lifting some? The night will favour us." The clansmen thought it too dangerous, and said so, but he laughed at them, saying that if the risk of the foray were the only argument to be set against it then he was quite willing to go himself. He had a princely knack of shaming men in this fashion, so four of the Highlanders slipped away down the hill and "brought off six cows without being in the least discovered". It was such small moments of schoolboy excitement that the Prince was to remember, years later in the brandy fumes.

Bligh's, too, came back to Fort Augustus after a fortnight away, with much plunder and many cattle. They returned to the news that Lord Lovat had been taken in Morar, hiding in a hollow tree, some said, but without the wit to cover his legs. Hughes saw the old man borne by on a litter, and felt no sympathy for him. "He had been a great courtier and a great knave: but how abominable for ever his character is represented in England tis not half so bad as his North British countrymen make it." Only MacShimi's Frasers were to mourn the moment when their chief's head was cut from his fat neck.

Hughes, and other volunteers like him, were being discharged at their own request. They had enlisted for the term of the Rebellion and that, quite obviously, was over now. They could have stayed, the Duke was offering two guineas to each man who did so, and the promise of a share in the Veteran's Fund which the citizens of London had subscribed. Four hundred pounds of this had already arrived in Fort Augustus, to be distributed first among those men who had been wounded in the battle. It was paid out over a drum-head, on the green one afternoon. Barrell's share, naturally, was the largest, being £165 8s. 2½d. The wounded of Munro's received £112 13s. 11½d., and the rest, but for two shillings and a penny overplus, was divided among ten other battalions "according to the nature of their wounds and their behaviour in the day of battle".

Hughes believed that, had he stayed, his share in the general bounty would have come to sixteen shillings or more, but he was homesick. "I made the best of my way to London, designing to resume my former employment, being that of a weaver."

"A warrant from heaven would not hinder me!"

THE ARMY HAD been camped at Fort Augustus for three days when Orders were published that sent Major Lockhart of Cholmondeley's on the first of his bitter raids: "Two captns 4 Subs 4 Serjts 4 Corpls and 80 Volunteers with Arms and Cartridge boxes only, with 2 Serjts 2 Corpls & 100 Volunteers without Arms to parade as soon as possible at the old barracks and proceed under the command of M Lockhart. They will be out 2 or 3 days, therefore will be provided with Meals accordingly. Howards, Cholmondeleys, Prices, Houghtons & Skeltons do not give to this detachments, the men of the detachment to be well shod."

No description of this Lowland Scot exists, and there is not even a record of his Christian name beyond the fact that it began with an I. He is described by his actions, and any imagined face that fits them would probably have fitted him. To the Army he was already well known, for the fact that he had broken his parole after capture by the Rebels at Falkirk, for the fact that Ninian Dunbar had been hanged in his scarlet coat, and for the fact that he had offered no reward for the return of his stolen horse. What Cumberland thought of the Major's ruthless zeal is also unrecorded, and perhaps there is room for believing that because Lockhart, and other Lowland officers, knew that the young man doubted the loyalty of all Scots they were that much more brutal toward their countrymen.

Lockhart had no difficulty in getting his hundred and eighty volunteers, for they were to harry the lands and farms of the Grants of Glenmoriston, and there would be no danger in this duty. Sixty-nine men from the narrow, crinkled valley were in prison at Inverness, having accepted the Laird of Grant's assurance of pardon, and their small farms at Inverwick, Dundreggan,

Blairy and Balnagarn were protected by women and children only. The glen had been raided already. Shortly after Culloden the Laird of MacLeod and Sir Alexander Macdonald of Sleat, both supporters of King George★, had marched its length with their militia. Laird and baronet had lodged for a night in the house of Grant of Glenmoriston, burning it to the ground in the morning, "destroying at the same time all the ploughs, harrows, and other such like utensils they could find". Chairs and tables were chopped into kindling, and the stone quarns by which the clansmen had ground their meal were rolled from the brae until they were broken.

But there was still much in the glen to be taken or destroyed. Lockhart's detachment left early in the morning, wading through the shallow run of the River Oich where the engineers were driving the first piles of a bridge. They marched by platoons, with pack-horses to the rear and the Major and his two captains in the van. They took the military road to the north-west, climbing a thousand feet in one mile to reach the saddle between two lonely hills known as The Roe and the Black Cairn. And there, at a cold spring of red water, the horses drank, before the detachment moved down into Glenmoriston at Dundreggan. They were still high on the brae when Lockhart demonstrated what the Highlands could expect of him. Three clansmen came out of the heather, and because the Major did not like their appearance or their manner he ordered them to be shot, their bodies to be thrown across the horses for hanging later in a suitable spot and a salutary fashion. By the fields at Inverwick Lockhart ordered two platoons of the unarmed soldiers to drive in the cattle of Grant of Dundreggan, and they were about to do this when Mr. Grant came up, holding a certificate of immunity. This, on the authority of the Earl of Loudoun no less, declared that he had taken no part in the Rebellion. "If you were to show me a warrant from Heaven," said Lockhart, "it would not hinder me!"

He ordered Grant to bring in his own cattle, a difficult order

---

★ The same Highland gentlemen who had sold one hundred of their clansmen for transportation to Pennsylvania. They had recruited their people for King George in much the same manner as the Jacobites had recruited theirs for King James.

for one man to execute, and Dundreggan had scarcely begun before Lockhart returned from burning the tacksman's house. He ordered Dundreggan to be stripped of all his clothes and taken to a tree by the burning house where he could be hanged with the corpses of the clansmen killed on the brae. Mrs. Grant was there, naked too, and some soldiers who had been unable to take her rings had drawn their hangers to cut off her fingers, but she managed to remove the rings herself. Dundreggan, a halter about his neck, was about to be pulled up with the swinging dead when one of the detachment officers, a Highland militiaman whose name was also Grant, stepped forward with his hand on his broadsword, daring Lockhart to continue with the murder.

The Major shrugged his shoulders, called the platoons into column and marched them deeper into the glen, following the twisted, tortured curl of the river. Beyond Inverwick they found a group of huts that had not been burned by the Laird of Mac-Leod, and this oversight was quickly remedied. Where the River Doe meets the Moriston in a black waterfall, Isobel Mac-donald was raped by five soldiers, and her husband, skulking high in the heather, watched this in agony. There were other women raped, too, and always before the doors of their burning homes. The soldiers marched on, shooting an old man and his son as they stood in their field, until the dark glen was burnt and despoiled from Loch Ness to Loch Cluanie. When Lockhart went away his soldiers left nothing of value behind them, and it took them a day to drive all the cattle back over the saddle to Fort Augustus. The women who had been ravished made pacts not to lie with their husbands until nine months were passed. "Which resolution," said the Laird of Glenmoriston, thinking of Isobel Macdonald and one other, "the husbands agreed to. But they happened (luckily) not to fall with child by the ravishing, nor to contract any bad disease."

Lockhart also harried Strathglass as terribly as he did Glen-moriston, and perhaps with more zeal because this was the land of the Popish Chisholms and Frasers. There, coldly and casually, his men shot a clansman who was wading a river toward them with his "protection", his warrant of immunity, held above his head. The soldiers moved on from this to rape a pregnant woman. In Glen Cannich, a dark and beautiful gorge, a farmer and his family were shearing corn in their small field when a platoon of Lockhart's soldiers arrived, marching with muskets slung and a drum beating out the pace. The farmer and his people ran to the rocks on the eastern wall of the glen, and had arrived there when a woman remembered that she had left her child in her house. They saw one soldier enter the house and come out, and then another went in, and when he came out the baby was spitted on his hanger.

When they could, which was not often, the Chisholms tried to recover their stolen property and kill the soldiers who had taken it. The raiding detachments marched by platoons or companies, and men were not often foolish enough to straggle from their commands. But sometimes it happened. The hills between Glen Cannich and Glenstrathfarrar were the natural boundary of Chisholm and Fraser lands, and through them one day passed two soldiers and a white horse, the animal loaded with booty taken from the Chisholms. High above the smoking ruins of the cottages they thought themselves safe, but by a place called Ruidlt-Bhacaidh, among desolate rocks and wind-pressed grass, they were met by two armed clansmen. The Chisholms killed one soldier before he could draw his hanger, and the other ran away. The white horse was slaughtered with a dirk-thrust, its body and that of the dead soldier dragged into a bog. The man who had escaped wandered for many days in the mountains, half-starved, lost and lonely, until he became insane. At nights his voice could be heard pleading for mercy, shouting prayers at the indifferent hills. Nobody helped him.

Captain Caroline Frederick Scott of Guise's Regiment was a better soldier than Lockhart, but no less harsh and brutal. He had shown great courage and skill in the defence of Fort William, and there is no record of Lockhart's performance in battle. Scott led one of the three columns that cut their bloody way through Badenoch and Lochaber. He was not liked by the officers of the Campbell militia who frequently served under him, and Major-General John Campbell of Mamore probably despised him for a Lowlander and a pathological sadist. Though Mamore was a Whig and King George's man, he was still a Highlander, and the militia of his name often stood between the regular soldiers and their continued brutality.

Caroline Scott would have fitted well into any age, as a medieval *condottiere* or a commander of the *Waffen-SS*. If there were more officers of his character in Guise's it is not surprising that more than forty soldiers of the regiment deserted to the Rebels. The more brutish of his men quickly saw that they had a commander who would condone, or at least overlook, their behaviour. Once the siege of Fort William was lifted, he took a party of men on a raid into Glen Nevis, a rugged fissure of rock, grass and timber less than three miles from the garrison. There was the home of Alexander Cameron of Glen Nevis, known as MacSorley the son of Samuel. Though his brother Alan had been killed on the bayonets of Barrell's at Culloden, and though another brother Samuel was a prisoner (and would soon turn spy and King's Evidence) Glen Nevis himself had stayed out of the Rebellion. To be on the safe side he had surrendered to Mamore and thus he was not at home when Scott's party came round the gentle shoulder of Cow Hill one morning, with bayonets fixed. Mist was dribbling down the welts in Ben Nevis's hide, and three of Mac-Sorley's tenants were surprised by the redcoats before they had time to run. Not that they would have fled. More naïve than their chief, they believed that they had nothing to fear, having stayed at home when other Camerons of Lochaber went out with Lochiel. Scott ordered them to be bound and taken to an oak tree. When the knots were tightened beneath their ears they still did not realise what was to happen to them, for they cried out to Scott as Murdoch McRaw had done in Inverness, saying that the soldiers had taken the joke far enough. "But they were mistaken," says the Reverend Robert Forbes, "for instantly they were hanged, and had not so much time as to beg God to have mercy on their souls."

Scott then returned to Fort William, but his command marched a mile and a half deeper into the ravine, moving through larch, birch and oak by the river's run until they came to Dun Dige. On this moated hillock in a clearing of deer-grass was the house of Glen Nevis. Whatever Scott thought of MacSorley's neutrality, if he gave it any thought at all, he knew that Lochiel and Keppoch had used Dun Dige as their headquarters when they had Fort William under siege, and, to his mind, this justified its sack. But the house was empty, the wind sighing through open doors. Mrs. Cameron, her niece, her seven-year-old son, and the women of her household, had fled as soon as they heard that the soldiers were coming. They went to Uamh Shomlairle, to Samuel's Cave high up the glen where the rock-walls close in on the roaring water of the Nevis. All her silver and her china, her small and pitiful treasures, she had buried by her garden wall, and the soldiers found nothing to reward them for the sweating march from the fort. Some went to drive in MacSorley's cattle from the grassy skirt of Meall an t' Suidhe, and the rest marched on to find Mrs. Cameron. They burnt any mean cottage they saw, fired their muskets and hallooed the occupants into the heather. Five miles up the glen the road narrowed to a stony bridle-path. The mist was thicker and the birch and pine wept with it, but the detachment found Samuel's Cave and the cowering women there.

All were stripped of their clothes, although a petticoat was returned to Mrs. Cameron so that she might, as the soldiers said, hide her nakedness from them. Her son's coat had gold buttons and fine gold loops, but the soldiers could not wait until the boy had taken it from his shoulders. They struggled about him, slashing at the threads with their knives and wounding the child in the neck.

Mrs. Cameron lived in the cave for six months, well into the harsh winter when the Nevis was black ice and the side of Ben Nevis furred with snow. She did not know what Scott might do if she tried to return to Dun Dige, and perhaps she was surprised when she received a message from him, ordering her to Fort William. On the advice of friends, she went, and in Scott's warm room at the barracks he handed back to her one shoe-buckle, a cloak and some of the gold buttons. This he did with a great show of magnanimity, saying that the robbery had taken place without his knowledge or approval. It was a quixotic gesture and there seems to be no plain explanation for it, unless it is that small tyrants flatter their vanity with small mercies. He had no equivalent mercy for an old woman whom his soldiers stopped on the Inverlochy road. They cut her hair from her head, saying that it would fetch a good price as a wig for a gentleman. When she asked for the return of a linen handkerchief they had also taken, hoping to cover her humiliation with it, they kicked her and told her to be gone for an old bitch.

Scott led a punitive expedition from Fort William into Appin, marching south by the Ballachulish Ferry to Ardshiel. The Campbells had already been there, driving off cattle which they sold for £200. But Mamore was not a harsh man and he had returned some milk-cows to Mrs. Stewart, together with six wethers and as many lambs, saying that he was sure that the Duke of Cumberland, whom he knew to have "as much humanity as any man on earth", would approve of this. Caroline Scott, who may have understood His Royal Highness a little better, quickly relieved Ardshiel's lady of this stock. Milk-cows, wethers and lambs were driven away, watched by Ardshiel himself from a waterfall cave where he was skulking on the brae of Beinn Bheithar. Scott demanded the keys to Ardshiel House, which Mrs. Stewart gave him. These were not enough. He asked for the "little keys" that would open her charter-chest, her desk and cabinets, and when she had handed them to him he took her to the door and told her to go, there being nothing at Ardshiel that was her's or her husband's any more.

Bewildered, she asked where she might go, and Scott suggested that she walk down the shore of Loch Linnhe to Appin House and ask her chief for help, for wasn't the feeble boy the father of her husband's clan? She pleaded for food for herself and her children, and, reluctantly, he gave her a boll of meal. He then began the gutting of Ardshiel House. He took the blue-grey Ballachulish slates from its roof. He removed all timber from the frames, and ordered that nails be withdrawn carefully and straightened. The walls were taken down stone by stone, the lintels and rabbits loaded on wagons. He cut down the ash trees and the fruit trees that had helped to make Ardshiel one of the most beautiful houses in the West, and he sold the timber and the slates and the nails, the lintels and the rabbits, and he scattered the stones of the house.

Clansmen attempting to surrender their arms to Scott were no more fortunate than those whom Hughes had seen surrendering to Cornwallis. Three men came to Fort William in June, offering their broadswords and firelocks, and expecting the pardon that Cumberland had promised. Scott ordered them to be hanged with the ropes of a salmon net, "which was done until they died". Hanging became so commonplace, and the life of a Highlander so cheap in the thoughts of Scott's men, that there may be some truth in the story told in *Letters from the Mountains*. This meandering book was written by Mrs. Anne Grant, wife to a minister who was chaplain at Fort William long after the Rebellion. While Scott was away from the Fort on one of his raids the garrison was commanded by a major of Houghton's Regiment. This man and his brother officers were drinking and gaming late one night when the Sergeant of the Guard came to them, reporting three Highlandmen at the gate with arms to surrender. The Major, flushed with wine and angry at the interruption, shouted "Hang them !", and this, it is true, may have been no more than an expression of his irritation. But the next morning, when he put his fuddled head out of his window, he saw that his Sergeant of the Guard had a literal mind.

Some of Scott's companions were officers of the Highland Independent Companies, and taking their example from him they had no mercy on the Jacobite clans. One was the son of Grant of Knockando who, with two hundred men, marched and burned and plundered his way from Moy to the head of Loch Arkaig. There, on the isthmus close to Achnacarry where Clunes Hill rises like a green pyramid from the pine and fir, he burnt the house of Cameron of Clunes, "stript his wife and some others naked as they came into the world, and deprived them of all means of subsistence except five milk goats". He marched toward Kintail, down the drover's road beside Loch Arkaig, and near the dark wood of Muich he was met by a Highlander, a Cameron kern who offered to surrender the arms he had at his feet. Grant asked why the man had not done so earlier, and the Cameron replied reasonably enough that when he had seen that men were being killed whether they submitted or not he had taken his wife and children high into the hills, to a "remote wilderness" he said, until it was safe to come in. It may be, too, that he thought it safe to surrender now to a Highlander like himself, but if he did he was mistaken. He was tied to a tree and shot.

Grant of Knockando then marched on to Kintail, where he met his friend Munro of Culcairn, the militiaman who had met Bligh's by Achnacarry and who had a taste for digging up fresh graves to see if any treasure had been buried with the corpse.

In July Scott was very busy in the Isles harrying the Catholic MacNeills of Barra and the Mackinnons of Mull. He was officially under orders from Campbell of Mamore but he did very much as he pleased. He was ferried from one bare island to another by Captain John Fergusson of H.M.S. *Furnace*, and the pair of them left bitter memories behind them.

Scott went to Rona, a blue and naked rock at the tip of Raasay. He was looking for the Prince, but there was nothing on the island but salt-dried stretches of white grass and a few crofters scratching a living. The Laird of Raasay, John MacLeod, said that Scott's men raped a blind girl on Rona, and "most unmercifully lashed with two cords two men, one of which soon after dyed, and the other, Malcolm MacLeod, has not recovered not till this day". Scott then had his party rowed across the Kyle of Rona to the island of Raasay where his men drove off the cattle that had escaped John Fergusson's marines, and where they ravished two women whose names were Kristie Montgomery and Marion MacLeod. "They so robbed the whole inhabitants," said the Laird, "both of their bedclose and even their bodyclose, that I am certain there was not the value of two shillings sterling of close of any kind left to any of the poor familys on the island."

The people of Raasay were MacLeods, and when Scott left they were raided and raided again by men of the Independent Companies, the Highland militia raised by the Government. And these, too, were MacLeods. They came from Skye, but common name and common tongue did not help Raasay. The island is a small thread stretched between Skye and the mainland, fifteen miles long and never more than five wide, and so protected from the worst of the Atlantic weather that flowers grow richly in its warm earth. The MacLeods of Raasay had ties of blood with the Glengarry Macdonalds, and perhaps they suffered for this as much as for the fact that, unknown to most of them, Prince Charles had spent one wet night on their island. According to their Laird, the MacLeod militia slaughtered two hundred and eighty cows, seven hundred sheep and twenty horses. They destroyed thirty-two boats and burnt three hundred houses. The Laird lost his house, his furniture and his cattle, all of which he valued at fifteen hundred pounds sterling.

The Laird's house had been burned by Captain John Fergusson's landing parties before the militia arrived. H.M.S. *Furnace* had been cruising off the Western Isles since March, when it came up from Belfast, and Fergusson had been very busy since then, burning and harrying. His ship was one of many which, like the *Raven* and the *Trial*, the *Trident*, *Triton* and *Happy Janet* were on careful watch for French ships that might come to aid the escape of the Prince and other Jacobite leaders. They were not always successful, as the skipper of a Glasgow merchantman proved. He said that when he was last in Morlaix an Irish wherry had put into the French port, and down its gangplank had come thirty Rebel officers or more, all singing "A-begging we must go!"

Most of the naval captains of Byng's squadron were simply sailors, tacking and cruising among the Isles and taking no part in the rape of them. Not Fergusson. He vigorously executed Cumberland's orders, believing that if a brigade of infantry could make laws in this country so then could a man-of-war. Nobody had a very high opinion of him, of his appearance or of his nature, and there is nowhere any contradiction of the Reverend Robert Forbes' description: "A fellow of very low extract, born in the country of Aberdeen, who, being naturally of a furious, savage disposition, thought he could never enough harass, misrepresent and maltreat everyone whom he knew, or supposed to be, an enemy of the goodly cause he himself was embarked in."

It was probably a great disappointment to this Lowland Scot that, for all his efforts, he never did capture the Prince. It would have made a glorious trinity of achievement, for he captured, or said he captured, Simon Fraser of Lovat, and for a while he was the gaoler of Flora Macdonald when she was a prisoner aboard the *Furnace*.

He began his activities in April, before Culloden was fought, when with Robert Duff, a brother-captain of the aptly-named *Terror*, he was wind-bound in the lee of Canna. This green isle of terraced hills to the north-west of Rum had once belonged to the monks of Iona, but it was now peopled with Clanranald Macdonalds, and some of its fishermen stood in the sleet of Drummossie Moor. Fergusson sent ashore an Irish lieutenant called Thomas Brown, with orders to round up fresh beef and mutton. The steward of the isle, John Macdonald, asked Brown for his authority, and the lieutenant, with a right-is-might flourish of his cutlass, indicated the eighty marines and sailors at his back. So the cattle were slaughtered and taken aboard the warships. Two days later Fergusson said the meat was bad, and ashore went Lieutenant Brown once more, and gathered twenty fat cows and many wedders.

Then, said one of the Macdonalds of Canna, the sailors and marines came ashore from the ships "to make ane attack upon all the girls and young women in all the Isle, married or otherwise". But one of the marines, who thought this proposal a little more than he could stomach, warned the islanders. The women took shelter in the caves and hollows of the hills. In the cottage of Evan Mor MacIsaacs, where there had been two young girls, the sailors found only the mother, a woman of fifty and in poor health. Evan Mor was put under guard of drawn swords, and the sailors made ready to rape his wife, but she escaped from them into the darkness. They pursued her drunkenly, shouting and waving their cutlasses, and passing by her where she had hidden in a bog. The Macdonald of Canna who told this story to Robert Forbes said that Mrs. MacIsaacs was pregnant, and that she died of a miscarriage before morning.

On the isle of Eigg, which was also Clanranald's and from which men had gone to fight with their chief's son, Fergusson declared that if all those bearing arms, or capable of bearing arms, did not surrender immediately he would burn the isle house by house until they did. A fugitive Jacobite, Dr. John Macdonald, gave himself up, hoping to placate the Captain. He was "stript of all his cloaths to the skin, even of his shoes and stockins, brought aboard the *Furnace*, barrisdall'd in a dark dungeon". In the pockets of this fool of a man was found a list of all the people of Eigg who had gone with young Clanranald or were sympathetic to the Prince, and Fergusson joyfully swept thirty-eight of them into the hold of his ship. Then his sailors and marines went ashore. They slaughtered cattle, pillaged houses, and "ravished a girl or two".

It was Fergusson who, with the militia, captured John Mac-Ginnis. This was the old boatman who had carried the Prince's shirts for twenty-four miles (though not his brandy-bottle). He was tied to a tree and flogged by the cat until "blood gushed out at both his sides". Also captured by Fergusson was Captain Felix O'Neil, an officer of Lally's Franco-Irish Regiment, and he was skulking in North Uist when he was taken. "Captain Fergusson," he said, "used me with all the barbarity of a pirate, stripped me, and ordered me to be put into a rack and whipped by his hangman, because I would not confess where I thought the Prince was." This order was about to be executed when Lieutenant McCaghan, commander of the detachment of Royal Scots Fusiliers aboard the *Furnace*, drew his sword and told his men to present their muskets. He dared Fergusson to continue with the flogging. Defiance of this kind always provoked in the sailor a frothing anger close to a stroke, but he never accepted the challenge. O'Neil received no whipping.

Fergusson's principal duty on the west coast and among the Isles was not to act as executioner or pyromaniac, but to be ferryman for the two thousand or more troops under the immediate command of Campbell of Mamore, Highland levies and the regulars of Scott and Miller. It was in this role that he attended a navy-blue and gold council of war at Tobermory, on the north-eastern tip of the Isle of Mull. Mamore had called the conference for the senior naval officers in the area—Fergusson, Captains John Hay, Richard Howe, and Robert Duff, and Commodore Thomas Smith, the sensible and just man who commanded all the King's ships in West Highland waters. They met in Mull on the evening of June 10, and the state of their nerves, their readiness to believe any story about the Prince, however fanciful, is clearly indicated by the reason for the conference. Mamore's intelligence service in the hills had reported

that Charles, and a number of other prominent Rebels, had taken
shelter on the Isle of St. Kilda, two thousand acres of rock and
gaunt grass forty-five miles west of the Outer Hebrides. It is
Scotland's furthest reach into the North Atlantic, a screaming
landfall for puffin and gannet, and in 1746 it was peopled by
a few wild and savage tenants of the Laird of MacLeod. Admittedly there seemed sense in the suggestion that the Prince had
gone there in the belief that no one would think of looking
for him in so remote a spot. But, on the other hand, once there
and once discovered he could never escape. St. Kilda's could
be less a refuge than a cage, and consequently no shelter at all.

The King's officers considered no arguments like this, but
prepared a grand expedition consisting of the *Furnace*, the *Terror*,
and a number of wherries for transporting troops. Commodore
Smith delegated command to Mamore, so that the Campbell
became, in his own delighted words, "a kind of Lord Admiral".
The Lord Admiral and his armada left Tobermory on June 13,
with ninety regular soldiers under the command of Captain James
Miller of Guise's, and one hundred and twenty Argyll levies.
The next day, at Loch Moidart, the wherries took aboard thirty
Royal Scots Fusiliers, and off the Isle of Eigg on the 15th the
flotilla was joined by *H.M.S. Trial* which had Caroline Scott
and more soldiers aboard. The expedition was now becoming
quite formidable, and grew larger still as it began to beat about
the Butt of Lewis. There it came up with two forty-gun men-of-
war, the *Loo* and the *Eltham*, Commodore Smith commanding.

It made St. Kilda's by June 19, and the redcoats and the clansmen below decks on the wherries may have been heartily glad,
for the weather off the isles of Uist can be something even
seamen are pleased to avoid. Boats went ashore on the afternoon
on the 19th, landing soldiers and levies, and they might have
been setting foot on some hitherto undiscovered South Pacific
island. The wretched MacLeods had taken to the cliffs and the
holes in the hills upon first sight of the sails, crying and wailing.
When some of them were finally driven into the open, and their
gabbled talk translated, they had little of interest to tell. They
knew nothing about a Prince, or a Pretender, or His Majesty King
George for that matter. They had heard that the Laird of MacLeod

their chief had recently been at war with a great woman somewhere, and that he had naturally got the better of her. But that was all they knew of the world beyond their sea-foamed perimeter.

As well as being ferryman for such comic expeditions as this, Fergusson was also a gaoler, and the hold of the *Furnace* was soon full and rotting with prisoners which he and others had gathered from the islands. Among them was Donald MacLeod, an old man of sixty-eight who had fought with Glengarry's Regiment and who had later become a faithful attendant of the fugitive Prince. "The prisoners," he said, "got only half-man's allowance in every respect. For one day of the week they had pease; but the common fellows of the ship behoved to be served first before the gentlemen got any at all; and if the pease happened to fall short, the fellows would have mixed them up with saltwater. The victuals were brought to the prisoners in foul nasty buckets, wherein the fellows used to piss for a piece of ill-natured diversion." Many of the Rebels taken stayed in the hold of the *Furnace* for eight months.

Fergusson's commission in the Isles ended without his getting closer to the Prince than the cat he ordered to be laid upon the back of old John MacGinnis, or the short hour that separated the departure of Charles in one boat and the landing of his seamen in another. It was generally assumed by those who were held in morbid fascination by Fergusson's behaviour that he would undoubtedly have hanged the young man, and offered the corpse in exchange for the £30,000 reward. A kinswoman, Mrs. Ferguson of Pitfour, once asked the Captain if he would indeed have done this. Fergusson was not an idiot. "No, by God!" he said, "I would have preserved him as the apple of mine eye, for I wouldn't take any man's word, no, not even the Duke of Cumberland's, for £30,000 sterling, though I knew many to be such fools as to do it."

To most of Commodore Smith's captains, life in the Western Isles meant routine work, patrolling and blockading such as that to which they were accustomed off the French coast, though a little more hazardous, perhaps, due to the rugged and angry nature of the islands. Their logs record the weather and the winds, and the sails set to meet the sea, a chronology of anchorages and landfalls, of sick men doctored and discipline maintained. The days were dreary and monotonous, and rarely relieved by excitement. Thus there was sharp activity aboard the twenty-four-gun sloop *Triton* when, at dawn on Thursday, May 29, the main-top lookout reported a strange sail three miles south-east by east of Kebock Head on the Isle of Lewis. Captain William Brett put his ship in pursuit. An hour later, in the lee of the colonnaded cliffs of the little Isles of Shiant, he was close enough to fire a shot. The strange ship did not bring to, and Brett ordered more shots to be fired. This time she came about, close to shore, and lowered a boat. The north wind prevented the *Triton* from closing rapidly, and in the irritating delay Brett saw the boat go ashore, loaded with men and women. It came back, and before it could be filled again the *Triton*'s roundshot began to drop about the stern of the vessel.

The boat was pulled inboard and the ship made off toward Lewis with the *Triton* in pursuit, firing an angry shot now and then. Two hours after noon, said Brett, he "came up with ye chase and she brought too with her head off shore and hoisted English colours. I saw their men ranged at their quarters, she having fourteen guns."

While Brett was wondering what to do next, a boat put off from the vessel and came alongside him. The man who climbed to the *Triton*'s waist said he was the mate of the ship, and he had a very odd story. His vessel was the snow *Gordon*, a merchantman of Glasgow, which had sailed from Dublin on May 1, bound for Virginia with a cargo of salt, bale goods, powder, shot and eighty-one men and twenty-six women all of whom were indentured servants, convicted criminals sentenced to the plantations. On May 13, when the *Gordon* was a hundred leagues westward of Ireland, they had risen, seized the ship and placed her master and mate in irons, together with most of the crew. The mate was later released, and given the choice between being shot or taking the *Gordon* to the Isle of Skye where the desperate men and women wished to land and join the Rebels. If the news of Culloden had reached Dublin before they sailed nobody had recognised it as the end of the Rebellion. Who these unhappy people were is not plain from any account, whether they were Scots or Irish, whether they were ordinary criminals or men and women transported for their Rebel acts and sympathies.

Twelve of them had got ashore on Shiant before the *Triton* came up, and nobody can now know what happened to them. The rest were brought aboard Brett's ship and shackled in his hold. With the *Gordon* in tow, he sailed south for Carrickfergus, dropping anchor there in Belfast Lough a month later. "Sent an express to Dublin," he recorded, "to know what should be done with the Prisoners." He received an answer on July 16. "Sent all ye Rebel prisoners ashore to Carrickfergus Goal."

And from there they were once more sent to the Virginias. Thus ended the last act of rebellion on behalf of Prince Charles, though no doubt he never heard of it.

"'*Tis William returned with northern laurels crown'd!*"

BY THE MIDDLE of July the Duke had decided that he could now leave the affairs of Scotland in the hands of another, preferably the reluctant Earl of Albermarle who, when he heard of this, prayed that he might be anywhere else but in North Britain. It was thirteen weeks since Culloden, and "all that will be necessary" had taken Cumberland twice as long as he had promised Newcastle. Even so, he had done remarkably well. The Chain now consisted of five large troop concentrations in the Great Glen, from the Moray Firth to the Firth of Lorne: at Fort George, Fort Augustus, Fort William, Castle Stalker in green Appin, and Dunstaffnage Castle in Lorne. There were also garrisons at Duart on the Isle of Mull, at Mingary in Ardnamurchan, and at Bernera on the Sound of Sleat. In addition to the regular battalions of the King's Army, and the Argyll militia, there were eighteen Independent Highland Companies raised from the MacLeods, Mackenzies, MacKays, Grants, Munros, Rosses and Macdonalds of Sleat, Whig clansmen soon to be uniformed in the black Government tartan and short smart tunics of scarlet. All passes to the mountains were stopped, and all ports watched by the Navy. Scotland had never known such a police force. The gaols were full, there were cold embers from Knoidart to Balquhidder, from Moy to the Outer Isles, and great droves of Highland cattle now grazed on Lowland hills or Yorkshire dales. Most of the chiefs had surrendered their persons and their arms, and those who had not were attainted and living in holes with the fox, or hawking their threadbare honour in France. True, the Prince had not been captured, but neither had he escaped, and any day now a bayonet might turn him from a mountain bothy.

On the day that Cumberland left Fort Augustus, Friday,

July 18, his cousin Charles was indeed hiding in a hut. It was all that was left of the estates of Aeneas Macdonald of Borradale in Arisaig, the country of priests. It overlooked the powdered-shell and whitesand shore of Loch nan Uamh, the loch of the cave where the young man had first landed fifty-one weeks before.

The drums beat for the Duke's departure, drag, stroke and paradiddle. Three young aides rode with him, Yorke, Cathcart and Granby. They were accompanied by a captain's escort of Kingston's Horse, to which volunteer regiment the Duke had become affectionately attached, proposing to re-muster it as regular cavalry under his own name. They all rode rapidly and without regret, although Sir Everard Fawkener, jogging along by horse too, found the pace most tiresome. They passed out of the mountains by Stirling, and on the 21st they were at Edinburgh where the Duke spent the night at Holyrood Palace, in Prince Charles's bed of course. The baillies of the capital were happy to see him. They had found another Rebel standard to burn, and they would have liked His Royal Highness to witness this, and grace a series of public dinners with his presence. But the bells of joy were still ringing when Cumberland and his escort rode post-haste to the south, a gold box of presentation flung carelessly into his baggage. At nine o'clock on the evening of the 23rd he arrived at York, in time for supper with the Lord Mayor and Corporation at the Precentor's House.

It was probably a very dull dinner, for the Archbishop spoke at length, exhorting His Royal Highness to continue in the path of virtue and glory, and remarking that "though the things he had done for the nation were singularly great, his manner of performing them was still more to be admired".

Cumberland gave York three hours of his time. By midnight he and his escort were horsed once more, moving through the great crowd that had gathered outside the Precentor's House with torches and cheers. The Duke galloped off with yet another gold box in his baggage. Sir Everard Fawkener, perhaps too tired or perhaps to wind up the last of Cumberland's affairs, had been left behind long ago in Edinburgh.

The sweat-lathered horses and dust-caked men rode through Kensington on July 25, seven days after leaving the Great Glen.

The crowds were thick by Knight's Bridge, Tyburn Lane and Devonshire House, and Londoners indulged themselves with a saturnalia as great as that by which they had celebrated the news of Culloden two months before. Their hero, the patriot boy of the news-sheets, was home among them. "ECCE HOMO!" declared Mr. Edward Cave in his *Gentleman's Magazine*, beneath a plump and smirking portrait of the Duke, though it was not he who wore a crown of thorns at this moment. There was a renewed spate of congratulatory petitions to the Crown, by which clergy, lawyers, butchers, skinners, haberdashers, carpenters, Justices of the Peace, Lord Lieutenants of forty-two shires, and the fish-mongers of Billingsgate begged leave to approach the sacred Throne. They wished His Majesty to know of his subjects' pleasure at so great a deliverance from tyranny, and of their delight that this had been secured by his splendid son, that Hector, that Achilles, that magnanimous Alexander.

Into some of these petitions there crept a hint of what might have been the real reason for the satisfaction of the signators. Thus a body of "Merchants, Traders and Others in the City of London" said of the Rebellion that "the fatal blow thereby attempted to be given to the trade and publick credit of this nation gave us the greatest concern; and it is with equal pleasure we find that blow averted, and trade and public credit (which has so long flourished under Your Majesty's auspicious govern-ment) again restored and secured to us". Mercantile capitalism, which had been climbing into the political saddle since 1689, was happy that the horse had not bolted.

There was also "A Humble Address of the People called Quakers" from their General Assembly in London. They, too, begged leave to approach the Throne (though they did not admit that it was sacred). Their particular concern, as the clans came south over the Border, had been with the religious intentions of the Popish young Prince in tartan and velvet. "As none of all thy Protestant subjects exceed us," they told King George, "in aversion to the tyranny, idolatry and superstition of the church of Rome; so none is under more just apprehension of immediate danger from their destructive consequences, or have greater cause to be thankful to the Almighty for the inter-position of his providence and our preservation." Lest the King should think they were giving too much credit to the Almighty and too little to the Duke, they added that "a preservation so remarkable makes it our indispensable duty also to acknowledge the king's paternal care for the safety of his people, of which he has given the most assured pledge in permitting one of his royal offspring to expose himself to the greatest dangers for their security".

They concluded their turbid petition with the hope that "an uninterrupted race of kings of thy royal Progeny" would continue to be a blessing for England, Ireland, Scotland and Wales. Briefly, King George assured them of his faithful protection.

The bulk baggage of the martial boy (which was how the playbills were now describing the Duke) had arrived in London some days before His Royal Highness. It was said to have contained the head of Rory Mackenzie, a red-haired young Highlander who, when shot by pursuing soldiers, tried to put them off the hunt for Charles by crying "You have killed your Prince!". Cumberland was supposed to have sent the head to London so that it might be identified by Rebel prisoners in Southwark Gaol. But the story is part of that enduring Jacobite romance in which all men are brave and all women beautiful. There were enough men in Scotland who could have said whether or not this was the head of the Prince, and the Duke left Fort Augustus knowing that his cousin was still very much alive.

The baggage contained something of more practical value than a bloody head: Cumberland's share of the general pillage, bedding, linen, furnishings, which his servants had gathered for him from the houses in which he had rested. Nor did they alone take up such considerate collections. Awaiting the Duke in London was a handsome set of table china which General Hawley hoped he would accept as an expression of affection and regard from an old hero to a young one. Hawley had acquired the china in Aberdeen from a Mrs. Gordon of Hallhead who, on February 23, was told that her house would be his quarters during his stay in the city. She did not feel honoured by this, any more than her neighbour, Mrs. Alexander Thomson, who had the Duke himself as her unwelcome guest. Mrs. Gordon had sufficient spirit, however, to insist that before the General took possession she should be allowed to lock all her cupboards and cabinets, leaving Hawley the use of her furniture only.

The cavalryman endured this restriction for a few surly days and then he demanded her keys, threatening to destroy everything in the house if he did not get them. Through his aide, Major James Wolfe, he informed her that he had confiscated all her property except the clothes she then wore. Although Mrs. Gordon thought the nervous young man was most rude to her, Wolfe probably did his best to reassure her, telling her that no one doubted her loyalty to King George. But she was a housewife outraged, and she wasn't thinking of King or loyalty. Her most prized possessions were now at the mercy of a man who liked to put his booted legs on the table when he drank, and whose language, bellowed at the top of his trooper's voice, was deeply distressing.

She asked Wolfe for the return of some of her property, her china for example. Wolfe agreed to ask the General, but got a blunt refusal. She then asked the Major for a pair of her son's breeches, a little tea, a bottle of ale, and some flour to make bread, there being none to be bought in Aberdeen. Once more Hawley refused, his reply tactfully paraphrased by Wolfe. Mrs. Gordon was now very worried about her china, although the aide-de-camp promised her that she would not be robbed.

"But General Hawley," she said, writing to her sister later, "packed up every bit of china I had, which I am sure would not be bought for two hundred pounds; all my bedding and table linen, every book, my repeating clock which stood by the bed in which he lay every night, my worked screen, every rag of Mr. Gordon's cloths, the very hat, breeches, nightgown, shoes and what shirts there was of the child's, 12 tea spoons, strainer and tonges, the japan'd board on which the chocolate and coffee cups stood, and put them on board a ship in the night time and directed to himself at Holyrood House at Edinburgh."

Mrs. Gordon's melancholy summary of her losses is an interesting illumination of an eighteenth-century household. What the General did not desire for himself, he gave to his staff officers, the good lady's "flutes, musick and cane" for example. He entertained lavishly and soon disposed of five and a half pounds of her tea, "seven loaves of fine sugar, half a hundred loaves of lump sugar, seven pounds of chocolate, a great stock of salt beef, pickled pork, hams, peas, butter, coals, peats, ale, verne jelly, rice and spice, some cheese, brandy, rum, sago, hartshorn, salop, sweetmeats, Narbonne honey, two dozen wash balls, with many things 'tis impossible to mention, all of which he kept himself, nor would he give me any share of them, even my empty bottles he took".

Nor was this the end of Hawley's grand plunder from one house. Mrs. Gordon wrote it all down for her sister. He took "the blankets and pillows of the beds, even the larding pins, iron screws, the fish kettles and marble mortar". Being an independent Scotswoman, she protested to the authorities of course, and Hawley sent a casual message through the Judge Advocate that all things would be paid for or returned. They never were. "In short," sister Jane was told, "he has left nothing behind him but the beds without covering. A house so plundered I believe I never heard of."

When the campaign was over, General Hawley (having no wife, no one closer to him than a housekeeper, though his will suggests she may have been his mistress) sent Mrs. Gordon's table china to the Duke. It was not even Mrs. Gordon's, since she had it on approval from a merchant. Cumberland thanked his general for the gift, though he had no particular liking for it, nor any desire to keep it. He gave it to a London prostitute who, since her entertaining was naturally on a small and intimate scale, could have no use for ten serving dishes, forty large plates and three dozen small plates. She sold them to a dealer, and it was in this man's salon, many months later, that a friend of Mrs. Gordon saw the china and learnt "through what clean hands it had come into his possession".

When Cumberland arrived in London he found that both Houses of Parliament had passed the Bill to increase his yearly income to £40,000. In addition, his father gave him the lucrative sinecure of Ranger of Windsor Castle. Nor were his soldiers being forgotten. The Veteran's Scheme had reached its saturation point of £6,000, and every unwounded man who had stood or ridden

on Drummossie Moor could expect at least twelve shillings and
sixpence from it. There was also to be a Culloden Medal, one of
the earliest campaign awards to be struck for the British Army.
Cast in gold for the officers it bore a Roman bust of the Duke
with the single word *Cumberland* in halo above it. On the reverse
side the nude figure of Apollo transfixed the neck of a dragon with
his arrow. The legend was in Latin, *Actum est ilicet periit*—The
deed is done, it is all over. In subscription was the exergue:
Prod:Cold Ap 16 1746. There were copper and bronze copies for
private soldiers, and it was ordered that upon ceremonial occasions
the medal was to be suspended from the neck by a crimson,
green-edged ribbon.

Cumberland's pleasure at such an award was simple and
sincere, for however hard and heavy was his hand upon his soldiers he was jealous of their honour. He was delighted, too,
when his officers formed a Culloden Society to meet once a year
on the anniversary of the battle for fitting celebration. The men of
Barrell's Regiment, whose bayonets had been broken and bent by
the Camerons, were granted their own peculiar honour. Beneath
the Lion of England on their regimental seal was engraved the
word *Culloden*, and it remained there for forty years.

During that autumn of 1746 Cumberland was the capital's
hero, with mobs running after his coach wherever he went, and
even the cartoonists managed to put some gentle good humour
into their gross caricatures of his fat body. Fat or not, he was a
handsome figure when he went to St. Paul's Cathedral for a
service of solemn thanksgiving. He wore his dress uniform of
scarlet, lapelled and cuffed in blue. The buttonholes were stitched
with gold thread, and his buff waistcoat was edged with gold
too. There was gold on his right shoulder, a tumbling aiguillette
of glittering cord, and still more gold on the crimson baton
in his hand. His breeches were snow-white, his pumps buckled in
silver, and his happy cheeks glowed within the neat white curls
of his wig. The service had been skilfully stage-managed by the
Dean, for as the young man stepped into the nave, sweeping off
his laced beaver, the organ pealed and the voices of the choir
rose in molten notes to the great dome. The congregation was
enthralled, and so it should have been, for what it was hearing

was "The Conquering Hero", specially written for the occasion by George Frederick Handel.

The sermon was a fitting application of Christian teaching to the matters in everybody's mind, and contained no confusing observations on the subject of mercy. The Archbishop of York had already made the Church's views plain on that point. "I hope," he had said, "that I am not a sanguinary man, but surely the proper time for mercy is when the Rebels have delivered up their arms and their mock Prince."

The mellow weather of August and September was kind to open-air manifestations. The Army, anxious to exploit the public's admiration and thereby win recruits for the next bloody brawl in Flanders, produced mock battles beneath the trees in Hyde Park. Thus, when twenty-eight companies of the First Regiment of Foot Guards were exercised there, the newspapers reported that "they went through their firing four deep, with their bayonets fixed, as at the last battle near Culloden House, and performed the exercise, though quite new to them, exceeding well". The mob, ready to enjoy such a show without feeling inclined to enlist as a result, got as much amusement as excitement out of the display. Most of their pleasure came from the fact that an enthusiastic Guardsman accidentally bayoneted the man in front of him. And more to the mob's taste, perhaps, was the sentence of death passed upon fifty-six deserters. They were reprieved of course; men were not so easily enlisted that they could be dispensed with so prodigally. They were marched up and down in St. James's Park for the due execration of the crowd, and then sent to Portsmouth. They arrived there footsore and hungry, "but the loyal folk refused to give them refreshments before they embarked". From Portsmouth they were sent to rot in a penal battalion on Cape Breton Island.

Here and there in the Army soldiers were charged with drinking the health of James III, although it is not easy to understand why they did this, whether it was in loyalty to the House of Stuart, or whether, as is more likely, they were making the most violent protest against military service that they could imagine. They were all flogged at the halberds. More severe was the punishment of a sergeant in the Third Regiment of Foot

Guards who had openly, and without the aid of a pint of ale, declared his attachment to the Stuarts. He was publicly shot in Hyde Park. He refused to be blindfolded, and before he died he declared that he bitterly regretted the part he had played in the suppression of the Rebellion. Cumberland is said to have been so enraged by this (his temper could be ungovernable) that he demanded that the Scots Guards should henceforth be known as The English Guards and that their drums and fifes should play nothing but English airs.

But occasional protests from mutinous soldiers were faint ripples against the general tide of rejoicing. At Sadler's Wells a ballet called "Culloden" was performed nightly to a packed house. The audience was delighted by "an exact view of the battle accompanied by a prodigious cannonade". There was also a new dance known as "The Culloden Reel", though when English officers of the Edinburgh garrison called for its performance at the theatre the Guard from the Castle had to put down the resulting riot. Tyburn Gate, at the north-eastern corner of Hyde Park, was renamed Cumberland Gate, and only a few people saw irony in this juxtaposition of the Duke's name and gallows. Less conventionally, a pretty, clustering flower was now called Sweet William, and this challenge to their imagination quickly pushed bad poets into print:

> "The pride of France is lily white,
>   The rose in June is Jacobite.
>   The prickly thistle of the Scot
>   Is northern knighthood's badge and lot;
>   But since the Duke's victorious blows
>   The lily, thistle and the rose
>   All droop and fade, all die away;
>   Sweet William only rules the day.
>   No plant with brighter lustre grows,
>   Except the laurel on his brows."

When Scotland heard of this horticultural compliment it named the more obnoxious of its weeds "Stinking Billy".

Mr. David Morier, the Swiss artist who worked on military

and equestrian subjects under the patronage of the Duke, was busy that August on a spirited canvas of the battle. He had chosen as his subject the left-flank grenadier company of Barrell's, as it received the charge of the Cameron men. For models, of course, he was most fortunate. Clansmen from Southwark Gaol and the prison-ships at Tilbury were brought to his studio and there asked to take up such positions as fitted the action. By Mr. Morier's vivid, if undistinguished brush they thus acquired a little immortality, one with broadsword raised and dirk held forward beneath his target, another taking a bayonet in his breast, and yet another turning away with his wounds. And beneath their feet the dead of the clan. It was Mr. Morier's most successful painting, and the memory of it may have given him some satisfaction when he died a debtor in the Fleet prison.

As the year moved on toward winter some Londoners became uneasy about the way in which the rebellious spirit of the Highlands had been suppressed. Letters in the newspapers, telling of what officers had seen, showed that somewhere a conscience was stirring. Smollett wrote lines of humane sympathy for the Scots in their present suffering, and when it was suggested that the Duke become a freeman of a City Guild an alderman muttered into his stock. "Let it be of the Butchers," he said.

Jacobite journalists were also active, in their own tracts or in the general news-sheets. One, signing himself "Tom : Curious", asked why more of the prisoners were not wounded. "I wish," he asked the editor innocently, "you would inform me what became of the Rebels that were left wounded in that Field of Battle." Another, writing above the sarcastic by-line of "A True Modern Whig", proposed the sterilisation of all Jacobite women "not past the age of breeding", and he went on with further ridicule: "I am also of the opinion that seed-corn and implements of husbandry in Scotland should be destroyed. That would effectually extirpate them and save us the expense of transporting them to our Colonies." However pedestrian this irony, it was matched by the genuine opinions of men like Richmond and Chesterfield. And the hide of the public was, in any case, too thick to be penetrated by sarcasm. More in keeping with general thought was one more bad poem:

"'Tis he! 'Tis he! the pride of fame,
WILLIAM returned! the shouts proclaim.
WILLIAM with northern laurels crown'd,
WILLIAM the hills and vales resound!
What numbers fled, what numbers fell,
CULLODEN's glorious field may tell:
CULLODEN's field the muse may fire,
To sing the sun and charm the fire."

5

THE PRISONERS

"We was all carried to the county gaol"

In the gaols of England and Scotland, on the transports at Inverness and Tilbury, there were at one time or another three thousand four hundred and seventy Jacobite prisoners, men, women and children. These were held as Rebels, and in addition there were several hundred prisoners-of-war, French and Spanish, or Scots and Irish in the service of foreign kings. For them, imprisonment was brief. Nationality was not yet something immutable, or determined by naturalisation papers. A Scot or Irishman had only to prove that he held a commission from the King of France for him to be regarded as no subject of King George at all, at least not in this context. The Rebel prisoners were much less fortunate. The charge against many of them was often no more than that they had been seen "to drink the Pretender's health", or were "known to wish the Rebels well", and, in the case of James Warden a Perthshire pedagogue, that "he sang treasonable songs". John Middleton, a gardener of Kincardine, spent eleven months in prison before a court accepted his plea that he had been "made prisoner by a party of soldiers, to whome he was showing the way, because he could not go the length with them". John Long was nearly a year in York Castle, desperately trying to prove that he had been merely carrying medicines for his employer, Dr. James Stratton, when that gentleman was arrested. There was a genial scoundrel called Donald Beaton from the Isle of Tiree who was in the Rebel Army for no more than two or three days, not long enough for him to remember which regiment had had the honour of his service. Since he was an habitual thief it was thought best to keep him in prison. The Reverend William Seton, non-jurant Episcopalian of Forfar, went to gaol because he had chosen to preach on Jeremiah 8: 4

shortly after the Prince landed: *Thus saith the Lord; Shall they fall and not arise? Shall he turn away and not return?* And there were young men whose crime may have been more idleness than treason. Archie Kennedy, aged eighteen and a jeweller's apprentice of Edinburgh, had put on a white cockade and joined Mr. Finlayson at the Prince's cannon because, he said, all the shops were shut and there was no work for him when the Rebels came to the city. But he was hanged for it.

Of all the prisoners taken, one hundred and twenty only were executed, and, of these, thirty-eight were deserters from the King's Army. The number is small, but it should not be considered on its own. To it must be added the six hundred and eighty-four whose exact fate was unrecorded, who died in prison from wounds, fever, starvation and neglect. To it, too, might be added the hundreds who were of course murdered in the glens, or who perished from hunger and exposure in the hard winter of 1746-47. Mrs. Jean Cameron, Lochiel's sister-in-law, said in later years that many Highland people died in this fashion. She told how the old women of Lochaber would follow the soldiers and beg from them the guts and the green hides of the cattle slaughtered. This offal the women cut into pieces and boiled for food, and while they were about their fires, said Mrs. Cameron, the soldiers sometimes shot them "for diversion and for wagers etc.".

Of those who were tried and executed four were peers of Scotland or England. They were thus entitled to, and duly received, the exclusive privilege of the axe. The rest died by the rope: thirty-eight deserters, two spies, twenty-four officers and men of the Manchester Regiment, forty soldiers of the clans, and twelve of no stated unit. The Manchester Regiment suffered most, perhaps, because it was English, the only formation raised by the Prince when he crossed the Border. He left it behind when he retreated, to defend the virtually defenceless castle at Carlisle, and it is to be hoped that he did not know what he was doing. The condemned were hanged at several places throughout England, at Tyburn and Kennington Common in London, at York in the county of York, and at Carlisle, Brampton and Penrith in Cumberland. The last to be executed was Lochiel's brother (and Mrs. Jean's husband) Dr. Archibald Cameron. He died without trial on Tower Hill, seven years after Culloden, leaving an un-finished letter to his son, unfinished because he had no knife to sharpen his pencil once it broke. He advised the young man to service God, honour King James, abstain from late and heavy suppers, and avoid drinking and whoring.

Some of the skulls of the hanged, spiked above the gates of the cities in which they were executed, were still grinning down on the streets thirty years later when another King George faced another rebellion, this time in his Colonies.

The laws under which the prisoners were arrested, gaoled, hanged, banished or transported, were many and confused. There were also Cumberland's frequent drum-head proclamations by which he promised that if he did not get exact obedience the guilty would be "pursued with the utmost severity as rebels and traitors by due process of law or military execution". But the simple meaning of all laws and all proclamations was this: any man, woman or child found in arms against the King, or helping such people in arms, or expressing sympathy with the Rebellion, was thereby guilty of treason. It was a wide net of small mesh, and it caught many fish. Their disposal was not so easily decided. Cumberland's solution, in May, was a soldier's solution, and was ridiculously impracticable, like most of the proposals made by victorious generals. He believed it to be "the only sure remedy for establishing Quiet in this country", and he urged its acceptance upon Newcastle.

"I mean," he said, "the transporting of particular Clans, such as the entire Clan of the Camerons and almost all the Tribes of the M'Donalds (excepting some of those of the Isles) and several other lesser Clans, of which an exact list may easily be made." He believed that prisons and mountains should be flushed clean of all Jacobites. As a precedent for blanket legislation against whole communities he quoted the severe Acts of proscrip-tion passed against Clan Gregor during the past hundred years, by which it lost land, title and even the name MacGregor. But although the Privy Council considered this proposal, when it was put before them on the Duke's behalf by a Mr. Kilby, it was not adopted. It was felt that the Acts of Attainder, passed or to be passed, by which the people named in them would "suffer and forfeit as a person attainted of High Treason" if they did not surrender within a given time, were sufficient to deal with the more obnoxious Jacobites in the Highlands and Lowlands. Where the rotting inmates of the gaols were concerned, the Council agreed that a selected number of them should be brought to trial as soon as possible. For this purpose there was a revival of instructions contained in an Order in Council of 1715 (when the Prince's father had made his unhappy descent on Scotland). A new Order in Council, published on July 23, declared that His Majesty had taken into account the great numbers of his rebellious subjects then in prison, and the need to make a speedy example of them. It was decided that, after some had been set aside as witnesses in the trials of others, those who were not Gentlemen or Men of Estates should draw lots among themselves, and that one in every twenty should thereby stand trial for his life. His Majesty further declared that he was willing to show mercy to the rest, if asked for it, and would pardon them on condition that they left his kingdom, never to return. To help them on their way he would be graciously pleased to see that they got transport to his Colonies, and indentured employment there with any plantation owner who bid high enough for their bodies and their labour. Other prisoners, more fortunate, would be banished, left to find their own place of exile.

The disposal in this manner of the three thousand four hundred and seventy has been carefully catalogued*

Executed	120
Transported	936
Banished	222
Died in prison	88
Escaped from prison	58
Conditional pardon	76
Released or exchanged	1,287
Disposal unknown	684

There were many Highlanders among the prisoners, of course, and as the eye passes over the lists the ear is caught by the music of Gaelic names, of Macdonald, MacQuarrie and Fraser, of

* "The Prisoners of the '45". See Acknowledgements.

Cameron, MacLean and MacKenzie, MacLeod, MacKay and MacGregor. These were men who had rarely left their glens until the Prince came, who spoke nothing but their Irish tongue, who now rotted in foetid English gaols, mocked for their tartan rags. There was Allan MacDougall, the blind piper to the Duke of Perth's Regiment who had marched sightless into the Royal troops at Falkirk. There was young Lachlan Macdonald from the grey isles of Uist where his father was admired as a sweet-tongued Bard. Thomas MacKay had been a wood-turner in Glenmoriston, and from the same valley there were many Grants like Donald, the pressed farmer of Ballintombuie, and John who was "a common Highland boy attending the Rebels". Duncan MacRievre was an oarsman of Benbecula, a Clanranald man who had helped speed that bonny boat over the seas to Skye. There was a deaf-mute, David Fraser of Glen Urquhart, who had charged with Lovat's, killing seven soldiers with his broadsword and dirk. Or so it was said. Another deaf-mute had no name at all, but was a Mac-donald who was put down on the gaol-roster as "Keppoch's Dumbie".

There were women among the prisoners, eighteen of them being accepted as ladies of quality. They included the Viscountess Strathallan whose husband had been killed in the rout at Culloden and whose crime was that "she put out illuminations on the Pretender's birthday in a most remarkable manner", the Ladies Mackintosh of Moy Hall of course, and Lady Frances Stewart the sister of the impetuous Lord Elcho. The ladies did not stay long in the common gaols. Rank was allowed privileges across political differences. When they had the money for it, both ladies and gentlemen of quality were moved from prison to the custody of Court Messengers outside.

The Regimental Women were not persons of quality. Although the leaders of the Jacobite Army had forbidden women to follow their men in the campaign, many had done so, and fifty-eight of them were imprisoned. Twenty-seven, many with babies, were ultimately transported to the American Colonies or the West Indies. They were almost entirely Highland women, with names from the hills, and they were registered under the regiments they had followed: Keppoch's, Lovat's, Clanranald's, Roy

Stewart's and Glengarry's. Mary Kennedy, of Glengarry's, was gaoled with her child, and when they were both transported it was said in her favour that she sewed and laundered well. Isabel Chalmers, who also had a man in Glengarry's, was tall and slender, and her master in Antigua was assured that she had excellent fingers for knitting. Barbara Campbell, who had Clan Diarmid's red hair, was advertised as being clever at most things, and Mary MacKenzie was "a lusty, healthy lass who knits and spins".

The youngest Rebel held in prison, other than the infants of the Regimental Women, was William Crosby aged seven, whose father was an Irish weaver. Both had taken service with the Manchester Regiment, and both were taken prisoner at Carlisle. Father William was sentenced to death, but was reprieved on the day set for his execution. There is no record of what happened to the boy, which means, perhaps, that he died in the filth and the rot of Carlisle prison.

Three boys, unlucky in the lotting, were tried and sentenced to death, though none was hanged. George Barclay, a soldier of Lord Ogilvy's Angus Regiment, was sixteen and he was reprieved on condition he enlisted in the King's Army, which he did with understandable alacrity. John Bennagah, also sixteen, had been pressed into the Prince's service when old Glenbucket went recruiting in Glenmachy. He was reprieved and sentenced to transportation, but he died of starvation and neglect before his weak body could be carried to a ship. The third boy was James Gordon, the fifteen-year-old son of the Laird of Terpersie, and he too had been pressed by Glenbucket. Perhaps he did not mind this, for his brother was an officer under Glenbucket (and was later to be hanged for it). James was on the Rebel Muster Roll as a lieutenant of artillery which, if nothing more, gives a clear picture of the nature of the Prince's cannoneers. He was reprieved, too, but he spent two years in prison before a transport took him to Jamaica and oblivion.

As there were young boys, so there were old men. Five per cent of the male prisoners were between seventy and eighty years of age. Patrick Fergusson was eighty, the oldest soldier among the Rebels and a labourer who had enlisted in the Duke of Perth's Regiment, though the imagination wonders why.

According to his gaoler he was "old and gray", and that is all that is known of him. There is no account of his release or transportation so undoubtedly he died one day in Lancaster Castle, his body buried unmarked in the common ground outside. Donald Cameron, a clansman who fought with Lochiel's, probably died too, for it is hard to see how a man in his seventies could have survived the Tolbooth at Inverness, the North Sea transports, and the foul hell of the hulks in the Thames.

Within a few weeks of Culloden there were twenty-five surgeons in prison, men who had served with the Prince's Army or who had been loose-tongued enough to declare their sympathy for him when doctoring loyal patients. Among them were Lauder and Rattray, of course, and a Donald MacIntyre of Argyll who may have been a Highland blooder like John Farquharson, for the gaol register declared him to be a quack. Alexander Abernethie was both a farmer and surgeon, of Tipperty in Banff, and he had chosen to be a captain-at-arms for the Prince rather than a doctor. He was sentenced to death in Southwark, and he pleaded bitterly for mercy, having no courage to face the rope and the disembowelling. He received mercy, though not from the court. He died in prison before Londoners could be given the pleasure of his hanging. Colin MacLachlan was a Highland doctor who had come from his practice in the West Indies to help the Stuarts back on the throne, and he seems also to have found it an excellent opportunity for remedying family injuries. Although he declared that he had not been concerned in the Rebellion, witnesses swore that he had taken a body of armed Highlanders to the house of a Mr. John Wedderburn, seeking revenge on that gentleman for the debauching of Miss Mac-Lachlan.

The courts wasted no time in discussing whether or not surgeons were non-combatants, or entitled to special clemency because of the humane nature of their profession. At the trial of Dr. James Stratton, who served the Jacobite garrison at Carlisle, Chief Justice Wills made the Law plain: "It is objected that it don't appear he had arms. All are principals in aiding or assisting; and are parties in levying war, and surgeons are necessary, so are drummers."

And if treating a Rebel's wounds was treasonable, so was any ministering to his spirit. In prison there were fifteen Catholic priests and ten members of the Non-Jurant Clergy. Of the latter, two were hanged: the Reverend Robert Lyon, young chaplain of the Angus Regiment, and the Reverend Thomas Coppoch of the Manchester Regiment whom the Prince had promised to make a bishop. Both died courageously, if only after voluble declarations from the scaffold. The crimes of the Non-Jurant ministers were often little more than "explaining the Pretender's Manifesto from the Pulpit", and at least one of them, poor fellow, had not even done that. The Reverend John Grant had been most circumspect throughout the Rebellion, whatever his sympathies. He kept close to his parish in Urquhart, for which lack of enthusiasm the Prince's Macdonalds helped themselves to his meagre property. In May 1746, the Laird of Grant, suspicious as usual of everything and everybody in Glen Urquhart, arrested the minister and sent him for trial, at which his remarkable eloquence happily secured him an acquittal.

The presence of so many Catholic priests in the prisons, four of them Jesuits, was probably an embarrassment to the Government, and it treated them with remarkable leniency, hanging none and releasing all in time. No one abroad was moved by the deaths of Mr. Coppoch and Mr. Lyon, but the execution of a Jesuit would undoubtedly have interfered with smooth and successful diplomacy.

Almost all the captive priests were Highlandmen, and some were sword-bearing chaplains to the clans, like Captain the Reverend Allan Macdonald, Confessor to the Prince and a kinsman of Clanranald. At Prestonpans and Falkirk he had ridden along the line of his tribe blessing their broadswords before giving them a spirited demonstration of how they should be used on the enemy. John Fergusson captured him in South Uist and sent him to London where Father Macdonald must have had a loss of memory. In an appeal for release he said that he had had no connection with the Rising. The Duke of Newcastle tactfully accepted the appeal and dispatched him from the country, on condition that he never returned.

With Medicine and the Church, the Law was also represented

among the prisoners, twenty lawyers of whom three were hanged and six transported. There were thirty-two seamen, some deserters from the Royal Navy, some French or Spanish officers, and some who were merchant skippers taken for aiding Rebel fugitives. There were seamen turned soldiers like Andrew Simpson who became, surprisingly, a drummer with the Angus Regiment, or John Williams who took to the saddle with Fitz-James's Horse. And there were the unfortunate boatmen like Lachlan MacVurich and John MacGinnis who had ferried the Prince from one sad isle to another during his wanderings.

The lotting of the prisoners for trial or transportation was conducted by their gaolers, by the officers of the soldiers guarding them, or by solicitors' clerks appointed for the purpose. The Highlanders who spoke no English can have had little understanding of what was happening. One day the door of the cell would open, the hatch of a ship's hold be thrown back, and there would be a man with an upturned beaver, roughly ordering each prisoner to take a slip of paper. Alexander Stewart, who had been footman to the Prince and who had ridden away from Culloden with him when the clans broke, left an account of how he was lotted on Sunday, August 17, at Carlisle:

"About two o'clock in the afternoon a rascall of the name of Gray, Solicitor Hume's man from Edinburgh, with his hatfull of tickets, presented the hat to me, being the first man on the right of all the twentie that was to draw together. I asked Gray what I was going to doe with that, and he told me that it was to draw for our lives, which accordingly I did and got number fourteen. So he desired me to look and be shure. I told him it was no great matter whether I was shure or not." The luck of the lotting fell against Alexander Hutchison, not because he had drawn the black paper, but because he had been groom to the Prince and it pleased Gray to see him go for trial. At five o'clock the same evening Gray returned with two other officials. "They came all out to the yarde where we was sitting on the grass, with a verie large paper like a charter, and read so much of it to us as they thought proper, and told us that it was to petition their king for mercy to us, and that it was to go off that night for London, and as soon as it came back we probably

might get hom or els transportation; for such mercy that was but
to hang only one of twentie and let nineteen go for transportation,
pointing to me in particular with his fingar and told me if that
Popish spairk had cairried the day he would have hanged nineteen
and let only the twentieth go free."

They were ordered to put their names to the foot of this
petition, asking for the King's Mercy and a shackled passage
to one of his Colonies. Stewart and some others refused, but their
names were written on the paper just the same, by Gray or another solicitor's man. "And about eight a clock," said Stewart,
"we was all carried to the countie gaol that was for transportation."

This happened wherever prisoners were held, at Lancaster,
York, Carlisle and London. At Tilbury Fort on the Thames, a
star-shaped battlement of brick, the Rebels from Inverness were
re-visited by an old acquaintance. This was Captain Stratford
Eyre, an Irish officer of Battereau's who had been Provost
Marshal in the Highland capital. He was a hard, resolute man,
full of what was being called "the Cumberland spirit", and he
had been responsible for the preliminary examination of prisoners
after Culloden.

Because he was the officer seen most by the prisoners in the
Tolbooth, and because it was he who gave orders in their hearing,
he became the subject of their anger and their bitterness. He was
sent to London as a reliable officer with experience of interrogation, and thus it was that he went aboard the transports at Tilbury
to supervise the lotting. From among the four hundred and
thirty stinking prisoners in the ships' holds he set aside three
women and twenty men who had turned King's Evidence,
and also fifty-two who were marked down for trial because
they had "an extraordinary degree of guilt" or because they were
Gentlemen or Men of Estates. The rest he divided into regimental groups, having a soldier's mind about these things, and
against the name of every twentieth man lotted he wrote the
word "JUSTICE" in red ink. Seventeen were thus chosen, the
last being an old ale-seller from Aberdeen who does not appear
to have served in the Prince's Army at all but had been arrested
upon information laid by a malicious neighbour. With no wish
to stand trial or die he quickly turned King's Evidence.

Among those whom Eyre had set aside as witnesses was the Laird of Mackinnon's old boatman, John MacGinnis, who felt, perhaps, that the bloody whipping he had received from Fergusson was as much as any man should be expected to suffer for the Prince. All over the Highlands the fabric of ancient loyalties was mouldering, and John MacGinnis had agreed to be a witness against his chief. Among the Gentlemen of Estates also set aside was John Gordon, old Glenbucket's son, who was half-blind from drink according to Lord Elcho. Another was Roderick MacNeill, the aging Catholic chief from the Isle of Barra who had not risen for the Prince but who had been arrested on suspicion. Like John MacGinnis he sensed the decay of old values. The warcry of his clan was *Buaidh no Bas*, Victory or Death, but he chose Life and turned King's Evidence against his people and friends.

When the solicitors' clerks drew up lists of the prisoners they splintered the mass of suffering into degrees of gentility and commonality. Delicacy of blood, to which musket-ball and bayonet had been indifferent, was now of statutory importance. The prisoners were divided into four categories:

1. Really gentlemen.
2. Not properly gentlemen but above the rank of Common Men.
3. A lower degree than the preceding.
4. Common Men.

Most of the prisoners were Common Men, landless, voiceless and very soon hopeless. They had no money and no friends nearer than the Highland Line, and because they were inarticulate and illiterate they left nothing on record but their names. The "excepted persons", that is the people of quality in the first three categories, or those turning King's Evidence, were blessed in their experiences compared with the Common Men, though perhaps they would not have admitted it. In time, most of the excepted persons came under the charge and care of the Messengers, officials of the Courts whose duty was to convey prisoners and witnesses from one place to another. The Messengers made handsome profits from this, turning their houses into private gaols, making every attic and cupboard a cell and extorting the final penny for every service they gave. Many petitions of appeal were written by prisoners in the custody of Messengers, accusing them of cruelty, neglect, blackmail, theft and starvation. There were no shackles, no irons in the houses of these officials, but since they were liable to suffer imprisonment themselves if their charges escaped they took no risks. The four principal Messengers were Carrington, Chandler, Dick and Vincent, and of them all Carrington was the most highly regarded by the Government. Not surprisingly he was also the most hated by the prisoners. John Sharpe, Solicitor to the Treasury, said of Carrington on one occasion "I think he will manage the prisoners and get out of them what they know better than any other."

Thomas Chandler kept a house in Windmill Street at the head of Haymarket, and was determined to make it pay as much as possible. One of his prisoners was John Hay, an Inverness man who was in London to give evidence against some of the chiefs. Mr. Hay found life in Windmill Street unendurable, and said so in a petition for removal to another Messenger's care. "We are all bolted up every night in one room like so many Hogs, without any Bedding save a Little Straw. Neither did he ever bestow Body Cloths on us of any value; and now we are run out of the few we have got . . . . May it therefore please Your Grace to take the miserable situation of your poor petitioner to consideration; and order me to be put under the Care of some other Messenger."

The Prince's banker, Aeneas Macdonald, eventually came under the care of Dick (who also had Flora Macdonald in his custody at one time), and although Mr. Macdonald did not like the experience at all he thought it preferable to Southwark Gaol, from which he had once written after many months imprisonment: "I was almost eaten up with vermin of all kinds last summer, though I did all possible to keep my ward clean. I would pay 6s. 8d. a day out of my pocket to get to a Messenger's House rather than stay in this cursed place." And 6s. 8d. a day is what he did pay Messenger Dick, but then he was a banker.

John Mackinnon of Mackinnon and his lady, against whom their boatman was to give evidence, were in the separate custody of Messengers, the Laird for three years. All their money was finally exhausted and they had to live on a small subsistence which the Government paid them, perhaps because they came under Category One of the blood groups. Lady Mackinnon wrote a petition of protest, of course, objecting to conditions in the house which Messenger Munie kept at Derby Court, Westminster. Attached to the petition was a subscription in an unidentified hand, saying that Lady Mackinnon had been arrested on mistaken information and that in Munie's house "there was no place for her except in a cockloft with a rotten floor and a hole in the roof for light, with no stove or any kind of firing, where she has lain all the preceding part of the winter, exposed to the inclemency of the weather".

Of those men who had turned King's Evidence, and who were held by the Messengers, the Highlandmen were most unhappy, having dark memories of how justice worked in their hills. William McGhie and Donald Stewart, who were to give evidence against Banker Macdonald and Lord Balmerino, thought a dirk-thrust as likely in Westminster as it was in the Highlands, and they made this plain in their petition for relief:

"Our lives are threatened, our dwellings marked, and there is danger of our being conveyed from giving evidence by a mock press gang. We are exposed to beggary, our persons known, and our enemies watchful. Giving evidence in open court, wher the criminal's friends will swarm, attended with such imminent danger we do not find ourselves under a necessity to run such a risk to be left to the miseries of want, contempt, rage, begarry, loss of character and life itself."

The appeal was disregarded. Donald Stewart had cause to be alarmed, having received a letter that threatened his life if he gave evidence. But he gave it, and seems to have survived.

But whatever the anguish and the suffering of the excepted persons at the houses of the Messengers it was nothing to what was being endured by the Common Men in the ships and gaols.

"This was done to us when we was not able to stand"

MOST OF THE prisoners taken in the Highlands came to London by sea. They were brought by the small merchantmen which, entering the inner basin of the Moray Firth once the guns had stopped on Drummossie Moor, were berthed alongside Citadel Quay or anchored inshore. Eight days after the battle, when the rot, stench and overcrowding of the Inverness gaols was becoming a problem, Captain Stratford Eyre went aboard all the ships to discover how many men they could conveniently hold. The embarkation began the following day, a file of soldiers and a sergeant attending every master as Guard, and as soon as a vessel received its miserable cargo it moved out into the Firth to await further orders, its bare masts and yards scratching at the Highland sky. None of the ships was more than four hundred and fifty tons in burden, and its only accommodation was the hold where the Rebels were told to lie as best they could on the earth and stones of the ballast. Five hundred and sixty-four prisoners had been thus loaded by May 30, and it was decided that they should leave on the next tide for England where they were to be disembarked, imprisoned and ultimately tried. They sailed under escort from H.M.S. *Winchilsea*, Captain Dyve R.N. commanding, in seven rolling, leaking, coastways tubs of which four had been named for the sweet innocence of their owners' kin—the *Margaret & Mary*, the *Alexander & James*, the *Jane of Alloway* and the *Jane of Leith*. The other three were the jolly *Dolphin*, the sober *Thane of Fife* and *Wallsgrave*.

The convoy beat down the North Sea in a foul wind until, three weeks later Captain Dyve brought it up the Thames to Tilbury. Newcastle told the Admiralty that three hundred of the prisoners were to be sent ashore to the Fort, and the rest were to remain on the transports that had brought them, or were to be transferred to other vessels there. The lotting would follow as soon as possible.

For the prisoners the voyage had been a hell of privation, hunger, typhus and persecution. Thirteen had died on the *Alexander & James*, eleven on the *Jane of Leith*, and there were corresponding deaths on the other ships before or after they sailed. William Jack, the merchant-soldier of Elgin, was aboard the *Alexander & James* and wrote bitterly of the sadistic treatment he received from the ship's crew. "They would take us from the hold in a rope and hoisted us up to the yard-arm, and let us fall into the sea in order for a ducking of us; and tying us to the mast and whipping us if we did anything, however innocent, that offended them; this was done to us when we was not able to stand."

John Farquharson, the Highland blooder, had the same experience of this yard-arm ducking, but he gave an explanation for it when he wrote to Robert Forbes (still assuming the desperate humour of an English officer). He said that the prisoners were so closely-packed in the hold that each had to arm himself with a twig or a rag for defence against the lice that crawled from one body to another. "There you woud have seen the lice marching and contre marching in order for an assault; but the moment the lice of the one came to the foresaid mark, he took his twig and beat them back, because they said their neighbours lice bit sorer than there own." This desperate and ceaseless battle between the prisoners and their parasites greatly amused the seamen, and they sometimes offered their own solution. "They'd take a rope," said Farquharson, "and tye about the poor sicks west, then they would hawll them up by their tackle and plunge them into the sea, as they said to drown the vermine; but they took specell care to drown both together. Then they'd hawll them up upon deck and ty a stone about on the leggs and overboard with them. I have seen six or seven examples of this in a day." Most of the prisoners treated like this were already half-dead from fever, so drowning may have been a charity.

Farquharson escaped from a Messenger's House in London, though he did not say how, but William Jack was eight months on one ship or another in the Thames. Of the hundred and fifty prisoners who were transferred with him to the *Liberty & Property* only forty-nine were still alive at the end of that time, the rest having died of starvation, typhus or persecution. Among the dead were most of Jack's friends. "There is none in life that went from Elgin with me," he said sadly, "but William Innes of Fochabers. James Brander Smith in Conloch dyed seven months agoe. Alexander Frigg dyed in Cromarty Road. Jo Kintrea that lived in Longbridge dyed also . . . but blissed be God I'm in a pritty good steat of health at present in spyte of my enemies."

The *Jane of Leith* brought James Bradshaw to the Thames. He was from Manchester, a warehouseman in the check trade who had found it more exciting to become a rider in the Prince's Life Guards. Unhorsed, he was taken prisoner at Culloden. He was unlucky, too, in the lotting, and still more unlucky at his trial, for he was condemned to hang on Kennington Common. Before he died he made a statement about the things he had seen and experienced aboard the transport, raising his voice above the heckling of the mob, which was demanding a more spiritual valediction from him.

"Several of the wounded were put aboard the *Jean*, of Leith," he said, "and there died in lingering tortures. Our general allowance while we were prisoners was half a pound of meal a day, which was sometimes increased to a pound, but never exceeded it; and I myself was eye-witness that great numbers were starved to death. Their barbarity extended so far as not to suffer the men who were put aboard the *Jean* to lie down even upon the planks, but they were obliged to sit on large stones, by which means their legs swell'd as big almost as their bodies. These are some few of the cruelties exercised, which being almost incredible in a Christian country I am obliged to add an asseveration to the truth of them; and I do assure you that upon the word of a dying man, as I hope for mercy at the day of judgment, I assert nothing but what I know to be true."

The *Pamela* was a prison-ship to which some of the prisoners were transferred once they reached Tilbury. Her master was Thomas Grindlay, a thick-hided skipper of the rope's-end and bilboes school. Even Government officers found him distasteful, though none of them enough to have him removed. The mortality aboard his ship was higher than on any of the others, and his treatment or indifference accounted for a large number of the forty-five prisoners whose deaths were officially recorded in the seven weeks after the convoy arrived in the Thames.

The Reverend John Taylor, a Non-Jurant minister from Thurso, was aboard the *Pamela* and might well have died with the others had not an Army officer insisted that he be brought on deck for fresh air. Taylor said that he and his fellow-prisoners were plundered of all they possessed, until three-quarters of them were naked but for loin-cloths of linen or tartan. They spent most of their time in the hold, in darkness, sucking air through chinks in the timbers. Drinking water was lowered to them by buckets, in which the sailors would urinate when they were drunk. To Taylor, Captain Grindlay was "a Libyan tiger", and his first officer Barker was no better. "A rank atheist of a most scandalous life and lost character; who had not the least tincture of the social virtues and a very shame to human nature itself. Cruelty was one of his darling qualities, and had he not been restricted by his commission he would probably have sacrificed all the poor prisoners to gratifie his impotent fury and madness."

On the *Pamela*, too, were many of the Grants whom the Laird had betrayed to Cumberland. They had been brought down from Inverness aboard the *Dolphin*. Other prisoners always spoke with respect for these naked men from Glenmoriston and Glen Urquhart, remembering how they lay and died on the ballast stones, their whispering voices answering in the language of their hills when Grindlay or Barker mocked them with English oaths.

In August the *Pamela* was visited by Surgeon Minshaw, with orders from the Commissioners for Wounded to report upon the state of the ship. He came aboard one Thursday evening between eight and nine o'clock and asked when he might examine the prisoners. The Captain of the Guard told him that this would be possible in the morning, and so, at six o'clock the next day, Mr. Minshaw was again rowed across the muddy flats. The hatches were taken from the 'Pamela's hold and Mr. Minshaw looked down. "Such an intolerable smell," he reported, "that it was like to overcome me, though I was provided with proper herbs and my nostrils stuffed therewith."

He retired to the quarter-deck where a seat was provided, and he asked that the prisoners come up from below, one by one, in answer to their names. Fifty-four men did so stagger to the deck, giving their names, their regiments and the homes of their birth. Mr. Minshaw was a gentle man, and, being very much moved by what he was seeing, he exercised great patience. Some of the prisoners could scarcely crawl, and were pulled over the hatchway by the soldiers. Eighteen men could not come up at all, not without the use of a sling, said Grindlay, and he was disinclined to go to that trouble. He said he would send soldiers below to get what information the surgeon needed. Mr. Minshaw told the Commissioners: "To hear the description given by the Guard who went into the Hold of the uncleanliness of that place is surpassing imagination, and too nautious to describe, so that that, together with the malignant fever raging amongst them and another odious distemper peculiar to Scotchmen, may terminate in a more dreadful disease."

The Commissioners do not appear to have been disturbed by Mr. Minshaw's report, any more than they were by a Memorial which they received from an unknown Frenchman among the prisoners. To prevent the spread of infection and disease among his fellow-prisoners he suggested that all their clothes and wigs should be at once burned, and that they should be issued with new ones. The sick should be taken ashore to a house of hospital on the Essex bank where there was a garden in which they could walk and take the air. The prisoners should be given proper facilities for washing and cutting their hair, and the issue of a quart of beer and a glass of brandy a day would do much to keep them healthy. All this, he thought, would cost no more than sixpence a day for each man. The Commissioners passed his Memorial to the Secretary of State and that was the end of it. Six months later, it is true, the commanding officer at Tilbury was told that since there was now room in his Fort for all prisoners still aboard the ships he should land them at once. But the motivation was economy, not humanity.

More attention was paid to complaints from the soldiers guarding the transports. They found the duty very hard. Major John Salt, commanding the detachments of Lord Henry Beauclerk's Regiment aboard the *Liberty & Property* and the *Alexander & James*, told the Duke of Newcastle's secretary that "the Stench is so great at present that the Soldiers are oblidged to lay on the Deck". They also grumbled that they had "nothing to Subsist upon but Bread and Cheese with hot fiery Brandy and Water". A considerate War Office agreed that the detachments should be relieved every forty-eight hours. Captain Cayran, commanding at Tilbury when the Frenchman wrote his Memorial, did have a moment's uneasiness about the three hundred Rebels crammed into the arched powder-galleries of his Fort. When the state of affairs there began to offend his sense of military decency he put in a request that the wards be cleaned. He got a tart reply. The Duke of Newcastle asked why any man of common sense should require an order to keep his station clean.

The officers at Tilbury were immediately answerable to Lieutenant-General Adam Williamson, Deputy-Lieutenant and Governor of the Tower of London. He was a very old man, much burdened by debts, and he liked nothing better than to be left alone with his manuscript book of *Wise Sayings and Moral Apophthegms* which he had been collecting since he was an ensign under King William and Marlborough. He enjoyed the personal favour of George II, and was a capable servant of the Crown, which meant that he let it do his political thinking for him. He was also honest within these conventional military limits, and when he gave in evidence words he had overheard one of his Jacobite prisoners say in private, he did so because he believed it to be his duty. He did not like Rebels and was sure that Providence brought all men their just deserts, so he was not too much concerned by reports of the suffering at Tilbury.

The Fort, where a red-wigged, raddled Elizabeth I had talked of honour and dishonour a hundred and fifty-eight years before, was a great attraction to Londoners during the late summer and autumn of 1746. They went down to the marsh-banked estuary by wherries or private boats. From Westminster, and for sixpence, it was possible to travel on the Gravesend tilt-

boat, the Long Ferry which the people of Gravesend had operated
for three and a half centuries under a charter granted them by
Richard II. It was rowed by five oarsmen, and could take forty
passengers who sat aft under the tilt, a canvas awning. The
trip was a jolly experience, particularly if the weather were
fine and there was a good wind to fill the sail and relieve the
oarsmen. At Tilbury they were brought in close to the transports,
and they held perfumed handkerchiefs to their noses. If one had
an entrée to Captain Cayran, or Captain Massey, it was possible
to land and enter the Fort across its tidal moat. Then a walk
over the cobbled parade for a brief but exciting glimpse of the
Rebels inside the powder-galleries. Even without such an entrée
the day could be made by the sight of the transports, by the
bright scarlet of sentries on the ramparts, the sun glinting on steel
bayonets, sea-fowl crying on the mud-flats and the noise of drums
rolling. But the real excitement of the journey, understood or
not, was that enjoyed by a man who can stand so close and yet
be so comfortably far from caged animals.

When, in January 1747, Mr. John Kirkes, Surgeon to the
Prisoners, was ordered to help Captain Massey with the transfer
of all men from the ships to the Fort ("so that the great Expence
of the Transports might be saved") the death-rate had become
monotonously high. By September, twelve weeks after the
convoys had brought five hundred and sixty-four prisoners
to the Thames, one hundred and fifty-seven were presumably
dead, there being no other plausible explanation for the blank
against their names in the column that should have shown their
disposal. Three months later still, the fog and the frosts of the
surrounding marshes must have accounted for many more.

Life aboard the Tilbury transports was undoubtedly the
worst that the Jacobite prisoners suffered, but elsewhere in
the country, in the gaols of York, Lancaster and Carlisle, they
also endured hunger, cold, disease and persecution. In what
some of them later wrote there is a bitter and bewildered failure
to understand the unprovoked cruelty of their captors. James
Miller, a soldier of the Manchester Regiment, said of the time
after he was captured at Carlisle: "We were barbarously treated,
the souldiers rifling us and taking everything of value from us,

both money and Cloaths; they did not offer us any Provisions for three days, and on the fourth but one small Bisket a man." He and others were taken to Lancaster by a troop of Lord Mark Kerr's Dragoons, and the riders prodded or dragged the staggering men into all the mud that was met. In Lancaster Castle the Rebels were put in irons, and what food they were at last thrown was offal and hides from the butchers' yards, which gave most of them the flux and bloody disorders. Miller said that eighty of his comrades died in Lancaster before the rest were herded back to Carlisle where, on "one pound of Brede a day", they were left to await their ultimate disposal.

In London, the Tower was reserved for the Jacobite leaders like Balmerino, Kilmarnock and the Earl of Cromarty. Newgate, the Marshalsea, and the New Gaol at Southwark housed the men chosen by lotting, the prisoners from Carlisle, and most of the excepted persons who were not in the hands of Messengers. They were largely gentlemen of small degree, Highland tacksmen and farmers, merchants and tradesmen. Many had been ensigns, lieutenants or captains in the Rebel Army. After bills of indictment were found against them, all those in Newgate Gaol were transferred to Southwark, for however grievous had been the Rebellion general crime was as active as ever, and Newgate's cells were needed for the pickpockets, foists, foot-pads, murderers, rapists and highwaymen crowded out of other gaols.

The first prisoners of all had arrived in London in February, from the Rebel garrison at Carlisle. They came through the streets from the north, some of them in open flour-wagons, but most of them walking and manacled in pairs. Two dragoons had the charge of five pairs, one leading them with a rope, the other driving them from the rear with his sabre. Their coming had been announced the day before in the newspapers, so there was a large crowd ready to welcome them. And by a remarkable coincidence there arrived on the same day, or the day before, the first wounded redcoats from the north, the defeated victims of the battle at Prestonpans. They were carried through the streets in open wagons, too, so that the city might see their armless bodies and slashed faces and know what the clansmen's broadswords had done. Thus the temper of the mob was indignantly high when the prisoners came. The Rebels were pelted with stones and filth, jeered at and spat at.

The New Gaol at Southwark was on Borough High Street south of London Bridge, between Distiller's Yard and the green plane trees of King's Bench Field. There were held the men, mostly officers, who were to be tried by the Commission of Oyer and Terminer at Saint Margaret's Hill, not far away on the fork of the High Street and Counter Lane. They were well guarded. In June iron-smiths were ordered to put double-bars on all the windows. Every morning at ten o'clock thirty soldiers marched across London Bridge from the Tower and mounted post on the gaol for the next twenty-four hours. The prison was a bleak, brick building of four storeys on each of which were placed sentries with fixed bayonets. There were fifty-six cells, each ten by eight and a half feet, more than enough room, it was thought, for two or three men. There was one small window high on the wall, and through this glassless opening during the evenings came the sweet mockery of the bells of St. George's Church next door. The building, originally intended for debtors, stood about a central quadrangle on which was a Beer Room and a Wine Room wherein prisoners might, if they had the money, entertain themselves and their visitors.

Keeper Richard Jones was the Saint Peter of Southwark New Gaol, and he had a suitable hierarchy of lesser angels. He welcomed visitors to his prisoners, but admitted them at a price, for, as he would no doubt have said, he had to live himself. There were many petitions (regularly refused) asking relief "from the cruel avarice of the gaoler and turnkeys". All visitors, whether they were friends or tradesmen, paid Jones sixpence at the door to get in and sixpence at the door to get out. Any prisoner wishing to go from his cell to the foreyard for exercise could do so if he had sixpence to pay the turnkey of his floor. The beer and wine concession was held by Jones, or leased by him to the turnkeys, and he was of course always open to bribery for other privileges. Most of his prisoners, being officers, had a little money or had friends outside ready to send them some. Being a wise man, Keeper Jones did not take all this at once, for that might have dried up the supply. Those who had no money at all, only the fourpence a day granted them by the Government, complained that they could not buy the strong beer necessary for their poor health, and that they could rarely afford the small beer hawked by their gaoler.

Father Allan Macdonald, the willing amnesiac and onetime Confessor to the Prince, was such a prisoner. "I'm loaded with irons and lying on a floor," he wrote to Messenger Carrington in the hope that the man would ask for the custody of him (he did not), "and I suffer several other hardships by which my already shatter'd constitution is almost entirely destroy'd . . . I hope they'll take into consideration what I have suffered for this year past, first aboard a man of warr, then for more than half a year in the hull of a transport in the River, after that at Tilbury and last of all here where I'm used as above since I have not money to pay for better usage." This was not the triumph of the True Church for which he had prayed when he blessed the broadswords of Clanranald's, so perhaps it is not surprising that he swore to Newcastle that he had had no part in the Rising.

Not all the prisoners were content to wait for whatever punishment or parole the Government might decide they deserved. Forty-five of the fifty-eight successful escapes were from prisons in Scotland, where conditions were easier and the gaols frequently no more than inadequate tolbooths or decaying castles like that at Dumbarton, from which nine MacGregors hacked their way one night. Scots gaolers, too, were understandably more lenient than those in England, either from genuine sympathy or in fear of Jacobite sentiment outside.

Escapes from the London prisons required skill and sudden courage. Toward the end of Aeneas Macdonald's long imprisonment he was lodged in Newgate where he frequently entertained his friends. One May morning the son of Keeper Richard Ackerman opened the door of the banker's cell to admit two visitors, and had no sooner done so that one threw snuff into his face and the other knocked him down. While the boy was still sneezing and rubbing his eyes, Macdonald ran down the stairs in his slippers, crossed the foreyard to the open gate, and passed through to the street. Pursuit was quickly organised and, with young Ackerman at the head, it came up with the footbare

Macdonald in Warwick Lane, halfway to Ludgate Hill. There the
banker emptied his own snuff-box into Ackerman's face, but the
young man angrily struck him down with the heavy cell-keys,
breaking his collar-bone. Carried back to Newgate, Macdonald
apologised with Highland courtesy. Ackerman accepted the
apology just as politely, but now the banker was shackled to the
floor.

Richard Jones lost at least one of his prisoners from the New
Gaol at Southwark. This was Alexander MacLachlan, a Major
of the Atholl Brigade and a former customs officer at Fort
William, the same MacLachlan who had been so tightly manacled
in the Inverness Tolbooth that his wrists swelled about the iron.
He was condemned to death in November 1746, but was reprieved
and sentenced to transportation. Two years later he was still
in the New Gaol awaiting execution of the sentence. One day he
asked Jones for permission to dine with three friends at the
Swan Tavern in Finch Lane by the Royal Exchange, saying that he
wished to borrow money from them, and it was undoubtedly this
that encouraged the keeper to give his permission. In his report
he said it was because the Major was "a person in years and
always well-behaved". A turnkey called Downes Twyford was
sent with MacLachlan as an escort. At first, Mr. Twyford had
a very dull evening, the four gentlemen speaking in the Irish
language only, and the turnkey must have wondered what it was
they were discussing so intently. He soon discovered. After
an hour or so MacLachlan complained of distressing diarrhoea.
Twyford accompanied him to the necessary house, up three pairs
of stairs at the back of the tavern, and felt satisfied that there
was no possibility of escape there. MacLachlan did indeed seem
ill, his complaint being common enough among prisoners.
So the turnkey left him upstairs. The Major soon returned and
continued his discussion with his friends. And then . . .

"Pretending a violent looseness he went up a second time,"
deposed Mr. Twyford in his unhappy report, "and then a third,
and at this latter did not return. On enquiry, found that he
had left by the back door in a great hurry, and dispite all de-
ponent's efforts he could not trace him. Denied absolutely that he
or the keeper received any reward for letting him go."

Only one man succeeded in escaping from the Tilbury transports, at least only one is so recorded. Stewart Carmichael of Bonnyhaugh had been captured in September 1745, while on his way to join the Prince. He was brought to the Thames and transferred to the *Pamela*. The prisoners aboard this ship were fed with the offal of diseased cattle and hogs supplied by speculators in Gravesend, and while most prisoners ate what they could of this Carmichael had the wit to see a further use for it. He saved the pig's bladders until he had four that could be inflated. One night he forced open a port, slipped over the side into the river, and, with the bladders beneath his arms, paddled his way to the Kent shore. He remained hidden in London until the Act of Indemnity.

The escape of Donald MacLaren was sudden, dramatic and successful. He was a drover from Balquhidder who had gone with other MacLarens to fight with the Appin Stewarts, holding a captain's commission under Ardshiel. For three months after Culloden he skulked with others of his name on the Braes of Leny, the wild and beautiful pass below Ben Ledi, until they were discovered by a party of soldiers on a rebel-hunt. Captain Donald fought with his broadsword, shouting *"Creag an Tuire!"* as the MacLarens had cried when the Appin Regiment charged against Munro's, but a musket-ball broke his thigh and he was captured. He was taken to Stirling and then to the Canongate in Edinburgh. In August he was sent southward for trial in Carlisle, strapped to the saddle behind a dragoon. Before the Border was reached, and when the detachment was riding down the vale of the Annan, he managed to free himself from the strap, or saw that it had become loose. It was morning, and the mist was thick above and within the green hollow on Erickstane Brae which local people called the Marquis of Annandale's Beef Stand. There MacLaren slipped from the horse and rolled into the hollow. Lieutenant Howison, the officer commanding, cried out "By God, I arrest you in the King's name!", which would not have stopped Donald MacLaren even had he been able to halt his descent. The dragoons dismounted, and came down into the bowl of mist, yelling and stabbing, but MacLaren buried himself in a bog, and covered his head with sods. He remained there for some days, keeping himself alive by eating the rotting flesh of a dead sheep. He finally made his way home to Balquhidder, where he disguised himself as a woman and lived thus for two years until he felt it safe to be Donald MacLaren the drover again.

Major Macdonald of Tirnadris, young Ranald's father, made a desperate attempt to escape from Carlisle while under sentence of death. He bribed a guard to allow him passage from the gaol once he had torn his starved wrists free of his fetters. But the guard changed his mind, or the Major was stopped by another foolishly left unbribed, and Tirnadris was once more ironed to the floor. No more successful were other condemned men in the same prison. Six of them, led by the Reverend Thomas Coppoch, made an ingenious tool to cut through their manacles. They laid a silk handkerchief over the edge of a wine-glass and struck it regularly with the blade of a knife until the steel was toothed like a saw. But they, too, were discovered, and there was nothing further they could do but prepare the last dying statements which, they hoped, might give some poor nobility to their judicial hanging and disembowelling.

"I declare death don't shock me in the least"

ON MAY 15, 1746, the Privy Council demonstrated its lack of faith in the Scottish courts by declaring that all Rebel prisoners then in Scotland should be brought to England for their trials. It was at first intended that these should be held in Newcastle or Carlisle, and it may be worth remembering that both were Border towns with no historical reason to love the Scots. When Mayor Smith declined the honour for Newcastle, and when it was realised that no one court could possibly deal with the two hundred and fifty-seven men, women and boys lotted or selected, it was decided that the cases should be heard in London, York and Carlisle. The trials were brief and uniform, held in small rooms among the sweet smell of sweat, old wood and anti-scorbutic herbs. The prisoners who appeared seemed uniform too, merged by circumstance and monotony into one suffering human being. The Manchester men were the first to be tried, and what happened to them was a pattern repeated again and again that summer, autumn and winter, so that the reading of one trial is more or less a reading of them all.

On Monday, June 23, at the Court House on St. Margaret's Hill, Southwark, true bills of indictment were found against thirty-nine Rebel soldiers captured at the surrender of Carlisle, and against a snuffling, confused Welsh lawyer, David Morgan, who had been the Prince's counsellor on English affairs and who had taken a leading part in the raising of the Manchester Regiment. The court then adjourned until the beginning of July when the prisoners were arraigned before it and when it announced that their trials would begin on the fifteenth of the month. Since the bills of indictment had been drawn there had been spirited talk and argument on the nature and definition of treason, on whether Scotsmen had the right to demand a trial in their own country (they had not, it was unanimously agreed), on whether the word alone of a prisoner was enough to prove his commission in the French Army (it was not), and on whether the acceptance of a Commission of Excise from the Pretender was an overt act of treason (it most certainly was, the levying of duties and taxes was the jealous privilege of King George's Government). There was one other subject that helped to pass the port about the tables in chambers at Lincoln's Inn and the Temple, and this was whether the Courts should accept a man's plea that he had been forced into the Prince's service. Chief Justice Lee, when such a plea was made before him later, said what had been in most legal minds for some time. Alexander MacGrowther claimed that he had been bound with ropes and taken from his home in Glenartney to serve in the Duke of Perth's Regiment. "The law as to force," said Sir William Lee, "must be a joining for fear of death, and returning the first opportunity. He might have redeemed himself for money. He has not proved any attempt to leave them. It must be a continuing force to mount to an excuse."

Alexander MacGrowther was 76 years of age, and he was sentenced to death. He would have hanged, had not the Scandinavian ambassador secured him a reprieve.

Of the forty-nine prisoners brought to trial at St. Margaret's Court that year, seventeen were executed on Kennington Common*, a short walk from the New Gaol through the flower and vegetable gardens at the end of Newington Butts. The fashion of their dying was soberly described for them by the Justice before they left the Court: "Let the several prisoners return to the gaol from whence they came; and from thence they must be drawn to the place of execution; and when they come there they must be severally hanged by the neck, but not till they be dead, for they must be cut down alive; then their bowels must be taken out and burned before their faces; then their heads must be severed from their bodies, and their bodies severally divided into four quarters; and these must be at the King's disposal."

Francis Towneley was the first of the seventeen to be so

* By the Oval, on a spot where the parish church of St. Mark now stands.

butchered. He was an English Catholic and he held a commission from the King of France. He was aged 38 and he had been living in Wales when the Prince landed. His devout Catholicism and the traditional Jacobite sympathies of his family naturally made him one of the Stuarts' most zealous supporters. He became the colonel of the Manchester Regiment and the commandant of the Rebel forces at Carlisle when the Prince retired to Scotland. He opposed the surrender of the garrison to Cumberland, swearing at Governor John Hamilton and saying "that it was better to die by the sword than to fall into the hands of those damned Hanoverians", and by his own experience he proved how true this was. He was admired by his regiment, but his humourless nobility was too cold for love.

He was brought to Saint Margaret's Hill on July 15, and was the only man tried that day. The mob outside the New Gaol, in Counter Lane and The Borough, had found it difficult to decide whether there would be more to entertain them there than at Tyburn, where six soldiers were to be hanged for murder, violence and robbery in the London streets. On the bench, in the sombre dignity of ermine, scarlet, black silk and grey wigs, were Chief Justice Lee, Justices Wright, Dennison, Foster and Abney, Barons Clive and Reynolds, and two magistrates of the area. The jury consisted of three gentlemen, three brewers, a baker, brazier, starch-maker, gardener and cloth-worker drawn from the parishes of Addiscombe, Bermondsey, Camberwell, Clapham, Croydon, Kennington, Lambeth, Putney, Rotherhithe and Southwark. This was a great day for Surrey.

Seven witnesses were brought to depose against Towneley, and their evidence was much the same as that brought against all the accused, that a prisoner had been seen here with a sword in his hand or there with a white cockade in his bonnet, that he had taken a party of armed men along this road or had drunk a toast to the Pretender in that tavern. Roger Macdonald, a King's Evidence man who had deserted from Strathallan's Horse, was the chief witness against Towneley, declaring that he had seen the Colonel at the head of the Manchester Regiment, wearing a white cockade, a tartan sash, sword and pistols. In his evidence the renegade Macdonald said as much about himself as he did about the accused, whining that he expected a pardon for this service, and that since he came to London he had been destitute and starving, which was no fit reward for a loyal subject of King George. He received his pardon.

Samuel Maddox, a Cheshire man who had been an ensign in the Manchester Regiment, was another witness for the prosecution, giving evidence against Towneley and against many more of his brother-officers. He was an apothecary's apprentice, and he seems to have given evidence less from a sudden loyalty to the Government than from a hatred of Towneley. On the retreat from Manchester he had told his Colonel that he had had enough of Rebellion and wished to go home, but Towneley warned him that if he took a step from the ranks he would have his brains blown out. Maddox the apprentice remembered this insult from Towneley the gentleman, and he took his revenge at Southwark. Witnesses who appeared for the accused tried to discredit Maddox, saying, and they were probably right, that he was a cheat, a thief and a liar, and that for all the good he had been to the Cause he might just as well have stayed in Manchester with his master's pestle and mortar. But such evidence, though heard, was of no help to Towneley, and the Court quickly rejected his plea that, as an officer of King Louis, he was entitled to be treated as a prisoner of war. He was sentenced to death and he wept a little. He whispered "I never thought it would come to this!" It was his only moment of weakness, but the public in the well of the Court was grateful to him for it.

On the following three days seven more officers of the Manchester Regiment and the lawyer David Morgan were brought to trial. They were marched from the gaol between files of soldiers and through a great crowd of Londoners. They were officers, but it is doubtful whether their patrician Colonel would have regarded them as gentlemen, and the meanest kern standing in the sixth rank of Clan Cameron would have thought himself their superior in blood and breeding. George Fletcher, aged 25, was a linen-draper of Salford, managing the business for his mother, but when he saw the white cockades on the woollen bonnets, the gay tartan swinging, he thought them a more exciting cloth. He told his mother that he would enlist, and she fell on her knees crying, offering him a thousand pounds if he would stay at home behind the counter. Instead, he borrowed a hundred and fifty guineas from her and bought himself a lieutenant's commission under Towneley. When he was found guilty, and sentenced to death, he straightened his shoulders and shouted "I would do it all again!"

Thomas Chadwick of Staffordshire was shown on the gaol register as "a gentleman otherwise a tallow-chandler". It was said of him that he could "look death in the face with as much serenity as he could a friend", and Chief Justice Lee gave him the opportunity to prove whether this were so or not. He had a sweet singing voice that was a constant delight to his comrades, and when the Rebel Army passed through Lancaster he went to the church to play the organ and sing "The King shall have his own again!" This was duly charged against him at Southwark. Sentence: death.

John Berwick was also a lieutenant in the same company as Chadwick, and like Fletcher he was a linen-draper. His friends called him "The Duke", because of his surname perhaps. He had well-to-do friends who kept him comfortably supplied when he was in the New Gaol. "Scarce a day passed," said the *London Magazine*, "but hampers of the richest wines and the best eatables were brought to him." He was a merry fellow, and young enough to know that he would never die. Sentence: death.

The middle-aged Thomas Syddall had been the Adjutant of the Manchester Regiment. He was the son of a blacksmith, and before the Rising he had been a reputable barber in Manchester. His family's devotion to the Stuarts was as strong as Towneley's, and its sacrifices probably greater. They were Catholics, of course, and Syddall's father had been out with Prince Charles's father in 1715, and had been hanged for it. Throughout Thomas Syddall's boyhood he had seen his father's skull whitening on top of the Market Cross in Manchester, and his desire for revenge had grown strong. When the Rebels came south to Lancashire in November 1745, Syddall left his wife and five children and bought himself a commission in the Manchester Regiment. Exactly one month later he was a prisoner. Sentence: death.

James Dawson was "Jemmy" to his regiment, the son of a

respectable Lancashire family. He was at St. John's, Cambridge, when the Rebellion broke out, "but not observing decorum he quitted it to avoid expulsion". Not having the courage to face his father, he joined the Prince instead, and for four weeks he found a tartan sash much more brave than a student's gown. Sentence: death.

Andrew Blood was a captain in the Manchester Regiment, coming to the Prince from Yorkshire where he had been steward to a landed family. He was a reserved, taciturn man, and in the New Gaol before and after the trials he kept to himself, refusing to join in the desperate revelry by which other young officers kept up their spirits. In Court he quietly contented himself with a plea of Guilty. Sentence: death.

Thomas Deacon was the eldest of the three sons of the Non-Jurant Bishop of Manchester who became officers under the Prince. Robert, the second son, died a prisoner at Kendal while on his way to London in January. Charles, a boy of seventeen but an ensign of the Manchester Regiment, was in the New Gaol with Thomas, and although he was to be sentenced to death later that July his youth saved him for transportation. Samuel Maddox had much to say in evidence about Thomas Deacon. He remembered that he had seen the young man sitting outside the Bull's Head in Manchester, enlisting recruits for the Prince, giving each a shilling and a cockade of blue and white which he tied to their bonnets himself. Sentence: death.

The ninth man was no soldier at all. He was David Morgan, aged fifty, a barrister from Monmouthshire whose career at the bar had been less spectacular than he had hoped when young, and he had been living in his country home when the Prince came to England. Nobody seems to have liked the poor fellow. His companions in prison said he was haughty, ill-natured, over-pious and quarrelsome. He was probably just frightened. He was completely without literary talent, but he wrote copiously, several religious tracts and a dull, satirical poem of six hundred and thirty verses which was reprinted and enjoyed a healthy sale after his death gave it a morbid interest. His defence was that of a confused and terrified man. He said that, yes, he had indeed joined the Rebellion, but did not the Court know that he ran away from it in loyal disgust? The Court did not know. The Solicitor-General said that if Morgan had deserted the Rebels it was only when the cause was obviously doomed. Mrs. Morgan came to the New Gaol every day for the comfort of her husband, and her devotion and tenderness was generally thought to be more than the unhappy man deserved. Sentence: death.

All these men were hanged on July 30. The magazines and the newspapers kept the public well-informed about the life the prisoners led from the day they were sentenced to the day they died. The reports appeared in tightly-printed, scarcely-paragraphed columns between advertisements announcing the arrival of "exceedingly good LIMONS and BITTER ORANGES, the Bitter Oranges are fit for marmalade; also fresh chestnuts and walnuts". The accused were heavily ironed, wrists and ankles locked together by manacles and bars, so that they seemed to move in constant modesty or prayer. At night they were fastened to the flags of their cells by staples. The waiting, the thinking and the dark of the night acted upon them according to their natures. Syddall prayed, and said that he thought unceasingly of his family, his five children for whom the best that he could wish was that they might end their lives in a martyrdom such as his. Jemmy Dawson and Berwick sang, all through the night sometimes, and hysterically. They were often drunk. David Morgan quarrelled with the turnkeys and with Keeper Jones, and this was always worse after his wife had been to see him. George Fletcher was cheerful most of the time, except when he remembered how his mother had gone to her knees to prevent his enlistment. Then he wept and became maudlin. Blood, of course, said little, even when Deacon and Berwick began to talk wildly of a reprieve and asked him to stiffen their silly hope by agreeing with them. "I can die but once," he said, "as well now as any other time."

But it was Towneley who fascinated the journalists who paid Richard Jones their sixpences for entering the foreyard of the New Gaol. The Colonel of the Manchester Regiment did not step out of character. He was grave and uncommunicative, and rarely spoke to anyone except a Catholic priest called Saunderson. From a tailor in Southwark he ordered a new suit of black velvet in which he proposed to die, and this, perhaps, was a characteristic gesture on his part and showed how he saw himself. His cold dignity, his calm distraction excited no sympathy among the journalists, and none in their readers when they wrote about him. Some men will carry illusion up to and beyond the point of death, making a reality out of it. It was as if Francis Towneley still saw himself at the head of his tragi-comic Manchester Regiment which had never had the chance to fight a battle, a pale, noble figure in plaid and cockade, doomed but assured of eternity. His sad lack of humour, of enflaming imagination, had been obvious in the slogan he had chosen for his regimental standard: LIBERTY AND PROPERTY, CHURCH AND COUNTRY. It would not have turned the head of a clansman.

Towneley had his unwelcome familiar, the warehouseman James Bradshaw who had suffered so much persecution on the *Jane of Leith*. For some reason he had hated Towneley from the day of his enlistment, and had transferred to Elcho's Life Guards to get away from the man's icy self-possession. Now they were together again in the New Gaol, and the animosity between them, or rather the hatred Bradshaw felt, made the journalists curious. They discovered, or invented, a reason for it. They said that colonel and lieutenant had quarrelled over a young lady with whom both of them had danced at a ball in Manchester. His experiences on the transports had made Bradshaw a little insane, and he felt a nagging need to fray the edge of Towneley's detachment. The night before the nine were hanged Bradshaw was drunk as usual, and he shuffled up to Towneley in the foreyard, saluting him as if both were soldiers still. "I find, sir," he said, "you must shortly march into other quarters." Towneley stared him down in silence.

That night Morgan, having said farewell to his wife, was more irritable than ever. He quarrelled bitterly with the prison cook, accusing the man of profiteering, and the sound of his lilting, complaining Welsh voice went on and on in monolgue long after he had been stapled to the floor. The fathers of Jemmy Dawson and Chadwick came to see their sons. Tears prevented much conversation between the Dawsons as they sat together with hands clasped, although the father was asked for and gave forgiveness of his son's profligacy. Chadwick, who until then had been in high spirits, also wept when he saw his father.

Then Keeper Jones cleared the prison of visitors. Before they got what sleep they could, the condemned spent a little while studying the speeches they intended to make from the gallows, which they had either written for themselves or bought from preachers who hawked such things about the gaol. Towneley prayed, almost all the night.

They were all awoken at six o'clock in the morning. The weather, said their turnkeys, was overcast with the promise of rain. Morgan awoke in a temper, and when he heard that the coffee the condemned had ordered was already made and growing cold his rage became more furious. He scalded the turnkey with boiling words in Welsh and English. But he drank the coffee just the same, keeping the barrier of his disagreeability between his thoughts and his coming death. All the prisoners drank their coffee together, in a small room off the foreyard, and still with wrists and ankles manacled. They said little to one another, though once Chadwick smiled at Berwick. "Ah, Duke," he said, "our time draws near, but I feel in good heart."

"I too," said Berwick, "I declare death don't shock me in the least. My friends forgive me, and they have done their best to save me. May God be merciful to us all."

When the coffee was drunk, Keeper Jones said "Gentlemen, if you please." Perhaps he was sorry to see them go, their stay had been profitable for him. When the irons were removed, each man was pinioned lightly, but in no way that impeded the use of their hands. Thomas Syddall, who had been very calm until now, was able to take snuff to still his sudden nervousness.

"If you please," said Jones again, and the nine men were taken out into the yard where three sledges were waiting, each harnessed to three shire horses that had been rented from a Surrey farmer. In the foreyard, too, were many other prisoners come to watch, and some to see a rehearsal of their own departure soon. Bradshaw was there, and drunk the newspapers said, but he was probably only light-headed. He inspected the sledges thoroughly and gravely, poking the straw that had been laid on the timbers.

There was not enough he said, and he clutched at Jones's arm, demanding more straw "or the lads will get their feet wet".

It was ten o'clock, and the condemned were strapped to the sledges, three to each and on their backs, their faces staring at the sky. On the first sledge were Towneley, Blood and Berwick. On the second were Morgan, Deacon and Syddall. On the third were Dawson, Fletcher and Chadwick. The hangman stood on the first sledge with a drawn sword, and with his feet astride. The gates of the prison were opened and the procession moved out, just as the rain began to fall. Its military escort joined it in the street, a squadron of dragoons and a company of Foot Guards to lead it, and a squadron of dragoons and a company of Foot Guards to follow it. Despite the rain, the chill temperature of a London July, there was a large crowd along both sides of The Borough, Black Street, Newington Butts and the Clapham Road. There were hot-pie stalls, brandy-sellers and apple-women in St. George's Fields, and boys were already crying copies of last dying speeches that had yet to be spoken. When the procession had passed the crowd closed behind it and followed it to the Common. The people were unusually quiet, and there were no rowdy cat-calls, no jeers, no pelting with filth. The mob was used to hangings, and jealous of its rights in the free entertainment thus provided, but to-day there was quiet. Perhaps it was because, with the exception of Towneley, the white-faced men lying on the jolting sledges might have been anybody's neighbours, a linen-draper, a barber, a soap-boiler, a warehouseman. But there was something else that stilled the enthusiasm of the crowd in expectant silence. The hangings were to be followed by something more usually to be seen in the Smithfield slaughter-pens.

The sledges arrived on the Common at eleven o'clock. The crowd here was many thousands, larger than anybody could remember for such a spectacle. Men and women and children had been there since yesterday evening, jostling and fighting for room at the front, and those at the back, whose view of gallows, block and fire was obscured, were complaining angrily. There was also some indignation because there was no minister or clergyman on the scaffold. When the sledges came to the gallows the crowd sighed and whispered, but still there was no rowdiness. The nine men were unstrapped, helped up the steps to the scaffold, and there left to make their last statements. This took a very long time, and at the back of the crowd nothing could be heard, and little seen but a distant figure waving his arms. Towneley spoke first, and shortly, the rain falling on his new velvet suit, and he seemed disinclined to waste any more time than was necessary. What he said has been lost, although it may be assumed that he did not ask the pardon of his Manchester Regiment for persuading the Prince to leave it behind in Carlisle when most of it wanted to go on with the retreat to Scotland. A man ready to give his own life for a Cause, is rarely considerate of the lives of others.

Morgan followed Towneley, his spectacles on his nose, his voice flustered and still a little irritable. He took a book of devotions from his pocket and read aloud for half an hour, which greatly tried the patience of the crowd. Now and then he looked up from the book, and plunged into a bitter and venomous attack on the Church of Rome to which the Catholic Towneley, standing beside him, listened without change of expression. Morgan then proceeded with an explanation of his misfortunes, a confusion of tortuous theology which none but he could have understood. In the end he raised his voice to a shout, advising everybody who could hear him to buy and read a book of his own composition, *The Christian Test, or the Coalition of Faith and Reason*, which his dutiful daughter Mary would shortly be publishing for the relief of his family.

The speeches of Syddall and Deacon had been written for them by a Non-Jurant minister called Creake, who was at this moment selling printed copies of them among the crowd. "My dear fellow-countrymen," said Thomas Deacon, "I am come here to pay my last debt to nature, and I think myself happy in having an opportunity to die in so just and so glorious a cause . . ." Mr. Creake's zeal for Non-Jurant Episcopacy was strong in what he had written for Syddall: "If any would enquire into its primitive constitution I refer them to our Common Prayer Book which is entitled *A Compleat Collection of Devotions, both Publick and Private*." Both men forgave their enemies, including King

George and the Duke of Cumberland, while pointing out that neither had a right to such titles.

The rest of the condemned men read shorter speeches, or closed their eyes and prayed aloud. One or two threw papers and their gold-laced hats into the crowd after they had spoken, to the annoyance of the hangman, who considered their clothing his property. And one man threw a prayer-book after his hat, a page turned down to direct the eye to some verses of the eighty-ninth Psalm: *With whom my hand shall be established, mine arm also shall strengthen him. The enemy shall not exact upon him, nor the son of wickedness afflict him.*

The last words were spoken. The rain was now falling heavily, and it spat upon the faggots burning below the gallows.

Then, not too soon for the growing impatience of the crowd, the hangman pulled a cap over each man's head, covering it from crown to chin with a darkness that anticipated death. Morgan muttered irritably as the cloth came down. Syddall trembled and whispered "Oh Lord, help me!" From the others there was no movement. They were turned off one by one, and they were hanged by a rope made from alternate strands of red and white. Later a curious journalist sought out the rope-maker and asked why he had woven such halters. No reason, said the man, the colours had pleased his fancy that was all.

When the bodies had hung for three minutes soldiers removed the shoes, white stockings and breeches, and the executioner's assistants took off the rest of the clothes. They were placed on one side in neat bundles, and protected from the rain. Towneley's naked body was then cut down and placed upon the block. Observing signs of life in it, or some reflex movement, the hangman struck it several violent blows on the chest. He then cut it open, drawing out the bowels and heart which he threw upon the fire below. The head he severed with a butcher's cleaver, holding it in the air for a moment before placing it in a coffin with the trunk. The second body to be treated like this was Morgan's, and then the rest, one by one. When the hangman threw the last heart into the fire (it was Jemmy Dawson's) he cried "God Save King George!", and the crowd yelled God save him indeed.

It was over. The coffins were drawn away on the sledges, black smoke rolled in oily clouds through the rain. Constables were busy, picking up the papers which had been thrown from the scaffold. They reported to the magistrates that these were of a highly treasonable nature, in that they claimed that their authors had died in a Just Cause and that they "did not repent of what they had done, that they doubted not but their deaths would be avenged, and several other treasonable expressions". Such papers made very distressing reading, though it was difficult for the magistrates to see what could be done about them.

A mob gathered at Temple Bar later in the day when the heads were to be placed on spikes above Fleet Street, and it was a great disappointment to all when only two were put there. The hangman and an assistant ran quickly up the ladders just before sunset, each with a head beneath his arm. The crowd began to lay bets on which was Towneley's and which was Fletcher's. There were counter-wagers that Towneley's head had in fact been sent to Manchester, and still more sportsmen were prepared to bet that head and body of the Rebel colonel were now in the care of an undertaker in St. Pancras who was sewing them together so that they might be buried as one. The hangman surlily refused to enter into the spirit of the evening, and would not say to whom the bloody heads had so recently belonged.

The bodies of the nine men were all buried within the parish of St. Pancras, Towneley in the churchyard and the rest in ground near the Foundling Hospital. His Majesty, who by law had heads and quarters at his disposal, may not have cared where any of them went, leaving such matters to his Ministers. The heads of Dawson, Blood and Morgan were charitably returned to their families, but of the rest a necessary example was made. Towneley and Fletcher to Temple Bar, of course, Syddall and Deacon for exhibition on the Market Cross in Manchester, Chadwick and Berwick to spikes above Carlisle. Thus the skull of Syddall rested where his father's had been impaled thirty years before. Bishop Deacon made a vow never to pass the Market Cross lest he see his son's head, but one day a twist in the narrow streets, taken inadvertently, brought him to the sight of it. He raised his hat and passed on. For this small act of sedition he was charged and fined by the magistrates.

The Whig Press was remarkably restrained in its comments on the accused and their deaths, admitting that all had died with courage and devotion, however misused. What distaste the papers felt was expended on the irritable little Welshman who had fussed and fumed his way right to the gallows. The *Penny Post* said "What his virtues and better qualities were, if he had any, have not come to our knowledge; if they had we should gladly have mentioned them, that the world might not run away with the opinion that Mr. Morgan was the only man who ever lived half a century without doing one good action."

But, all the same, his family mourned him grievously, and it is to be hoped that his daughter Mary sold many copies of his bad book.

"Good people behold the quarters of a traitor!"

THERE WERE OTHER trials on Saint Margaret's Hill at which the same meticulous regard for the bloody letter of the bloody law was observed, until seventeen Rebels had been hanged and disembowelled in public and all the spikes at Temple Bar were threaded with skulls. For some prisoners there was unexpected pardon, and in one case the pardon showed the enduring paradox of Man, his reliance on brutality and his respect for brains. James Gadd was a typefounder, a young captain of the Duke of Perth's Regiment more actively employed during the Rebellion as a printer of the Prince's proclamations. He was the son of William Gadd, the Edinburgh goldsmith who had invented the art of stereotyping twenty-one years before, and who had recently published an edition of Sallust by this means. The boy pleaded guilty at Southwark, but the Master of Trinity College, Oxford, urged that he should be spared in recognition of his father's contribution to science. It was a pleasing thought and the King's Ministers were glad to show their clemency. James Gadd was unconditionally freed, although the compassion of society did not extend to his father, then dying in poverty.

There was no pardon, of course, for the witless warehouse-man James Bradshaw who was brought to trial soon after the first nine, and who appeared before the sober Court in a gay suit of green. It was pleaded on his behalf that he was not responsible for his actions, that while he was still an apprentice "he did several things like acts of lunacy, such as getting out of bed in the night, doing himself damage and abusing his comrades, upon which he was fastened down in his bed with straps". But the Solicitor-General, the great William Murray who was later to urge the coercion of rebellious Americans, asked witnesses if this were not merely the behaviour of an habitual sleep-walker, squeezing out of them an admission that indeed it might be so. Thus, like Towneley, James Bradshaw marched shortly into other quarters, but before he did he made a dying statement of simple sanity and moving sincerity, describing the sufferings he and others had endured on the transports.

Bradshaw and his companions died as those who had preceded them died, drawn in procession to the same barbaric ritual on Kennington Common. Before taking their places on the sledges they enjoyed a little refreshment in the foreyard of the New Gaol, calling for some white wine in which they drank the health of King James III and his family, giving each and every one of them their proper title, or at least what a Jacobite considered to be their proper title. All the condemned declared that they did not fear death, and they all prayed for the Prince. Three more men were to have been executed with them: Francis Farquharson of Monaltrie, the fair-haired "Baron Ban" who had stood with his clan at Culloden; Thomas Watson, a tobacconist and magistrate of Arbroath and a lieutenant of Ogilvy's Angus Regiment who had been at Culloden too; and James Lindsay a shoemaker and ensign of Strathallan's, the man who, when robbed of his clothing in Inverness, made himself garments of straw. The night before the execution Farquharson and Watson were granted conditional pardons, and in the morning, when James Lindsay was already strapped to a sledge, word came that he too was reprieved. He was unable to speak, and he wept as others were pulled away to the Common, the hangman and the cleaver and the faggots.

There were Highlandmen who died at Kennington, like Donald Macdonald, a young captain of Keppoch's who had remained behind with the garrison at Carlisle. He was very merry in prison and haughtily insolent in Court, declaring that if the Solicitor-General wished to know his name it would be best to ask his mother. And he laughed. In prison he joked about his fetters, holding them up and shaking them. But for them, he said, he would be happy to entertain the turnkeys with a Highland reel. Now and then, in the damp darkness and the silence of night, he thought that he could hear the pipes. "I was delighted by that music," he said sadly, "when the Army marched behind the Prince . . ." Such memories could change his merry humour to despair, and he would say bitterly that if he had known the Prince to be as unwelcome as he was, and as unlikely to win the throne, "then devil take me if I would have stayed behind at Carlisle!"

In Cumberland and Yorkshire there were also trials and executions. Nineteen men were hanged at Carlisle, and twenty-three at York. Seven at Penrith and seven more at Brampton. The Scots at Carlisle and Brampton were hanged within a short ride of their own country, and from the death of one of them, taking the low road home by the grave, came the lovely ballad of Loch Lomond. The trials at Carlisle began in August. There were three hundred and eighty-five prisoners in the Castle and they were lotted soon after Culloden. By the time the Commission of Oyer and Terminer met one hundred and nineteen were brought before Lord Chief Baron Parker. There were inn-keepers and excisemen, tailors, printers, watchmakers, goldsmiths, drovers, farmers and apprentices. Among them was a boy of fourteen, Hugh Roy from Aberdeen. He had marched beside his father in the Duke of Perth's Regiment, though neither had gone willingly. The father, John Roy an innkeeper, had been pressed into the Prince's service, and the son had gone along with him for company. John Roy died before he could be brought to trial, but Hugh appeared before the Lord Chief Baron and was condemned to death. He was pardoned on condition that he enlisted in the King's Army.

The trials lasted fourteen days. Thomas Coppoch, the tailor's son to whom the Prince had promised the Bishopric of Carlisle, the onetime student of Brasenose who had been chaplain to the Manchester Regiment, appeared before the Court in his cassock. It was charged against him that, clergyman though he was, he had marched in the Rebel ranks with a hanger at his belt, a tartan sash across his breast and a white cockade in his hat, and that he had further acted as Quartermaster and Billeting Officer to the regiment. He called his father and a Miss Humphreys to prove that he had been forced into Rebel service, but nobody believed this, least of all he perhaps. When he was condemned he called out boldly to his fellow-prisoners, "Never mind, boys, for if Our Saviour were here these fellows would condemn Him!" And when one of them began to weep he shouted, "What the devil are you afraid of? We shan't be tried by a Cumberland jury in the other world!"

Donald Macdonald of Tirnadris also pleaded that he had pressed into the Prince's Army, by Keppoch his chief, but he must have made the plea in contemptuous mockery of the Court, for he was a resolute Jacobite and a loyal clansman from his brogues to his bonnet. He had been the first to draw blood in the Rebellion, and he would have been at Culloden with Keppoch's had he not wandered into the Government lines during the gun-fog of Falkirk. He was a bold and bonny man, twice-married and with an eye for a handsome woman. In prison he was as gay as that other Donald Macdonald in Southwark New Gaol, talking of the pipes and the reels. He wrote to a lady of Carlisle that she might come and dance with him if she had no objection to his fetters. He dreamed of his northern hills and his burned house in the land of sweet briar, and sometimes, perhaps, of his son Ranald at Warwick Hall nearby. He dressed himself in tartan for his death.

The executions took place in October. The hangman was "an execrable rogue" called William Stout, a Hexham man who had bargained for the job until he got twenty guineas and all the clothes of the hanged. The prisoners died as others had died in London, with protestations heavily weighted by theology. Now and then one of them said something, or behaved in a manner that shaped him in simple nobility. John MacNaughton was a watchmaker of Edinburgh, a Quartermaster of Kilmarnock's Regiment, and a modest man of humble ambitions. He had been employed by the Rebels as a courier, and he was also accused of killing a dragoon colonel at Prestonpans, though the man had actually been cut from the saddle by the swinging scythe of a Cameron. MacNaughton was frequently pressed to turn King's Evidence against his comrades, the last effort being made when he was already tied to the sledge for execution. He was offered a pardon and an annual pension of £30. He refused. He said that the Government had honoured him by ranking him with gentlemen that day, and he hoped that he would be left in peace to suffer as one.

On the scaffold Thomas Coppoch spoke for half an hour, spiking his statement with shrewd texts in Latin, and asking God to bless all his enemies "especially that corrupted judge Baron Clarke". It is doubtful whether the mob understood one half of what he was saying, with his allusions to Aesop, Caesar and the Lernaean Hydra, but his fine pulpit voice was much admired.

In York, before the judges opened their commission and began the trials on October 2 they attended a solemn service at which the High Sheriff's chaplain preached on Numbers 25, verses 4 and 5: *And the Lord said unto Moses, take all the heads of the people and hang them up before the Lord against the sun, that the fierce anger of the Lord may be turned away from Israel. And Moses said unto the judges of Israel, slay ye every one of his men that were joined unto Baal-peor.* The judges of Israel did their best, they sentenced to death seventy of the seventy-five prisoners brought before them. Among the five unexpectedly acquitted was John Ballantine of the Atholl Brigade. Witnesses said for him that "he was forced unto the service by a party of Rebels who took him by violence out of his bed, threatened to stab him if he did not go with them, and did not allow him time even to put on his cloaths and that afterwards they placed guard on him to prevent him making his escape". This evidence was accepted, and the delighted John Ballantine threw his bonnet into the air, crying "My Lords and Gentlemen, I thank you. Not Guilty! Not Guilty! Not Guilty!"

In the end only twenty-three of those sentenced were hanged, the rest were transported or pardoned on condition that they enlisted, and the romantic legend of Jacobite loyalty takes a hard blow from the fact that thirty-one of these prisoners, lately soldiers of the Prince, now eagerly became recruits for King George. The twenty-three condemned were dragged in batches to the gallows on the first frost-sharp days of November. Many of them were Highlandmen, a MacLean and a MacGregor, a MacKenzie and a MacGinnis, a Fraser, Macdonald, MacKellar and MacInnes. From the scaffold some threw papers to the crowd, justifying their rebellion. Others were silent. But the end for them all was the same as it was for Captain George Hamilton of Baggot's Hussars. The hangman held up sections of his severed body and cried "Good people, behold the four quarters of a traitor! God save King George!"

The last to die at York, on the fifteenth day of November, was James Reid from Angus. He had been the Piper of Lord Ogilvy's Regiment, and on his behalf it was argued that he had never carried arms and never struck a blow against the King's soldiers. The jury recommended him to the mercy of the Court, but Lord Chief Baron Parker corrected their mistaken compassion. "No regiment ever marched without musical instruments," he said, "such as drums, trumpets and the like; and a Highland regiment never marched without a piper, and therefore his bagpipe, in the eye of the law, is an instrument of war."

The trials of the Rebel peers had begun in July, two days before the first executions on Kennington Common. "You will be in town for the eight-and-twentieth," Horace Walpole wrote to a friend, "London will be as full as at a Coronation. The whole form is settled for the trials, and they are actually building scaffolds in Westminster Hall." The scaffolding was for the spectators of the trials, since most of London Society wished to be present when Lord Balmerino, Lord Kilmarnock and the Earl of Cromarty were brought before their peers. Two-thirds of the ancient hall were filled with stands and seats, and fifty workmen had also erected boxes for the Prince and Princess of Wales, the Duke of Cumberland and his friends, the ambassadors and ministers of foreign powers. One hundred and thirty-six dukes, earls, viscounts and barons sat in coronets and ermine to try the Rebels. The President of the Court was young Colonel Yorke's father, the first Baron Hardwicke, a conscientious jurist and an implacable enemy of the Stuarts.

He left his home in Great Ormond Street early that Monday, riding in a procession of six coaches. He sat in an old, faded state carriage that had once belonged to an illegitimate daughter of the last Stuart king, James II. Ten bare-headed footmen were clustered about it, and it proceeded with the slow dignity the

Law deserved. The trials were to begin at nine o'clock, and each man was to be disposed of within an hour so that the whole business could be over before noon. The Rebel peers came in three coaches from the Tower, Kilmarnock hiding his fear behind a cold face, Cromarty almost swooning with terror, and Balmerino brave and jesting. They were kept waiting until eleven o'clock when they were brought before the Court, lectured shrewishly by Hardwicke, and then asked how they pleaded. Cromarty and Kilmarnock both said "Guilty!", but Balmerino made a fight of it. The others were removed while his trial proceeded. He fenced with the Court, objecting to the way it described him in the charge, questioning its right to try him under the regulations it had chosen, and once making room beside him for a small boy who was having difficulty in seeing what was going on. He was, of course, found guilty.

Two days later all three were brought back to Westminster Hall to hear their sentence. Before they set out there was some question as to which coach should carry the executioner's axe, and Balmerino settled this. "Come, come," he said, "put it in here with me." He flirted with the weapon throughout the morning, fingering its edge, and once saying to the executioner "Take care, or you'll break my damned shins with that thing!" They were all sentenced to death by hanging, and were asked what they had to say to that. They said little to the point. Kilmarnock said poverty, not will, had driven him to join the Prince. Cromarty mumbled in craven fear, and Balmerino said a few words of contempt and no more. After the sentence they were taken to a small room off the Hall for refreshments. They knew that they would be separated when they got back to the Tower, and Balmerino said that because of this they might as well have another bottle of wine. 'We shall not meet again," he said, "not until . . ." And he grinned and pointed to his neck. He tried to cheer Kilmarnock who was dolefully depressed, saying that they would not be hanged but beheaded (this being their right by rank), and he advised Kilmarnock how to take the axe, that he should not wince lest the edge cut his shoulders or skull. It would be a good idea, he thought, to bite one's lips before the blow fell. And then they were taken back to the

Tower, passing Charing Cross where Balmerino stopped his coach to buy some "honey-blobs", as the Scots called gooseberries.

Kilmarnock and Balmerino were beheaded, as the old man had expected. Cromarty's wife went to the Royal Family, and swooned effectively at their feet, winning her husband a reprieve and an ultimate pardon. Kilmarnock died with great courage, considering his fear, and Balmerino as if he had no fear at all. He walked about the scaffold, examining it with interest. Once more he fingered the axe, weighing it in his hands, and all this so upset the executioner that he had to strike three blows before he could strike off the valiant old fellow's head.

Horace Walpole, who did not like Cumberland, said that on the day the three peers were condemned the Duke had planned a ball at Vauxhall in honour of a whore called Peggy Banks, and was persuaded to defer it for a couple of days lest the mob thought it an insult to the Rebel lords. Certainly the ball was held, on August 4, though the Duke did not enjoy it overmuch. He was nearly crushed by cheering crowds when he came ashore from the Royal Barge, and nearly deafened by the bands that blared the National Anthem.

Two more peers were beheaded for their part in the Rising: Simon Fraser, Lord Lovat, who was executed in April 1747, and Charles Radcliffe, *de jure* fourth Earl of Derwentwater, who died on Tower Hill in December 1746. The Radcliffes had lost title, fortune and estates for the Stuarts. James, the third Earl, had been out in the 'Fifteen and had been beheaded for it. Charles had also been out, had been captured, but had escaped from Newgate before George I could take his head. He went to France, assumed his brother's attainted title, and became a secretary to Prince Charles. He was on his way to join the Rebellion in November 1745, when a British ship captured him off the Dogger Bank. He was very conscious of his blood, his nobility and his rank, and in demanding respect for them he worried the wits out of Governor Williamson at the Tower. He demanded a trial by his peers, but did not get it. He was placed at the bar of the Court of the King's Bench, and from there he stepped across to the jurors, raising the hand of one. "Here," he said indignantly, "is the hand of a man among the lowest class of mechanics. Is this a proper person for trying a peer?"

The Court did not say whether it thought so or not. It said that Charles Radcliffe should have no trial at all. His original sentence of 1716 should stand against him. And so it did.

"*I would sign non for no man that ever was born!*"

ELEVEN MONTHS AFTER Culloden the Government had not yet disposed of those prisoners who had applied for, and been granted, the King's Mercy of transportation and perpetual banishment to his Colonies. The pace of affairs had, of course, long ago fallen into the jog-trot of bureaucracy. Mr. John Sharpe, Solicitor to the Treasury, was immediately concerned, having been instructed to do something about the matter in September. In January 1747, the Privy Council nudged his elbow, ordering him "to get all the common highlanders who are pardoned on condition of transportation, exclusively of the Gentlemen and officers, transported forthwith". But, as Mr. Sharpe may have complained in private, giving orders was easy enough, getting nine hundred and thirty-six men, women and children to the Americas was quite a different matter. The greater part of this number, eight hundred and sixty-six, were to go under indentures, as bound servants to merchants, plantation owners, or anybody else from New England to the Windward Islands who wanted cheap labour.

The problem was to find ships and ship-owners who would take the prisoners, and until this was settled they were left to rot in prison. Newcastle occasionally urged the Commissioners for Wounded to honour their responsibilities, saying that "the remaining prisoners ought not to be worse treated than consistent with their security". Among the public there was little sympathy. "They will be transported for life," said the newspapers, "let them be of what quality and condition soever." There was also a strong feeling that transportation was too mild a punishment. Philip Carteret Webb, the Crown Solicitor who had supervised much of the lotting and who had been prosecuting counsel at some of the trials, joined in the general discussion of this subject. "If they are to be transported," he said, "you may be assured that most of them will return again in a short time. It happened so in 1716. Suppose a law was made for transporting them, and marking them on the face with a hot iron and making it a felony if they return; without such a mark, every law will be ineffectual."

A law regulating the transportations was passed, though fortunately for the already threadbare honour of the Government it contained nothing about branding. In this Act the King declared that "being moved with compassion of our especiall Grace" he had pardoned the Rebels on condition they submitted to transportation simple, or under indentures, and that any who returned without permission would suffer death as a felon without benefit of clergy. This was his Mercy.

The possibility of turning a profit on nearly a thousand marketable human beings early excited the cupidity of English merchants trading abroad. In September 1746, Mr. Sharpe began his lengthy negotiations with them, settling at last in favour of Mr. Samuel Smith of Cateaton Street, London, and Alderman Richard Gildart of Liverpool. For an agreed payment (to be made by the Government) both gentlemen said they would be happy to act as carters once the Rebels had been placed under indentures. "By which indentures," said His Majesty, "they shall bind and put themselves An Apprentice and Servant to the said Richard Gildart and Samuel Smith to serve them or their assigns in our Colonies in America during the term of their natural lives." The two merchants did not, of course, want several hundred apprentices and servants; they proposed to transfer the indentures, at a price, once the prisoners reached the Americas.

There had been some initial haggling over how much the traders wanted for this service, and when Mr. Sharpe had a figure which he thought might be acceptable to the Treasury he put it before the Board. "Read a report from Mr. Sharpe," say the Minutes, "informing My Lords (Mr. Sharpe also attending) that Alderman Gildart and Mr. Smith propose to Transport the Rebells at £5 10s. per Head to any of His Majesty's Plantations. My Lords agree to the proposal at £5 per head, and the persons to be taken at the respective Ports appointed by My Lords."

Alderman Gildart and Mr. Smith had won the lottery. For the transporting of each prisoner the Government would pay £5. For the transfer of the indentures in the Americas the merchants hoped to receive at least £7 a head. The prisoners were thus worth £12 gross, and from this amount had to come the cost of feeding them and carrying them from port to port. How the merchants made a worthwhile profit only the inarticulate and long-dead prisoners can have known.

Not that Mr. Smith and Alderman Gildart found it easy to get their money from the Treasury, and the pigeon-holes were filled with plaintive petitions from them. The warrant for payment declared that the £5 would be given in two parts, and only for a man or a woman or a boy actually transported. The Duke of Newcastle's quixotic clemency was a great trial to Alderman Gildart in this respect, and nearly two years after Culloden the merchant was petitioning the Treasury "for full allowance of 14 prisoners discharged by warrant from Duke of Newcastle after they were shipped for transportation". Moreover, he had already sent one hundred and fifty-seven Rebels to America before the Treasury made its first half-payment of £2 10s. The shipping of the prisoners was still going on in 1749, which means that many of them had been in gaol for three years, and they must, from the point of view of Smith and Gildart, have been very sorry merchandise by then.

For its part, the Government did not trust the merchants, and the Duke of Newcastle sent several letters to Governors of the King's Colonies, telling them that the prisoners were on the way, and asking them to make sure that none had escaped *en route*. Sir William Pepperell, Governor of Massachusetts, was as anxious to acquire some of the prisoners as were Messrs. Gildart and Smith, though for other reasons. "Could it be thought expedient," he asked Newcastle, "that two hundred of the rebel prisoners who may have been unwarily seduced should be sent over for Mr. Shirley's and my regiments? It might be a means of making good subjects of them." It might also, had the request been granted, have been the means of making corpses of them. The Governor's unhappy soldiers were dying of fever, eight or ten every day.

Some of the prisoners were shipped as drafts for disease-thinned battalions abroad. Thirty-eight went from Carlisle, and thirty-seven from York were sent to serve under Admiral Boscawen in the East Indies. These were men who had chosen enlistment as a condition for their pardon. Very few of them, already weakened by prison life, survived the service.

The indentured prisoners ready for transportation began their long journey in the spring of 1747. They were sent from gaol to Liverpool, handcuffed in pairs, and once aboard the ships they were locked in the holds. They were a considerable worry to Gildart, who complained petulantly about them in letters and petitions, for like most businessmen he did not wish it to be thought that his trade brought him profit or pleasure. On one occasion, however, he did have a serious loss, though it was less serious for him than for the prisoners involved. A boat, carrying eight men from the quay to one of his vessels, ran against a hawser and capsized. The prisoners, manacled together, were all drowned. Mr. Gildart, ever hopeful, told the Treasury that he expected to get £40 for them, just the same. He received nothing, not even when he explained that the dead men had involved him in great expense for bedding and provisions.

Mr. Smith also had his disappointments. He shipped one hundred and fifty men and women aboard the *Veteran* and dispatched them to Antigua, having been told that indentured servants would fetch a high price there, as well as in the islands of Jamaica and St. Kitt's. The *Veteran* was within landfall of Antigua when a French man-of-war, the *Diamond*, captured her and took her to Martinique. The prisoners were set at liberty. Mr. Smith wrote bitterly to the King's Ministers, asking that they insist upon the French returning to him his valuable cargo. Since the Kingdom of England was then in a state of war with the Kingdom of France nobody quite knew what Mr. Smith expected. He explained that his servants should be returned to him under the next exchange of prisoners, a suggestion which the French had the dignity to ignore. In his letter to the Government, Smith gave a list of all the men and women aboard the *Veteran* and across two centuries this still throws a faint illumination upon them. There was Elizabeth MacFarlane, a black, lusty, ruddy woman.

There was Daniel MacGillis, a brown, well-made, stiff boy of twelve. There was Peter Summerall, a shoemaker aged fourteen, slender, straight and with fair hair. There was John Macintosh from Inverness, who was sixteen and who played the fiddle. There were carpenters, shoemakers, labourers and bakers. There were maltsters, tailors, bookbinders, gardeners, ploughboys, drovers and goldsmiths. There were sempstresses, knitters, and weavers. They were all Common Men and Common Women, with the exception of John Mackenzie of Ross and John Ostler of Lincoln, and these were described in the list as having no trade but "are well-made and genteel". And they were for the most part Highlanders, Grants and Macdonalds, Stewarts, Campbells and Macintoshes, Camerons and Mackenzies. If such servants aboard the *Veteran* were typical of those carried by other transports, and they most probably were, then the colonies of America were not the worse for receiving them.

One of the indentured servants who left the Mersey in May 1747, was Alexander Stewart, the Prince's footman who had refused to sign his name asking for the King's Mercy at Carlisle, but had had it written down just the same. On the last day of April he was put aboard the *Gildart* at Liverpool with eighty-seven other men and women. "When we went aboard," he said, "we were all stript and searched that we hade no armes about us, or any instrument for taking of our irons, and thene we put on our cloths again, and then we was desired to go aft to the steirreg until we got on the Hanoverian pleat on our leags, and went to se the apartment where we was to ly." It was not pleasant. It was dark, noisome, and deep in bilge. The *Gildart* lay off Liverpool for some days with a second transport, the *Johnstown*, until they were joined by other merchantmen bound for America. Their masters were timid men, putting out to sea and putting back, putting out and putting back again, for fear of French privateers. They slipped across the Irish Sea to Belfast, speaking other vessels and asking news of the French, until at last they found the courage to set out across the Atlantic. The voyage took two months. On July 18 they entered Chesapeake Bay.

"We came to ane anchor at the port called Wecomica where we was to be put ashore at, and as soon as the shipe came to ane anchor we was all ordered below dake, for Robert Horner the super-cargor wanted to speak a queet word to us, which accordingly went all doun between daks, and Horner came down and made a verie fine speach concerning the goodness of the countrie that we was going to; and if we would atest for seven years, the men that would by us, if we pleased them well, would probably give us doun two years of our time, and a gun, a pick and a mattock, and a soot of cloths, and then we was fre to go thorou any place of the illand we pleased."

But Stewart was no more inclined to promise anything here than he had been at Carlisle. He told Horner that he was wasting his time, and the other prisoners looked at him and asked him for advice. "I told them they might doe as they pleased, but for mee I would sign non for no man that ever was born, though they should hang me over the yard arme. Then says they, We will sign non neither. So I told them, Gentlemen, stand by that then."

The little rebellion was spirited and courageous, but of short duration. Horner, who was Gildart's agent in the Colonies, waved two letters before Stewart's face. One, he said, was from the King to the Duke of Newcastle, and the other was from Newcastle to Gildart, and both empowered him to go to the Governor of Maryland and Virginia and "get a sufficient guard to keep us all in prison untill we should all sign". The prisoners wavered, but Stewart boldly replied that he and his friends had been under worse guards in England and had survived. Horner went ashore in a temper, and set out for Annapolis and the Governor. He returned without any soldiers, the Governor having said that so far as he knew he had no power to coerce the prisoners to sign themselves away to new masters. But Horner had brought some help in the form of "buckskins", as the native-born Americans were contemptuously known.

"And upon Wednesday, the twentie second of July, Horner returned back and all the buckskins in the countrie with him, and Cornel Lee, a monstrous big fellow, in order to bulle us to assign; and this Lee said to us he would make us sign. And we told him God Almighty hade made us once, and he neither could nor should make us again, for which he said no more." Colonel Lee, who was probably Thomas, one of the progenitors of

Virginia's aristocracy, thus got a small lesson in human nobility. It had nothing to do with blood lines and plantation acres.

In the end it did not matter whether the prisoners signed themselves away or not. Perhaps Horner did it for them, for he posted notices about the country saying that the Rebels would be handed over to the highest bidders. The master of the *Gildart* was a reasonable and compassionate man called Holmes who seems to have had no liking for Horner. When the agent was away in Annapolis, Holmes "sent letters to all the Roman Catholick gentlemen and others, who was our friends, so that we might not fall into the common buckskin's hands". These men, most of them from Prince George County, took up the indentures of all the prisoners aboard the *Gildart*, with the exception of four whom the buckskins bought. Their motives were simple and humane, to give the prisoners a good home and to release them as soon as possible.

Stewart's indentures were bought by two Scots brothers of Annapolis, and they may have chosen him rather than another because their name, too, was Stewart, and because their father had come from Appin. They paid £9 6s. sterling for him, and having paid it they promptly set him at liberty. Six months later he was home in Scotland, drawn there irresistibly, though he risked death as a felon if he were discovered. He was one of the very few who came back, who escaped or who had the money and courage to return once they had worked out their indentures. Of the eighty-one men of Glen Urquhart and Glenmoriston whom the Laird of Grant had handed over to Cumberland, a few are known to have returned. Alexander Grant of Inverwick, though in his fifties, came back from the Barbadoes to be a boatman on Loch Ness again. Donald Grant, who had gone to the West Indies with Alexander, was over sixty, yet he too found a way home to Blairy in Glenmoriston. And William Grant of Carnach came back to farm in Glen Urquhart.

The Colonies of North America and the islands of the Caribbean swallowed up the prisoners. They sweated in labour or died in fever. They worked under indentures for the rest of their lives or were given a conditional liberty after seven years. In the West Indies their Highland blood was often mixed with

African, and two centuries later their descendants brought back to Britain the lost names of Lochaber, Badenoch and the Isles. In the Americas the prisoners moved westward to the frontiers of Virginia and Pennsylvania, with their masters or on their own. They became Americans by residence, but in almost all of them there was kept alive a memory of their homeland. Their children inherited this nostalgia and its loyalties. When the American Revolution came it would have been understandable for them to be among the most zealous opponents of George III. In fact they formed a Royal Highland Regiment, and they fought for the Crown that had banished them.

6

THE SHARP ROCK

'They say they will never go again into the plaine'

WILLIAM ANNE KEPPEL, second Earl of Albemarle, succeeded Cumberland as Commander-in-chief of the King's Army in Scotland. Hawley had wanted the appointment, and thought it his due, but the Duke sent him south before he himself left Scotland. The problems of the kingdom needed a soldier and an administrator, not a hangman. Yet Albemarle was a harsh man, and the Scots could not claim that there was any comforting difference in affairs after Cumberland went. The Earl had been born forty-four years before in Whitehall Palace, the son of Arnold Joost van Keppel and Geertruid Johanna Quirina van der Duyn, and Scotland was to say that what a German had begun a Dutchman finished. Albemarle's father had come to England as a page of honour to William III, and his advancement followed naturally from that promising start. He was a peer by the time he was twenty-seven, and a major-general at twenty-eight. The boy, William Anne, was named for so generous a King, and for his godmother the Queen who followed. His career was less spectacular than his father's, he was forty before he became a major-general, and the manner in which he drove a carriage and six through his fortune inevitably earned him the nickname of "The Spendthrift Earl".

He did not like Scotland. It was "this cursed country" in almost every letter he wrote. It was cold, barbarous, inhospitable, and, so far as his knowledge went, never successfully governed by anybody. "I know ye people," he wrote to Newcastle in June 1746, when it was first suggested that he take Cumberland's place, "I know ye country and that my predecessors have split against a sharpe rock." But he was a soldier and a dutiful man, and he accepted the appointment when the Duke insisted, reserving the right to complain whenever he thought that this might speed his recall. On the whole he behaved with tact and judgment, but his views on what should be done to suppress the rebellious spirit of the Scots were conventional and matched his general disapproval of the country. "Nothing but fire and sword can cure their cursed, vicious ways of thinking," he told Newcastle, "therefore, for God Almighty's sake don't spare those whom you have in your power."

As much for his own comfort, as from a realisation that there was no longer any need for a large army in the Great Glen, he moved his headquarters to Edinburgh, and he divided Scotland into four military districts. The first stretched from Inverness and Fort Augustus to the mouth of the Spey. The second was the country between Strathspey and the east coast. The third was the country westward from Perth to Fort William. The fourth was all the shires south of Stirling. The horse regiments were sent to grass, and most of the Culloden battalions were posted to Flanders where a new campaign had been mounted against the French. The policing of the Highlands and the hunt for fugitives and arms now became work for small detachments under the command of subalterns or senior non-commissioned officers, patrols that lived for a week or two weeks in hillside bothies. It was unusual work for the men of British line regiments, but they did it as efficiently as the Highlanders of the Independent Companies. They had not, however, captured the Prince. When Albemarle went to Edinburgh, thanking God for a warm fire in a Scots August and for passable food at dinner, Charles Stuart was hiding on the braes of Glenmoriston, soaked by rain and mist and in a poor way for food until a fine stag was shot by one of the men sheltering him.

There was also a chain of small posts about the throat of the Highlands, from Stirling westward to the shores of Loch Linnhe. This had been established before Culloden, but it was now of greater importance, for it locked all the passes to the mountains. It also kept the MacGregors in check, as far as that were possible. After the 'Fifteen, a military fort had been built at Inversnaid where Loch Lomond poked a finger into Clan Gregor's country, but the nameless ones had of course burnt it. Now Albemarle decided to re-occupy it, telling Newcastle that it "would prevent a most licentious Clan (vizt) the MacGregors, from Robbing, plundering and laying waste the Country about them, which they have done for many years with impunity". Brevet-Major James Wolfe, now returned from Hawley's staff to duty with his regiment, was ordered to take some of Barrell's to Inversnaid and there reactivate the fort. He did the work well, setting up sub-posts in the wild hills, arresting lonely reivers, and sending soldierly reports every fortnight to General Bland at Stirling. He hated the mountains and the Highlanders, who, he thought, were "better governed by fear than favour".*

Few officers of the Army were enjoying their enforced stay in Scotland. It was not, to their mind, a proper way for a gentleman to campaign, living in a granite cell or dank hovel, with every chance of being dirked or shot should he take a ride in the evening when the damned rain lifted a little. Humphrey Bland wrote sardonically to Albemarle of the number of requests for leave he was receiving from his officers. They all claimed, he said, to have pressing business in England, but "the greater part of them, like Colonel Walgrave, want only to buy a Hatt or some such trifle". The men were just as bored and rebellious, and made the Scots suffer for it. They plundered the country, stealing peas and beans from vegetable gardens. They got drunk in St. Ninians, and stayed out of barracks long after nine o'clock when Tattoo was beaten. They were rounded up by the Provost Guard and flogged.

Howard's Old Buffs were the permanent garrison in Stirling, and their officers made plain their opinion that there was no difference between a decent Lowland tradesman and a thieving MacGregor. On July 29 William Pollock, a wigmaker of the town, sent his journeyman William Maiben to the barracks with a new wig for Lieutenant Stoyt. Mr. Stoyt was not pleased with it, and said so most rudely. Going downstairs from Stoyt's quarters Maiben was heard to mutter that he would welcome an

---

* Six years later, when he was again on duty in Scotland, Wolfe proposed a plan which, if it had been successful, would have resulted in the deliberate massacre of Clan Macpherson. "Would you believe I am so bloody?" he wrote, "'twas my real intention."

opportunity of kicking the lieutenant's backside. Stoyt called his batman and both set out for Pollock's shop where Maiben was struck over the head with a cane until it broke.

While the lieutenant was busy belabouring the journeyman, other officers of Howard's came into the shop and began to beat Mr. Pollock with their canes. Maiben was then dragged to the Guard Room where Mr. Stoyt complained to Colonel Thomas Howard that the regiment had been grievously insulted by him. Howard ordered that Maiben be tied to the halberds and whipped to the beat of a grenadier's drum. The poor fellow was yelling under this punishment when the baillies of Stirling came to Howard with a protest, but he told them to go about their business, for he and his regiment were the Law in the town, and "he spoke otherwise indecently to the magistrates".

They were stout men, however, and went to the Court of Judiciary charging Colonel Howard and Lieutenant Stoyt with *hamesucken*, with most barbarous and cruel abuse of the persons of William Maiben and William Pollock. Before Howard, or any of his officers could be brought in front of the magistrates, the Buffs were ordered away to Glasgow by General Bland, and there the cautious baillies entertained them to a grand dinner in a public hall, and complimented them with the freedom of the city. They had no time to discover whether this bribery would work, for a few days later the regiment marched to England. Mr. Pollock never did get any redress for the injuries suffered by himself and his journeyman, nor, presumably, did he ever get any payment for Mr. Stoyt's new wig.

In Aberdeen, where Lord Ancrum and Major-General Skelton commanded the second military district, the Reverend John Skinner complained that some dragoons and men of an Independent Company had burnt his meeting-house and plundered his home. They had been led there by a man called Hardy, an informer who earned himself a little fortune that summer, smelling out suspected Jacobites and Non-Jurants. "I was that day at Rora," said Mr. Skinner, "baptising a child or so, and came not home till pretty late, when to my surprise I found 7 armed men at my wife's bedside, who had lien in about 10 days before and not left her bed." Skinner was arrested under no charge that he could understand (except that it was upon information laid by Hardy) and the soldiers "packed up all my shirts and stockings, most of my books, with several other bits of portable furniture, and 10 shillings sterling of money".

Aberdeen, which had always considered itself a loyal city in a doubtful shire, was beginning to wonder if the soldiers were aware of this. English officers argued that since all Rebels were Scots (or appeared to be), then all Scots might well be Rebels. The logic was weak, but it served as a justification, and the Scots were advised to be that much more demonstrative in any manifestations of love for King George. The people of Aberdeen were invited to display their loyalty on August 1, the day on which the British Army traditionally celebrated the accession of the Hanoverian dynasty. Lord Ancrum told the civil authorities that the city must be illuminated, that candles must burn in every window, and here the trouble started. The baillies said that, while they understood and respected the reason for the celebration, it was their custom to celebrate the accession of a reigning monarch, not of his family. They would ring bells, they said, and they would hoist flags, but at this time of the year to put candles in all the windows would mean that the citizens would have to stay up very late indeed. Would Lord Ancrum please excuse them? He would not.

On the evening of August 1 the officers of Fleming's Regiment gathered in the city's largest tavern, and their companies were drawn up on the cobbles outside for the ceremonial drinking of King George's health. All were greatly surprised to see that no candles glowed in the citizens' windows. Captain Hugh Morgan was more than surprised, he was angry. He asked the soldiers whether they were men to take this sort of insult. According to some people of Aberdeen, he was the first to pick up a stone and hurl it through the nearest window. Within a few minutes the men of Fleming's were yelling through the dark streets, smashing windows, hammering on doors and looting where they could. Mr. George Forbes said that his warehouse was plundered by these men, who broke several valuable looking-glasses and stole or destroyed other property to the value of £130 sterling. The riots went on for several days. On August 7, sixty men under Captain Morgan (who was in no good humour because the magistrates had demanded his arrest) marched to the house of Alexander Grant, Sheriff of Aberdeen. Mr. Grant was dragged out of bed and accused of harbouring Rebels, and was told that he must accordingly have forty soldiers billeted upon him. Officers and soldiers then went to a nearby tavern, drank seventy Scots pints of ale and left without paying. They returned to their barracks loaded with Mr. Grant's "blankets, sheets and pullivers".

For a month testy letters passed between the Town Clerk, the Sheriff, Lord Ancrum and the Earl of Albemarle. Albemarle kept the Duke of Newcastle well informed, and said that to his mind Grant and four other worthy sheriffs were "in their hearts all Jacobites". He also passed on to Newcastle a handsome testimonial to Captain Morgan's virtue which had been written by Lieutenant-Colonel Jackson of Fleming's. Jackson said that the baillies had brought charges against the good fellow because he was "very active in Ferriting Gentlemen who were and are lurking, some of whom are of this neighbourhood; I take that to be one of their reasons of spleen". Albemarle finally agreed to pay some damages for things stolen or broken during the rioting (the Town House appears to have been a particular target for the soldiers' stones), and he hoped that if Morgan and other officers were brought before the magistrates those gentlemen might know where their best interests lay.

Fatigued by the campaign in the Highlands, weary of his office and longing to be in London, Albemarle was irritable and over-worked. His troops felt the edge of his temper, and the whip was as busy under his command as it had been under Cumberland's. It came down on the backs of suspected Rebels as well as disobedient soldiers. In a regular report from the first military district General Bland wrote: "One of Lord Fortrose's tenants has seized a Rebel who was taken with two letters which he was carrying to some of the Rebel chiefs, but he will not confess anything, tho he received this morning one hundred good lashes with a Catt of Nine tails." In Banff, Louis Dejean, the Huguenot colonel of Munro's, captured Hugh MacKay, an under-cook in the Duke of Gordon's household, and he flogged the man ("a little encouragement" he called it) until "he told me where some Rebels were lurking about this Town".

And so it went on through August into September, with riots and plundering, with lonely patrols struggling through the mountains, with ragged men shot as they ran from the heather, or flogged until they betrayed their friends. That he had not captured the Prince was particularly galling to Albemarle, and he assured Newcastle that for the chance of laying his hands on Charles he would "with infinite pleasure walk barefoot from Pole to Pole."

On September 24 he had to report that he would never have such a pleasure. "Just as I imagined, the Pretender's son is gone; the French ships heard on ye Western Coast took him and some of his people aboard them." Four days before Albemarle wrote this, the *Prince de Conti* and *L'Heureux* had sailed from Loch nan Uamh under cover of a dawn mist. They took with them the Prince, Lochiel, Lochgarry, John Roy Stewart, Dr. Archibald Cameron and some others. The Prince is said to have wept as the hills of Moidart fell astern. He had cause to weep.

That Albemarle received news of the young man's escape within a few days of it happening was due to his excellent intelligence service. He had at least one spy who skulked in the hills with prominent Jacobites, who boasted that he was held in great trust by Lochiel, and who is understandably never named in any of Albemarle's papers. Fear of a dirk-thrust probably prevented this man from betraying the Prince when he had the opportunity, but he kept Albemarle well supplied with information. "If I see or hear anything that is worth communicating to your lordship," he wrote, "I'll not slip one moment to acquaint you of it."

Two other spies were also Highlanders. They frequently worked together, a Macdonald and a Campbell, making an interesting association of names that must embarrass romantics. Donald Macdonald was an islander from Uist, one of Macdonald of Sleat's people, who had set up business as a tailor in Edinburgh, making clothes for most of the chiefs in the west. He became a spy and an informer before Culloden, when he went to Lochaber and Clanranald's country to collect some debts. He first sent what information he had to the Campbells at Inverary, but in August and September Albemarle was receiving frequent reports from him. The fugitive Jacobites were naïve, it did not occur to them that a Macdonald, even a Macdonald of Sleat, would betray them. They allowed the tailor to go where he wished, and even asked him for help at times. On their behalf at the beginning of September he kept watch for the French ships that were to come for the Prince, and he did this faithfully, not forgetting to keep the Earl of Albemarle informed as well. His reports were somehow passed to the deputy-governor of Fort William, who sent them by courier to Edinburgh.

Patrick Campbell, the other spy, is a more shadowy figure, his only public appearance being that of interpreter at the Carlisle trials. He must have been a skilful, brave and resolute man, for he moved among the hills far from his own Campbell country. He sent Albemarle shrewd analyses of the strength and character of Rebel sympathies, of the absence or plenitude of arms and food, and towards the end of the year he and Macdonald travelled together in the Highlands. In October snow fell on the high ground, and the winter that followed was hard. There were black frosts, ice in the sea-lochs, and a white shroud from Cape Wrath to the Isle of Mull. Yet Albemarle still fretted about another Rising. The reports he received from Campbell or Macdonald sometimes seemed to justify this fear and sometimes to prove its absurdity, and very often did both in one dispatch. "The common people," wrote Campbell in late October, "such as are herried and their cattle driven, especially among the Camerons, Clanronalds, Glengarrys and Glen Morrisons, are all ready to espouse the smallest opportunity to appear in Arms again, and for that purpose have certainly concealed some arms, tho' the number cannot be determined . . . . Keppoch's men and the people of Appin are determined never to rise in Arms again, nor can the Macphersons be prevailed upon to engage, notwithstanding Clunie's interest. The smallest encouragement from the Government or a shew of lenity has more effect upon the Cameron people than the greatest severity."

But Albemarle had nightmares. He dreamed he saw French frigates off the Isles, even in a West Highland winter (about which he knew nothing). "Though twenty thousand French should land to-morrow," Campbell reassured him, "they would not get one single Highlander. These are the present sentiments of the Highlanders."

Then the Commander-in-chief began to worry about Cluny Macpherson and the money the chief was believed to be distributing among the clans on condition they took to arms again. Campbell or Macdonald investigated this for him, and once more reassured him. "They say, whatever they may do at home in the Highlands they will never again go into the Plaine."

In November the two spies made a long and difficult journey through the West, going northwards from Tobermory to Moidart, to the Isles and back to Kintail and Lochaber, from Fort Augustus through the snow-deep passes of Badenoch. They reported that some MacLeans had hopes of help from France, and had hidden guns and swords against that day, but they were exceptional. In the Braes of Atholl "such of the inhabitants as we conversed with seemed to be weary of rebellion, and complained much that they were forced out by Lord George Murray". Everywhere the wretched people were gathering what food they could for the winter, and repairing their destroyed homes if possible. No one glen was like another, and if there were some cattle in one there was not even meal in the next. The chiefs were away, dead or gone to France, and the clansmen were leaderless. Every family mourned its dead. "The Highlands in general has suffered much where we travelled with regard to the loss of men. And particularly the Camerons have lost upwards of 460 men, and never had above 800 in the field. The Steuarts lost about 150, and did not exceed 260 from the beginning of the rebellion."

There was French gold in the hills, and there was rum and brandy, but these were small comfort to the glens that were without food or firing. In some parts of Moidart and Lochaber the people were being supplied with meal, butter, cheese and salt by boats from Ireland, and so long as these supplies lasted, or so long as the clansmen had French gold to pay for them, men went about with swords at their waists, said Campbell, and talked boldly of fighting. But nobody did fight, and the talk lasted only until bellies were empty. He was very much a Campbell when he allowed himself a little dissertation on the problem of civilising such people. "It is past the power of men to bring them into working in factorys while they are in hopes of a landing, and can have anything to steal, which is the only trade they incline to at present."

Albemarle continued to worry, though he should have realised that, with the Highlands in this ambivalent state, winter was going to settle most of his troubles for him. He was convinced that the mountains were full of Jacobite agents from France, men who were passing among the clans with money, orders, and plans for a rising. There were such agents, of course, though they were usually men whom the exiled chiefs had sent to collect rents from their impoverished peoples. When the agents were caught they were barbarously used. Evan MacKay, taken with letters in French and cipher upon him, was given five hundred lashes to persuade him to say where he was going, from whence he had come and whom he represented. He said nothing. A few days later he received five hundred more lashes, and still he would say nothing. He was thrown into a pit, probably the Bridge Hole at Inverness. He was given a pound of coarse meal a day but was too weak to eat it. When he was finally dragged out, his back raw and festering, he was taken to the Tolbooth and there beaten to death with musket butts. Before the beggars buried him a bayonet was thrust several times into his breast.

Among other reasons for Albemarle's concern, actual or imagined, was the very real state of affairs in his command. At Fort William, men of Houghton's Regiment were dying every day from fever, distemper and loneliness. Winter terrified them and destroyed their morale. The world was white, and choking mists rolled down the sides of Ben Nevis. The miserable, inadequate hospital at the Fort was crowded with two hundred sick men. Whatever his weaknesses, Albemarle was a considerate soldier. He bullied Newcastle for permission to remove the sick by sea, and he asked for medicines, surgeons and hospital stores to be sent to all garrisons in the Highlands, including "vinegar and brimstone to sweeten their barracks".

Not surprisingly, the Board of Ordnance in London had

sent no blankets or bedding to equip the garrisons for a Scots winter, and the soldiers were making what use they could of the few supplies sent them by the City of London as a reward for suppressing the Rebellion. Beyond this they used their wits. Albemarle's desk was covered with complaints and petitions accusing his soldiers of plunder and pillage in all the towns south of the Highland line (north of it there was nothing left to steal). Farmers said that their stock was being driven off in the night, their fields dug up, their straw stolen, and sometimes their houses looted. Merchants complained that armed bands of soldiers broke into their factories and stole clothing and bedding. Tradesmen said that officers refused to pay their debts. While they were in such a sullen temper few citizens delighted in the official celebration of the King's birthday. Edinburgh, however, since it was under Albemarle's cold eye, did its best to look happy. The Cross was richly dressed and flags were displayed. The magistrates held an official reception for Albemarle in the Parliament House (which some anti-Unionists found unbearably ironic). The city guard fired volleys below the Castle, and at night music was played while bonfires burned.

Albemarle wanted to go home. He wrote to Newcastle, saying that he hoped His Grace would intercede for him and send a relief soon, "for no Englishman can wish to be in Scotland above a twelvemonth together". Newcastle said soon, very soon, and meanwhile Albemarle had to endure the northern capital which, once it had paid its respects to the King's birthday, began to behave with remarkable insolence.

One night somebody burnt down Hawley's gibbets, which had been left in the Grassmarket. This was impertinent enough, though Albemarle may have been pleased to see the things go, but then there was worse. There were reports that at night many gentlemen went singing through the wynds, shouting treasonable words and wearing white cockades. This was the beginning of the safe and sentimental Jacobitism that was to drench the Lowlands and drown the memory of the fact that its people had done little or nothing to help the Prince when he had come. To Albemarle, however, tired and depressed as he was, it was naturally alarming. Thus, with suitable gravity, he reported to Newcastle on

December 24 "a surprising, audacious and impudent attempt to celebrate the Birthday of the Pretender's son".

This was Saturday, December 20. Earlier in the week the Lord Justice Clerk, a sober and intelligent man who should have known better, had warned Albemarle of what he believed was to happen. Forwarding an open warrant of arrest for Albemarle's signature, he said that for some time there had been rumours that a number of Jacobite gentry proposed to celebrate the birthday by a meeting (in Leith, he thought) at which their women would wear tartan sashes and white cockades. He thought that this should be regarded as an insult to the Government, and he asked that all officers of the law be given the power to seize and secure the men and women found at such a meeting.

The night of December 20 was remembered in Edinburgh for its humour rather than its terror. Where Scotland was well-fed and safe it was beginning to laugh at the English. Five companies of Lee's Regiment were paraded at dusk at the Canongate, equipped with cartridge, ball and bayonet, and they stood at the secure while their orders were read to them. It was too dark for anyone to be sure that the soldiers were not smiling. They were to discover and apprehend any woman or girl, of gentility or commonality, who was wearing a tartan gown, stockings, sash or cape, or who wore white ribbons in her hair or at her breast. The orders read, they marched to Leith.

Guards were posted at the corners of the streets, and files of soldiers called at all the houses named in a list drawn up by the Lord Justice Clerk and General Blakeney. Most of them took the duty philosophically and without ill-humour. When Lieutenant John Morgan entered Lady Bruce's house he "behaved with very great discretion, making a joke of the farce". He showed his warrant to Lady Bruce, inviting her to laugh with him, and he shrugged his shoulders when she pointed to a sentence which said that a Jacobite Ball was to be held at the house of a Widow Morrison. There was no Widow Morrison in Leith, said Lady Bruce.

The only woman arrested that night was Mistress Jean Rollo, an old spinster of Leith, who was discovered alone in her house and in a tartan gown. She had no knowledge of any ball, and apparently no knowledge of the proscription of the tartan (unless she was being pig-headed). She was brought before Albemarle who, after some trifling questions, stuffily dismissed her. He would not, however, withdraw his troops from the streets, and the soldiers' good humour soon froze in the ceaseless winds of the city. Before dawn a patrol angrily arrested some gentlemen who were returning from a late party. They were taken to gaol, and when they heard why they had been arrested they laughed and treated the whole affair as a great joke, refusing to give their names.

General Huske, officer commanding, received the raw edge of Albemarle's tongue the next morning, and in his turn he passed on the abuse to a Lieutenant Trapaud of Bligh's who, for his own amusement, had started the rumour. Albemarle did his best to keep his temper against the smiling faces he met when next he went abroad, and he turned his attention to a search for those Non-Jurant Ministers he believed to be hiding in Edinburgh or Leith. They were educating children in defiance of the Law, he told Newcastle, and he sent the Minister a list of their names. He had caught none yet, "but I shall continue to be on the watch".

In London emotions were cooling. Cumberland had gone to the Low Countries, driving to Harwich by fast post-chaise at four o'clock one morning, and without its martial boy the city seemed able to discuss rebellion and rebels without the whetting of knives. "I must own," wrote a correspondent to the *Westminster Journal*, "I am neither for killing wretches in cold blood, nor for some people's extravagant schemes of transporting them into plantations where, in the spirit of resentment remaining, they may possibly be more serviceable to the French and dangerous to us than in the Highlands."

But, said the *Daily Advertiser*, "the blow fallen upon the rebels, if not followed by the greatest severity, may only serve as a lesson of caution, not terror".

Not necessarily, thought the *Westminster Journal*, and while it was true (everybody knew) that the Scots were savages one should take a civilised attitude toward them. "The children of savages are capable of as much improvement as the children of Englishmen." This, however, was too revolutionary a view-point for most of the *Journal*'s readers, and one said that the Government should not concern itself with the education of the children of savages, but with the fruitful employment of such savages in, say, the scandalously neglected herring industry.

The year was ending, the year which people in the Highlands were now calling *Bliadhna Thearlaich*, Charlie's Year. It was as good a name as any. Few men have achieved as much in twelve months, though little of it can have been what he intended when he landed on the Isle of Eriskay. And with the year died two more men who had followed him. The first was in the High-lands. Just before Christmas a shivering patrol from Fort William, acting upon information, came to a hut in a wood five miles from the garrison. They knew whom they hoped to find inside—Hugh Cameron, a native of Erracht, a captain of Lochiel's. He was a giant, six feet seven inches in height, and since Culloden he had been at large in Lochaber, fully armed with broadsword, dirk and dags, and declaring his eternal defiance of the Elector. The lieutenant of Houghton's, who commanded the patrol, kicked down the door, and there was their man on his bed of heather. Hugh Cameron leapt naked from his plaid and seized his sword, but he was overpowered. He was taken to Inverness in fetters and there he was hanged.

The second was in London. Despite the December cold a great crowd came to Tyburn to watch the hanging of Sergeant Smith. He had deserted his regiment to join the Jacobites, from political and religious convictions rather than simple discontent with the King's Army. Throughout his imprisonment and trial he had been obstinately unrepentant. He marched from Savoy Barracks to Tyburn, his wrists and ankles hampered by gyves, and no drum beat to give him the step. He was dressed in a scarlet coat with white breeches and hose, white vest and shirt, and because his officers respected his courage they had allowed him to wear a knot of tartan ribbons at each knee, and a rosette of tartan on his breast. He smiled at the nervous hangman and asked him to be quick, for the morning was cold. When he was dead his body was cut down and buried in the earth beneath the gibbet, where it still may be.

"Their backs should be to God and their faces to the devil"

REPRISALS BY THE Highlanders were rare, and their response to brutality was curiously mild in so warlike a people. This might be put to the credit of their nobility had they not a savage history of murder and revenge. The truth is that for six months after Culloden they were probably numbed by shock and immobilised by hunger and fear, which, of course, was what Cumberland had intended. No one seems to have made any attempt to kill either Lockhart or Caroline Scott, and when a Cameron tried to take traditional vengeance on Grant of Knockando it was Munro of Culcairn whom he actually killed. It was an isolated act of desperation, committed in grief and pain, but it gave Albemarle some days of uneasiness for he thought it might be the beginning of murder and assassination. This uneasiness is evident in the bald account of the affair which he sent to Newcastle.

The cause of the murder was murder itself, possibly the killing of that Cameron who surrendered to Grant's Independent Company near the dark wood of Muich. Other Camerons, watching from the hillside, saw that it was ordered by an officer who rode a white horse and wore a long blue cloak. Some days later Grant's friend Munro came by Loch Arkaig at the head of a mixed party of Munros, MacLeods and Rosses. The weather was bad and he was wearing the cloak which Grant had lent him. He was also, by some accounts, riding a white horse. When the road passed between a thick wood and the loch, Munro saw a woman and a boy standing in the rain, the woman with her plaid drawn over her head. Since neither ran, as most people were inclined to run when they saw soldiers or militia, Culcairn halted to speak to them. At this moment there was a musket-shot from the wood and Munro fell out of his saddle.

"The advanced guard immediately crowded about the body," wrote Albemarle to Newcastle, "the ground where the shot came from being perpendicular from the road and the guard being obliged to go about ere they entered the wood made it a few minutes ere there was made any pursuit after the Murderer." The trees, the thick bracken and heather further delayed pursuit, and it was soon abandoned. The woman and the boy were arrested, although they said they knew nothing. Then a man came round the bend of the road, carrying a gun, and when he was seized he too said he knew nothing. "The man declared," said Albemarle, "that he had gone into the wood to shun the detachment because he had no pass or protection, and that on his seeing the party sent into the woods he came out rather than he should be taken there." This explanation was surprisingly accepted, perhaps because the stranger, anxious to please, said that the father and brother of the Cameron whom Grant had killed, Dugald Roy and Donald Roy MacOllonie, were skulking in the district.

The murder of Munro of Culcairn was never solved, any more than one can now say who killed Campbell of Glenure in Appin six years later.* Lochiel is said to have believed that the murderer was one of the MacOllonies, perhaps the father, waiting by Loch Arkaig day after day until he saw a blue-cloaked rider on a white horse. The search for him, or someone else, continued through the autumn and into winter, and Culcairn's clansmen talked wildly of coming down upon Lochaber and killing every Cameron they could find. There is a story that, before he left Scotland, Lochiel called a meeting of some of his clan, and that they sent a message to the MacOllonies urging them both to surrender before their people suffered more outrages.

A man of the name gave himself up, or was captured. At the beginning of December Albemarle received a dispatch from Patrick Campbell or from Macdonald the tailor: "I doubt not your

---

* The Appin Murder is, of course, a hinge in the story of *Kidnapped*. There is a similarity between Stevenson's fiction and the fact of Culcairn's death. He describes how Campbell was shot at the moment he halted his horse to speak with David Balfour. Munro was killed when he stopped to talk to the woman and boy.

Lordship has been informed that one McOloney was delivered up to my Lord Loudoun as the murderer of Culcairn, but lest you should be misled in this particular I think it my duty to give your Lordship the account I had of it. Ye McOloney delivered as the murderer is nicknamed in the Irish language Am-Biatach, that is to say Hospitable; this name was given to him in contradiction to his real character, being that of a Churl; which imputation joined to that of his being accounted a Coward; and not going to the rebellion, are the Crimes for which he was given up as a sacrifice, and not as concerned in Culcairn's murder, of which he is allowed by common fame to be innocent. One Donald Roy McOloney is said to be the actor of this murder, and father to the man who was shot by the Command on their march to the head of Locharkeg when this wicked deed was committed."

Time has confused the incident. Certainly no one was hanged for the murder. A Donald Roy MacOllonie and a Dugald Roy MacOllonie (which was father and which was son is not clear) were both out in the Rebellion with Lochiel's Regiment, and both were prisoners at one time. But the records indicate that they were released before Culcairn was shot and were not taken again. Two things only are certain, that someone shot Munro of Culcairn by the shore of Loch Arkaig, and that it was an act of revenge.

There were other killings, the dirking or shooting of men believed to be traitors. One victim was Robert Grant, a Strathspey man who had served in the Black Watch before the Rising and who became "a most villainous spy and informer against all that had been in the Prince's army". Whether he was or not, he was summarily executed. He was walking one evening by Inverwick in Glenmoriston and was suddenly surrounded by wild figures that leapt yelling from the heather. When his body was found the next morning his head had been cut from it and placed high in a tree as a warning for all.

Those responsible for this may have been the band known as The Seven Men of Glenmoriston. They had been out in the Rebellion, some with the Grants and some with other clan regiments, and when it was over they took to the heather with their arms, refusing to surrender. They lived in a cave called Corriedhoga, high in Glenmoriston where the valley closes toward Loch Cluanie. The cracking of the earth's crust had created it from three great rocks, and a stream of water ran across its gravel floor. Here the Seven Men sheltered the Prince at the end of July, and took an oath among themselves: "That their backs should be to God and their faces to the Devil; that all the curses the Scripture did pronounce might come upon them and all their posterity if they did not stand firm to the Prince in the greatest danger . . . ."

They were Patrick Grant, John Macdonald, Alexander Mac-Donell, the brothers Donald, Alexander and Hugh Chisholm, Gregor MacGregor, and for some period an eighth man Hugh Macmillan. The Prince stayed with them for a week and in all of his confused and wretched life he probably never had such devoted and undemanding friends. When he was too melancholy to eat, they too would go without food. When he found some gaiety from the little black bottle they danced and sang for him. They said he was one of their band and they called him Dugal MacCullonoy. To supply him with fresh clothes they raided a military baggage train, bringing back a scarlet coat and lace. They told him how they had become outlaws after Culloden, and had sworn that "if danger should come upon them they would stand by one another to the last drop of their blood". And the Prince, sitting on the couch of heather they had made, eating collops of the stag they had shot, called them his Privy Council, the first he had had since the battle. He said that with them he was as comfortably lodged as if he had been in a royal palace, "with the finest purling stream that could be running by his bedside within the grotto".

The Seven Men of Glenmoriston had a youthful bravery and arrogance, and would occasionally amuse themselves by walking abroad before their enemies, and when one day two of them were met by the Laird of Grant they faced him boldly, and were innocently stupid when he asked them what they had been doing and whether they had seen the rascally Pretender. They were not afraid to fight if they had to. At noon on a day toward the end of summer a party of one hundred redcoats and three officers marched into Glenmoriston, led by a spy called Donald Fraser. They began to drive off what few cattle were left in the valley.

"Upon which," said Patrick Grant, "we the Seven Glenmoriston Men made up directly with all speed to the party till we came within musket-shot of them, and then roared out to them with a volley of oaths that made all the rocks about us resound not to advance one step farther but to leave the cattle to us and to march off." The soldiers were drawn up into line and Fraser was sent up the brae to ask the Seven what the devil they thought they were doing. They were commanded to surrender at once and ask for protection. "Upon this I, Patrick Grant, cocked my piece and swore by Him that made me that I should give them all protection that would serve them to the day of Judgment."

Then began an extraordinary battle, with seven cunning men firing their muskets from the rocks above to the soldiers in the narrow pass below, wounding some and demoralising the others. In the end, if Patrick Grant is to be believed, the officer commanding the detachment not only surrendered the cattle his men had gathered, but handed over bread, cheese and whisky which the Seven declared they must have. "We bade them farewell, and desired them when they should come that way again, they might fetch more provisions with them."

They lived like schoolboys playing Robin Hood. One morning they came out of the rocks with swords swinging, bounding down on seven soldiers who were travelling from Fort Augustus to Glenelg with two pack-horses loaded with supplies. The Chisholm brothers, with Macdonald and MacDonell, dropped behind the cover of rocks and shot two of the soldiers, while Grant and the others went hurrahing on with their broadswords. The frightened English threw away their firelocks and ran. The dead were buried with decent respect, the pack-horses turned loose, and the Seven climbed back to Corriedhoga, their shoulders loaded with wine, sweet loaf-bread and meat. "And O!" said Patrick Grant, remembering the day, "we made a bonny fire of the two sogers' red coats."

Time dispersed them in the end, and it is impossible to know what happened to any of them with the exception of Grant. In 1759 he was pressed into King George's Army and sent to Canada, and so he may have been one of the Highlanders who, kilted in the Government's black tartan, climbed the Heights of

Abraham for James Wolfe. He died in 1761 or 1762, an out-pensioner of Chelsea Hospital.

Iain Dubh Cameron, known as Sergeant Mhor or Big John, led a band of freebooters in Lochaber for seven years after the Rebellion. He had been a non-commissioned officer in one of King Louis's Scots regiments, but he returned to Scotland for the Rising and to serve with men of his name in Lochiel's. After Culloden he wandered for a while on his own, in the mountains above Loch Arkaig, and then he gathered about him a number of young men who refused to surrender their arms or their tartan. He took them on forays into Perthshire, and sometimes into the heart of Campbell country in Argyll, and there were songs sung about him. In time he probably abandoned his Jacobitism, except as an excuse, and lived as broken men had always lived in the hills, by blackmail, robbery and cattle-stealing.

Although the MacGregors were of course blamed, it may have been Big John who kidnapped Alexander Garden of Troup and provoked a flurry of letters to and from Albemarle's desk in September and October 1746. About ten o'clock on the evening of August 31, Mr. Garden was aroused by a hammering on his door. He opened it to find a dozen armed Highlanders, led by a young man who politely demanded £2,000. Mr. Garden said that he had not that much money in the house, whereupon the Highlanders entered and made themselves comfortable. They told Mr. Garden to write to his friends for the money, advising him to make the letter convincing, for if the money did not arrive within three days they would, regrettably, cut his throat with a dirk. While the desperate man was composing his appeal, the Highlanders wandered through his house, taking £100 sterling and all the papers from his charter-chest.

They then left for the Hills of Renny, carrying Mr. Garden along. His terrified wife was told to send the letter with a servant and to waste no time, for they were impatient men. They also warned her against sending soldiers, but the local garrison commander was indifferent to Mr. Garden's safety. He sent a troop of dragoons into the hills, and it would seem that the outlaws were more bloodthirsty in threats than they were in action. The dragoons found Mr. Garden on the moor, bound with thongs and greatly distressed, but otherwise unharmed. The soldiers patrolled the hills for a week before they gave up the hunt for the robbers.

Big John entered a legend, and there were stories told about him that had been told about Rob Roy a quarter of a century earlier. It was said that an English officer, carrying gold to Fort William for the payment of soldiers there, was afraid to travel at night, and asked a traveller whom he met at an inn to ride part of the road with him. On the journey the officer talked about Sergeant Mhor, calling him a robber and a murderer. At this the stranger put a hand on the Englishman's bridle and softly said "Stop there, I never shed innocent blood!" The officer was too surprised to protest or resist when Big John took his saddle-bags. "That is the road to Inverlochy," said the outlaw, "and tell the Governor at Fort William to be more cautious next time he sends a courier for his gold." In England men told the same story about Robin Hood and Claude Duval.

Big John was captured in 1753, while he slept in a barn on Rannoch Moor. Brought before the Court of Justiciary at Perth he was tried for the murder of a man in Braemar. He did not deny the charge, but said the man deserved his death. He died bravely at the end of a rope, and there were many people in Lochaber who mourned him, not because he was a bandit but because he had not surrendered.

For the rest, resistance was a small matter of passion and anger. In Appin a young girl, whose cow had been shot by a soldier, killed him with a stone when he attempted to rape her. The body was buried secretly at Airds, but was afterwards exhumed by the girl's brother who made himself a dirk-sheath from the skin of its arms. In Aberdeen a Sheriff's officer, who had given aid and information to Cumberland, was found one night with his throat cut. Sometimes, in the glens, travellers asked for and were given escorts of soldiers to protect them from highway robbery, and this practice continued for many years.

"No man or boy shall put on the philebeg"

A NEW YEAR, and in February Albemarle was permitted to leave Scotland and hand his office and duties to Humphrey Bland. His letter of thanks to Newcastle was a confused confession of happiness and failure. "My joy at leaving this country is inexpressible, for tho' I have aimed at strictly doing my duty and pleasing these people I have found every day more and more difficulty in my attempts, the spirit of disaffection in the generality, and that of partiality and of skreening the most guilty in others (even amongst those in employment) is too much rooted to make it possible for an honest and zealous man to remain with them and at the same time preserve his character; this and the desire to serve under HRH The Duke had made me press your Grace and Mr. Pelham so very strongly to be removed."

The difficulty and disaffection he spoke of was a sickness among the people of Scotland (and among some of his officers) that seriously hampered the policy of repression. Albemarle was himself unhappy about the value of this policy. "Upon the whole," he told Newcastle in one of his long and discursive reports, "I think this Kingdom can never be kept in awe but by a sufficient military force, and at the same time I think it is a shame that the pay of so many men should be spent among them, for it is enriching this country at the expense of England. I am further of the opinion that very few now employed deserve the King's favour, and very few out of employment fitt to replace them. I mean as to principals, for craft and cunning they all abound with." All Scots were rogues, even those loyal to King George II.

To the last of his days in Scotland Albemarle's spies sent him contradictory reports from the hills. Patrick Campbell said that agents were going through the Fraser country dressed in women's clothes and distributing letters and papers from France. In Badenoch, he said, "they still have plenty of arms, for when they surrendered they gave up only some rusty, useless arms". In the Mackenzie country people were talking of the Rising that was to come with the spring, and although food was scarce there was so much French money about "that they have raised the price of whisky from 12 to 18 and 20 shillings, and also meal to a very high price". All through the Isles there was talk of another Rebellion at Patrick Mass, but the truth was that the Prince was never coming again, and perhaps all knew it. The truth was that a broadsword hidden in the peat was no comfort to the empty bellies of a man's children. "The inhabitants of the Rebellious countries," reported Campbell, "begin to be in misery for want of Provisions; steal they must or leave their country, which is as bad as death."

Such information was studied by Newcastle when he and the King's Ministers considered the legislation necessary for punishing the clans and making further rebellion impossible. In the three years following Culloden Parliament revised some of the laws that had been passed after the 'Fifteen and enacted new ones that were to destroy for ever the Clan System and the feudal power of its chiefs. The Lord President Duncan Forbes, if the jottings in his papers are a guide, advised leniency, not from compassion alone but also from common sense (so he thought). "Unnecessary severity," he wrote, "creates pity. Pity from unnecessary severity is the most dangerous nurse to disaffection, especially if continued for any time. And therefore it is the outmost consequence on this Occasion to weigh well what is necessary to be done in the way of just punishment; to the end it may be speedily done; and to consider whether, and how far, it is consistent with the future tranquility of the Kingdom to restrain merited punishment and to extend unmerited mercy." Great numbers of the disaffected, he said, "were compelled to join the active Rebells, by threats which were justly terrible to them".

He meant well, but he was a political child. In the end it was harshness, not mercy, that succeeded. By brutality the Highlands were subdued, the glens emptied, the clans destroyed, and the

Hanoverian dynasty made so secure that sixty years or so later the Prince Regent could indulge his romantic fancies by paying for the tomb of Prince Charles. Jacobitism was taken over by the sentimental song-makers, and the warrior spirit of the clansmen was usefully expended in England's wars.

The Ministers may have listened to Duncan Forbes with yawning patience, but more to their taste were memorials such as that drawn up by General Bland and Lord Justice Clerk of Scotland Fletcher. This argued that "could we but at once get rid of all Chiefs of Clans in these barbarous and disloyal parts of the Highlands, it would facilitate all other operations both in point of difficulty and time. And therefore, so far as we can get rid of them, we ought; and where we cannot get rid of them that such regulations be made and carried into execution as to make the common people as free and independent of their chiefs as the nature of their case can admit."

Bland and Fletcher also suggested that the Government should buy or sequestrate the lands of the chiefs, and send to the Barbadoes any who objected. Such lands should also be cleared of clansmen who grumbled, and the country settled with decent, law-abiding, God-fearing Protestants from the south. The Highlands should, in fact, be colonised. It was a proposal that created considerable interest, but it was not accepted, at least not in detail.

There had been much legislation during and immediately after the Rebellion to determine the nature of treason and the punishment it deserved. Quite early the Government had, of course, suspended the Habeas Corpus Acts which governments pass to protect the individual and withdraw to protect themselves. There were Acts to settle the place and procedure of the trials, and to regularise the transportation of those who drew the King's Mercy from the lotting. There were Disarming Acts and there was an Act to compel suspected persons of property to lodge substantial bail against their loyal and peaceable behaviour. And there were Acts of Attainder against notable Rebels, chiefs, lairds, tacksmen and lords who were known to be skulking abroad or in their own glens. Finally, six years after Culloden, there was the Act of Grace by which King George II once more showed his royal inclination to mercy and "resolved to grant his General and free Pardon in a large and bountiful manner, not doubting but that it will raise a due sense of gratitude in all who had been artfully misled into treasonable practices against his person and government". There were some who were still excepted from this pardon: those who had committed treason or felony after June 15, 1747, others who persisted in serving the Kings of France and Spain when told to come home, and of course, lastly and inevitably, the unhappy people of Clan Gregor. Not until 1775 were the penal statutes lifted from the shoulders of the MacGregors, and they were once more allowed the right to use their own names.

But the legislation which most immediately destroyed the Highland way of life was that which took from its people the kilt, plaid and clothing of tartan weave. Duncan Forbes was doubtful of the wisdom of banning the Highland dress, though he agreed that it fostered a warlike spirit among the Highlanders. He thought that only the Jacobite clans should be forbidden to wear the tartan, and he tried to explain how useful the philebeg, the little kilt, was to people living in the mountains. "The Garb is certainly very loose, and fits Men inured to it to go through great fatigues, to make very quick Marches, to bear out against the inclemency of the weather, to wade through Rivers and shelter in huts, woods, and rocks upon occasions; which men dressed in Low Country garb could not possibly endure." Such an argument, thought the Government, was a very good reason for proscribing the dress. The tartan banned, the kilt gone, their raw legs put into breeks, and Highlanders would become as other men. Colonel Belford's artillery had begun the business, a bolt of broadcloth would finish it.

So to the market-crosses throughout Scotland, from Caithness to the Border and from the Firth of Forth to the Isles, nailed to church doors and the doors of Town Houses, went the words of both Houses of Parliament:

"And it is further enacted. That from and after the 1st of August 1747 no man or boy within Scotland, other than such as shall be employed as officers and soldiers in the

King's forces, shall on any pretence whatsoever, wear or put on the cloaths commonly called highland cloaths, that is to say, the plaid, philebeg or little kilt, trowse, shoulder-belts, or any part whatsoever of what peculiarly belongs to the highland garb; and that no tartan or party-coloured plaids or stuff shall be used for great-coats, or for upper coats; and if any such persons shall, after said 1st of August, wear or put on the aforesaid garments, or any part of them, every such person so offending, being convicted thereof by the mouth of one or more witnesses, before any court of judiciary, or any one or more Justices of the Peace for the shire or stewartry, or judge ordinary of the place where such offence shall be committed, shall suffer imprisonment, without bail, during six months and no longer; and being convicted of a second offence, before the court of judiciary, or at the circuits, shall be liable to be transported to any of His Majesty's plantations beyond the sea, for seven years."

For those Highlandmen who had no English, and to whom the nailing of another piece of skin to a church door was something best forgotten, there was an added compulsion. Wherever possible they were made to swear an oath, in the Irish tongue and upon the holy iron of their dirks:

"I do swear, as I shall answer to God at the great day of Judgment, I have not, nor shall have in my possession any gun, sword, pistol or arm whatsoever, and never use tartan, plaid, or any part of the Highland Garb; and if I do so may I be cursed in my undertakings, family and property, may I be killed in battle as a coward, and lie without burial in a strange land, far from the graves of my forefathers and kindred; may all this come across me if I break my oath."

No Englishman, and perhaps no Lowlander, could have composed an oath so obviously Highland in feeling.

The mountain people had no other clothes but the tartan plaid and kilt. Without them they would go naked. They did the only thing they could do at that moment. They dyed the tartan black and brown. They sewed their kilts between their legs to make breeches. Nor, perhaps, were they comforted by the distant sympathy of their absent lairds. One of these, the Laird of Cawdor, preferred to live on a softer estate in Wales than among his lands along the Nairn Water where many of his people were members of Clan Chattan. When his factor wrote to him, telling him how angry the clansmen were with this law that drove them into breeks, and how difficult they were finding it in their poverty and their pride, he wrote back with words of cheer and intelligent advice:

"I have thought that the poor Highlanders who are distressed by wearing breeches might be very agreeably accommodated by wearing wide trousers like seamen; made of canvas or the like. Nankeen might be more genteel. But I would have them cut as short as the philebeg, and then they would be almost as good and yet be lawful."

Thus Bonnie Prince Charlie's rebellion ended in a bad joke, with his clansmen in ragged breeches and their women dipping tartan plaids into vats of dye and mud. As Forbes had expected (though not as seriously) there was resistance to the Act. Some Highlanders ignored it, a few taking to the hills rather than abandon the dress or accept humiliating compromises. Others carried tartan plaids beneath their coats, draping themselves with them when there were no soldiers about. Some wore strips of coloured cloth about their waists, blue, green and red, pleated like the kilt and worn over comic trews. When caught they were of course imprisoned. Caught again they were transported. Some were shot by the soldiers who had once hunted for the Prince, for fugitives or for arms, but who now searched the glens for rags of woven cloth.

The military posts and the moving patrols were kept in the Highlands for many years to see that the Disarming Acts and the Act against the tartan were strictly observed. For the soldiers the life was poor and unrewarding. It was once suggested that they be paid £5 for every fugitive or outlaw brought in dead or alive, "and what is meant by dead is in Case of their being shot or killed upon making resistance". The soldiers thought highly of the proposal, but it was not adopted. Officers

commanding the detachments submitted regular reports of their
work, and that written by a Captain Molesworth of Guise's, one
week-end in 1751, is typical of them all:

> "The party at Strathglass apprehended Archibald Chisholm
> in Glencannick of Strathglass, wearing the phillibeg and
> he is, at my instance, committed to Inverness Gaol for
> six months. The day following a young fellow in full
> plaid was pursued by the said party on their patrole, and to
> avoid them attempted swimming a loch and was drowned."

So, in the beginning, the law against the wearing of Highland
dress or the tartan was firmly imposed and the penalties were
scrupulously applied, but as the years passed it staggered and
died beneath its own inertia. It had served its purpose, however.
When the proscription was lifted in 1782 there was no enthusiastic
return to the tartan or the kilt. A Proclamation went round the
glens:

> "This is declaring to every man, young and old, Commons
> and Gentles, that they may after this put on and wear the
> Trews, the little Kilt, the Doublet and Hose, along with the
> Tartan Kilt, without fear of the Law of the Land or the
> jealousy of enemies . . ."

But the old attachment to the Highland dress had died in
a generation, the old patterns (if they had ever had more than
an area significance) were forgotten. Forgotten, too, was the
skill of making dyes from the herbs on the hills. The clans were
no longer, their true identity had gone with the broadsword
and their chiefs, and the wearing of the kilt was an affectation
for gentlemen or for those who joined His Majesty's Highland
Regiments. It was not until forty years later still, when George IV
(a post-Rebellion Jacobite) came to Scotland and dressed himself
in a ridiculous uniform of scarlet kilt, plaid, bonnet, eagle feathers,
broadsword, dirk and *skene dhu*, that a romantic and extravagant
interest in the Highland dress was born. Walter Scott was hard at
work creating his Gothic picture of the Highlands, helped by many
Lowland gentlemen whose ancestors had regarded the clansmen
as savages. Tartans were invented and ascribed to this clan or

that, a religious devotion being paid to setts that would not have been recognised by any Highlander who charged at Culloden. Sentiment spins enduring lies. When Victoria's humourless German consort designed a tartan that was used on the carpets, furnishings and wallpaper at Balmoral all interest in the parti-coloured cloth should have been killed by a giggle. But it was not.

The banning of their dress took from the clans their pride and their sense of belonging to a unique people. The abolition of the hereditary jurisdictions of their chiefs, which followed, destroyed the political and social system that had held them together. By these jurisdictions the chiefs had had the "power of pit and gallows" over the clans, and it might be argued that the abolition of them liberated the Highlanders from feudal and tribal tyranny. So indeed it could have done, had it not been preceded and accompanied by battle and the gallows and the harrying of the glens. When the English heard of the chiefs' power of life and death over their people they asked themselves if they were still living in the Middle Ages. The removal of such an injustice gave to the suppression of the Rebellion the satisfying flavour of a crusade.

Since both friend and enemy of the Hanoverian dynasty possessed these jurisdictions, a Campbell chief as much as a Cameron, the Government benevolently considered and approved payment of compensation, and naturally enough the Duke of Argyll, the greatest chief and greatest Campbell, got the greatest cash payment. He received £21,000. The Earl of Eglinton was paid £7,800, and the Earl of Morton £7,240. And so on down to the £25 paid to the Duchess of Gordon. The attainted Jacobite chiefs and lords were paid nothing, of course, but lost their jurisdictions all the same.

Once the chiefs lost their powers, many of them lost also any parental interest in their clansmen. During the next hundred years they continued the work of Cumberland's battalions. Land which they had once held on behalf of their tribe now became theirs in fact and law. They wore the tartan and kept a piper to play at their board, but profit and land-rents replaced a genuine pride in race. So that they might lease their glens and braes to sheep-farmers from the Lowlands and England they cleared the crofts of men, women and children, using police and soldiers where necessary. The descendants of those who had fought for the Prince, or against him, were sent in thousands to Canada. It was a new transportation, but this time the laird was responsible not the Government.

From the green saucer of Glenaladale, dipping down to Loch Shiel, Alexander Macdonald had taken one hundred and fifty men to serve in Clanranald's regiment. Within a century there was nothing there but the lone shieling of the song.

7

THE LAST VICTORY

IN AUGUST 1748, before the Town Council of Aberdeen, eleven men and women swore to the truth of a vision which they said they had seen in a valley five miles to the west of the city. On the fifth of that month, at two o'clock in the afternoon, they saw three globes of light in the sky above, which they first took to be weather-galls but which increased in brilliance until twelve tall men in clean and bright attire crossed the valley. Then were seen two armies. The first wore clothing of dark blue and displayed Saint Andrew's Cross on its ensigns. The other was uniformed in scarlet and was assembled beneath the Union Flag. Twice the red army attacked the blue, and twice it was beaten back. When it rallied and attacked for a third time it was routed and scattered by the Scots army. Those who watched saw the smoke of the cannon, the glitter of steel, and the colours waving, but they heard no sound. When the blue army was triumphant the vision passed.

A lost cause will always win a last victory in men's imaginations. And no British regiment now has Culloden among its battle honours.

Appendix

THE KING'S ARMY AT CULLODEN

BEFORE THE MIDDLE of the eighteenth century British regiments were known by the names of their Colonels. The system of numbering them came later, and later still their district appellations. There were some exceptions to this custom. Campbell's were known as the North British or Royal Scots Fusiliers, and St. Clair's, the oldest foot regiment in the British Army, were referred to as the Royal Scots or the Royals. I have used these titles. One of the many ironies of Culloden is that there was a regiment of "Royal Scots" on both sides. The Jacobite regiment, composed of Scottish exiles raised by the Drummond family, I have called Scots Royal to avoid confusion.

Sometimes a British regiment would get a new colonel in the middle of a campaign, and would change its name accordingly, to the confusion of anybody trying to follow its history. Thus, after Culloden, Bligh's became Sackville's when Lord George Sackville became its Colonel, and Munro's became Dejean's when Lt.-Col. Louis Dejean was promoted. I have endeavoured to keep the names consistent in this narrative. A Colonel of a regiment did not necessarily lead it in action. He was frequently of general officer rank. The Colonel of Wolfe's was Brigadier-General Edward Wolfe, the father of James. The Colonel of Blakeney's was Major-General William Blakeney. And so on. The regiments of Culloden are as follows, with the numbers they were later given, and the names they later assumed. Many of them have been recently amalgamated. Barrell's, for example, are now joined with Cholmondeley's in the King's Own Royal Border Regiment.

FOOT

The Royals	1st	The Royal Scots
Howard's	3rd	The Buffs, Royal East Kents
Barrell's	4th	King's Own Royal Regiment
Wolfe's	8th	King's Liverpool Regiment
Pulteney's	13th	Somerset Light Infantry
Price's	14th	West Yorks Regiment
Bligh's	20th	Lancashire Fusiliers
Campbell's	21st	Royal Scots Fusiliers
Sempill's	25th	King's Own Scottish Borderers
Blakeney's	27th	Royal Inniskilling Fusiliers
Cholmondeley's	34th	The Border Regiment
Fleming's	36th	Worcesters
Munro's	37th	The Hampshire Regiment
Conway's	48th	Northants Regiment
Battereau's		Disbanded
Argyll Militia		

HORSE

Cobham's Dragoons	10th Hussars
Lord Mark Kerr's Dragoons	11th Hussars
Kingston's Horse	Disbanded

ARTILLERY

Captain Cunningham's Company Disbanded

Acknowledgements

IN THE YEARS following Culloden the Reverend Robert Forbes, episcopal Minister of Leith and later Bishop of Ross and Caithness, assiduously collected letters, memoirs, journals and eyewitness accounts of the Rebellion and its aftermath. These ultimately filled ten black manuscript volumes which he called *The Lyon in Mourning*. Nearly seventy years ago Henry Paton edited them for the Scottish History Society, and allowing for their evident Jacobite sympathies they are still an invaluable source of information. This book is in debt to them, as it is greatly in debt to the painstaking scholarship of Sir Bruce Gordon Seton and Jean Gordon Arnot. Thirty-three years ago the Scottish History Society also published their analysis of the prisoners taken during the Rebellion, *The Prisoners of the '45*. The three volumes of this work list the names of all prisoners who could be found in State Papers, gaol registers and elsewhere. Jacobite historians have not used it as they might have done, and Chapter Five of this book would have been impossible without it.

I WOULD LIKE to offer my deep thanks to people who have helped me in my search for the material for *Culloden*, particularly the following: Donald A. Anderson, Burgh and County Librarian of Inverness; Brigadier B. A. Burke, D.S.O., Secretary of the Regimental Association, The King's Own Royal Border Regiment; Sir James Fergusson of Kilkerran, Keeper of the Records of Scotland; Dr. C. T. McInnes, O.B.E., Curator of Historical Records at the Scottish Record Office; Lt.-Col. M. E. S. Laws, O.B.E., M.C.; Lt.-Col. I. B. Cameron Taylor of the National Trust for Scotland; W. A. Thorburn, Curator of the Scottish United Services Museum, Edinburgh Castle; and Miss Katharine

Tomasson. I am also, of course, grateful to the staffs of the British
Museum Reading Room, the War Office Library, the Public
Record Office, London, the Scottish Public Record Office,
the Edinburgh Castle Museum, and the Maritime Museum at
Greenwich.

PRINCIPAL SOURCES

MANUSCRIPTS

Duke of Cumberland's Order Book	Scottish Public Record Office
The Hardwicke Papers	British Museum
The Newcastle Papers	British Museum
Order Book of the Appin Regiment	Edinburgh Castle
Order Book of Cholmondeley's	Edinburgh Castle
Order Book of Barrell's	Bowerham Barracks, Lancaster
The Log of H.M.S. Triton	Maritime Museum
WO 10/28-34, WO 55/408-9	Public Record Office

CONTEMPORARY PUBLICATIONS

The British Magazine	1746
The Gentleman's Magazine	1746
The London Magazine	1746
The Scots Magazine	1746
The Caledonian Mercury	1746
The London Evening Post	1746
St. James Evening Post	1746
Jacobite Tracts	1746
An Authentic Account of the Battle of Culloden	1746
BOYSE, Samuel	An Impartial History of the Late Rebellion. 1748
BURT, Edward	Letters from a Gentleman in the North of Scotland (Fifth Ed. 1818)
HENDERSON, Andrew	The History of the Rebellion. 1753 The Life of the Duke of Cumberland. 1766

HUGHES, Michael	A Plain Narrative. 1746
JOHNSTONE, Chevalier de	A Memoir of the 'Forty-five. 1820
MARCHANT, John	The History of the Present Rebellion. 1746
RAY, James	A Compleat History of the Rebellion. 1752

PUBLISHED PAPERS

ALBEMARLE, Earl of	The Albemarle Papers. Edited by Charles Sanford Terry. New Spalding Club. 1902
FORBES, Duncan	The Culloden Papers. 1815
WHITEFOORD, Charles	The Whitefoord Papers. 1746
WILLIAMSON, Adam	The Official Diary of Lt.-Gen. Adam Williamson. 1912

REGIMENTAL MANUALS

Exercises for Foot Forces. 1739
A short course of Standing Rules for the government
and conduct of an Army in the Field. 1744
The Manual Exercise, with Explanations. 1748
A System of Camp Discipline. 1757

OTHER SOURCES CONSULTED

ALLARDYCE, James	Historical Papers relating to the Jacobite Period. 1895
BLAIKIE, Walter Biggar	Origins of the Forty-Five. 1916
BLUNDELL, Dom Odo	The Catholic Highlands. 1909
BROWNE, James	A History of the Highlands and the Highland Clans. 1838
CHAMBERS, Robert	History of the Rebellion. 1869 Jacobite Memoirs. 1834
CHARTERIS, Evan	William Augustus, Duke of Cumberland, 1721-1748. 1913

CUNNINGHAM, Audrey	The Loyal Clans. 1932
DUKE, Winifred	Prince Charles Edward and the Forty-Five. 1938
ELCHO, Lord	Affairs of Scotland. 1744-1746. Edited Evan Charteris. 1897
FERGUSSON, Sir James of Kilkerran	Argyll in the 'Forty-Five. 1951
FORBES, J. Macbeth	Jacobite Gleanings from State Manuscripts. 1903
FORBES, Robert	The Lyon in Mourning. Edited by Henry Paton. 1895
FORTESCUE, Sir John	History of the British Army, Vol. II. 1899
GRANT, Mrs. Anne	Letters concerning Highland Affairs. Scottish History Society. 1896
HOME, John	The History of the Rebellion in Scotland. 1822
KELTIE, John S.	A History of the Scottish Highlands, Highland Clans and Regiments. 1875
LANG, Andrew	Prince Charles Edward. 1900 A History of Scotland, Vol. IV. 1897
MACLACHLAN, A. N. Campbell-	William Augustus, Duke of Cumberland, a sketch of his life exhibited in the General Orders of HRH. 1876
MUNRO, R.	Recollections of Inverness. 1870
PETRIE, Sir Charles	The Jacobite Movement, the Last Phase. 1950
ROSE, D. Murray	Historical Notes. 1897 The Mystery of Culloden Battlefield, 1904 Captain Caroline Scott's Diary of the Siege of Fort William. 1900

SETON, Sir Bruce Gordon, and ARNOT, Jean Gordon	The Prisoners of the 'Forty-Five, edited from the State Papers. 1928
STEWART, David	Sketches of the Highlanders. 1825
TAYLER, Alistair and Henrietta	1745 and After (O'Sullivan's Narrative). 1938
TERRY, C. Sanford	The Rising of 1745. 1890
	The Forty-Five, a narrative of the last Jacobite Rising by several contemporary hands.
THOMSON, Mrs. Katharine	Memoirs of the Jacobites. 1846
TOMASSON, Katherine	The Jacobite General. 1958

And also, of course, the many published histories of the regiments engaged at Culloden. The histories of the clans and the septs of clans which were consulted are too numerous to be named here. But I am more than grateful. In my views on the tartan and the exaggerated importance that has been given to its various setts since 1820 or so, I am unrepentant.

The Index which follows is the painstaking work of Roger Senhouse, to whom I am deeply grateful. Not only does it guide the reader through a thorn-hedge of place-names and patronymics, but it may also be used as a valuable appendix of further information.

Index

Certain bracketed abbreviations are used to distinguish members of one clan or family in which political or religious interests were at variance or divided. Thus (H) denotes Hanoverian (Royalist or Whig) in contradistinction to (J) (Jacobite or Rebel). (C) denotes Catholic, (NJ) Non-Jurant, (Pr) Presbyterian. After Culloden and the suppression of the clans, (P) denotes Prisoner, (PT) prisoner transported to the colonies, (KE) those of the Rebels who turned King's Evidence, (MR) the Manchester Regiment. The main regiments are listed under ARMIES (H) and (J), as drawn up in line of battle, followed by other units employed in Scotland after Culloden: further reference to (J) units, other than the French, will be found under CLANS, together with all those who bore the patronym of clan or sept. All place names north of the border are grouped under SCOTS TOPOGRAPHY, cross-referenced by bracketed clans.